CONSUMER GUIDE®

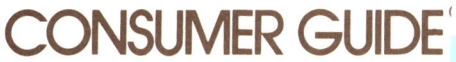

Rating & Raising Vegetables

A Practical Guide For Growing

Vegetables • Herbs • Fruits • And Sprouts

By Virginia L. Beatty And The Editors Of Consumer Guide®

PUBLICATIONS INTERNATIONAL, LTD. • SKOKIE, ILLINOIS
Distributed by Simon and Schuster

Copyright© 1977 by Publications International, Ltd.
All rights reserved.
This book may not be reproduced or quoted in whole or in part by mimeograph or any other printed means or for presentation on radio or television without written permission from Louis Weber, President Publications International, Ltd.
3323 West Main Street
Skokie, Illinois 60076

Manufactured in the United States of America
1 2 3 4 5 6 7 8 9 10

Library of Congress Cataloging in Publication Data
Beatty, Virginia L.
    Consumer guide rating and raising vegetables.
    1. Vegetable gardening. 2. Consumer education.
I. Consumer guide II. Title
SB321.B37   635'.0973   76-10266
ISBN 0-671-22362-3
ISBN 0-671-22361-5 pbk.

Trade distribution by Simon and Schuster
A Division of Gulf & Western Corporation
Simon & Schuster Building
Rockefeller Center
1230 Avenue of the Americas
New York, New York 10020

Rating
& Raising
Vegetables

About The Author
Virginia L. Beatty is a consultant in environmental education and urban horticulture. She was born into a plant growing and collecting family and her long-time interest in vegetable growing was encouraged by an uncle who was an extension horticulturist at Purdue University. For ten years, Mrs. Beatty has been gardening in the heart of Chicago where she helped start the flower and vegetable gardening programs in Chicago Housing Authority developments and has served as a consultant to their Residents' Gardening Committee. Mrs. Beatty is the first woman to serve on the Cook County Agricultural Extension Council and is a member of the American Society of Horticultural Science and many other organizations. She hosts "Plant Talk," a daily radio program, and is the author of *Consumer Guide® Rating and Raising Indoor Plants*.

Contents

Why Grow Eatables? 10

Planning and Planting 12
    Planning 13
    Starting from Seeds 19
    Planting 23

Extending Your Garden 28
    Extending Garden Space 29
    Extending the Growing Season 34
    Extending Your Garden Indoors 36

Growing Essentials 39
    Light 40
    Temperature 42
    Water 43
    Soils and Mixes 48

Growing Aids 52
    Fertilizers 53
    Compost Piles 55
    Mulches 58
    Soil Analysis 62
    Tools 64
    Where to Get Seeds 68
    Cooperative Extension Service 71

Growing Challenges 75
    Weeds 75
    Pests 82
    Diseases 90
    Pesticides 93
    Common Vegetable Gardening Problems 94

Rating Eatables 98

Catalog of Eatables ...106
   Apple ...110
   Artichoke, Globe ...111
   Artichoke, Jerusalem ...112
   Asparagus ...114
   Basil ...116
   Bean, Four-Angled ...117
   Bean, Lima ...118
   Bean, Mung ...120
   Bean, Snap ...121
   Beet ...123
   Broad Bean ...124
   Broccoli ...126
   Brussels Sprout ...127
   Cabbage ...128
   Cabbage, Chinese ...130
   Carrot ...131
   Cauliflower ...132
   Celeriac ...134
   Celery ...135
   Chard ...137
   Chayote ...139
   Chicory ...140
   Chive ...142
   Collard ...143
   Corn ...144
   Cress ...146
   Cucumber ...147
   Dill ...149
   Eggplant ...150
   Endive ...151
   Fennel ...152
   Garlic ...154
   Grape ...155
   Horseradish ...156
   Kale ...158
   Kohlrabi ...159
   Leek ...161
   Lettuce ...162
   Marjoram ...164
   Muskmelon ...166
   Mustard ...167
   Okra ...169
   Onion ...170
   Parsley ...172
   Parsnip ...173

Pea, Black-Eyed 175
Pea, Sweet 176
Peanut 177
Pepper 179
Potato, Sweet 181
Potato, White 182
Pumpkin 184
Radish 185
Rhubarb 187
Rosemary 188
Rutabaga 189
Sage 191
Salsify 192
Soybean 193
Spinach 194
Spinach, New Zealand 196
Squash 197
Strawberry 198
Tarragon 200
Thyme 201
Tomato 202
Turnip 204
Watermelon 205

Favorite Crops Step by Step 207
   Bean 208
   Cabbage 210
   Corn 214
   Cucumber 218
   Grape 220
   Herbs 224
   Lettuce 228
   Onion 230
   Pepper 234
   Root Crops 237
   Squash 240
   Strawberry 243
   Tomato 248
   Tree Fruit 254

Glossary of Gardening Terms 263

Planting Dates for 68 Eatables 269

Personal Gardening Calendar 282

Index 283

Why Grow Eatables?

A garden is a perfect place to show your individuality. It is your garden, those are your plants (and your weeds), and the feelings of excitement, creativity, and power that you have when gardening are very real. What is more practical and rewarding than growing something good to eat? Or learning to like something you didn't like before because you grew it yourself?

In this book "eatables" include vegetables, fruits, herbs, weeds, and other plants that produce parts or wholes you can eat. If you are a gourmet, growing your own special eatables is sometimes the only way you can find the flavor, appearance, or combinations that you want. This often takes some effort; the rewards are usually in proportion to the labor. But the hard work can seem insignificant when you contemplate the results, and working close to the ground in the sun and fresh air is by far the best kind of labor there is. It is fun to dig into the earth with your bare hands, getting soil under your fingernails and into your shoes before the eatables go into your mouth.

The gardening experience may turn the whole family into fruit and vegetable connoisseurs. A fresh sprig of green from the garden can make a world of difference in that tiresome lunch box or that diet salad. The "not another casserole" reaction at the dinner table can change to anticipation, especially if everyone in the family has helped grow the ingredients.

One of the beauties of growing your own eatables is that you can grow only what you need and harvest it as you need it. You don't have to buy a whole box or basket and then wonder what you will do with the rest. Don't let the lack of a big outside plot stop you from growing your own eatables. You can use hanging containers, window boxes, roofs, terraces, and all kinds of unconventional containers — fixed, movable, or in-between. You can even grow eatables indoors, with or without artificial lights. You will harvest the satisfaction — both spiritual and gustatory — that only your own home grown eatables can give.

This book explains practical gardening to beginners and reminds seasoned gardeners of some tips they may have forgotten. In gardening, it is a good idea to plan before you plant, and then make haste slowly. Do your own thing and do not let anyone try to stop you. If it is what you want, and if it works, then go ahead. If it does not work, then you have learned something and you can continue from there. While there are some useful rules to follow, there is also plenty of room for experimentation. Remember, too, that the results are often in the hands of the fates in the form of rabbits, raccoons, or small people on tricycles. There are such things as partial failures and almost successes. Plant growers belong to a secret society whose members always expect the worst, but hope for the best. Keep cheerful, keep your eyes and ears open, and keep your growing records up to date.

Plant people are always happy to share information, plants and the final product. They are found next door, down the street, at a garden center or on the family tree. Unusually knowledgeable plant people can be found at your local Cooperative Extension Service. Extension services are the best source for information on varieties that do best in your area, what is attacking your eatables and what to do about it.

Growing something to eat teaches you more than just the growth pattern of the plants and the nearby weeds and insects. You also begin to ask questions about where the plant comes from, how it grows, what happens to the light, water, and food. There are fascinating interrelationships in nature that will show you new ways of looking at things. Experiment, have fun, and ask yourself, "How does that plant fold itself up in that seed?"

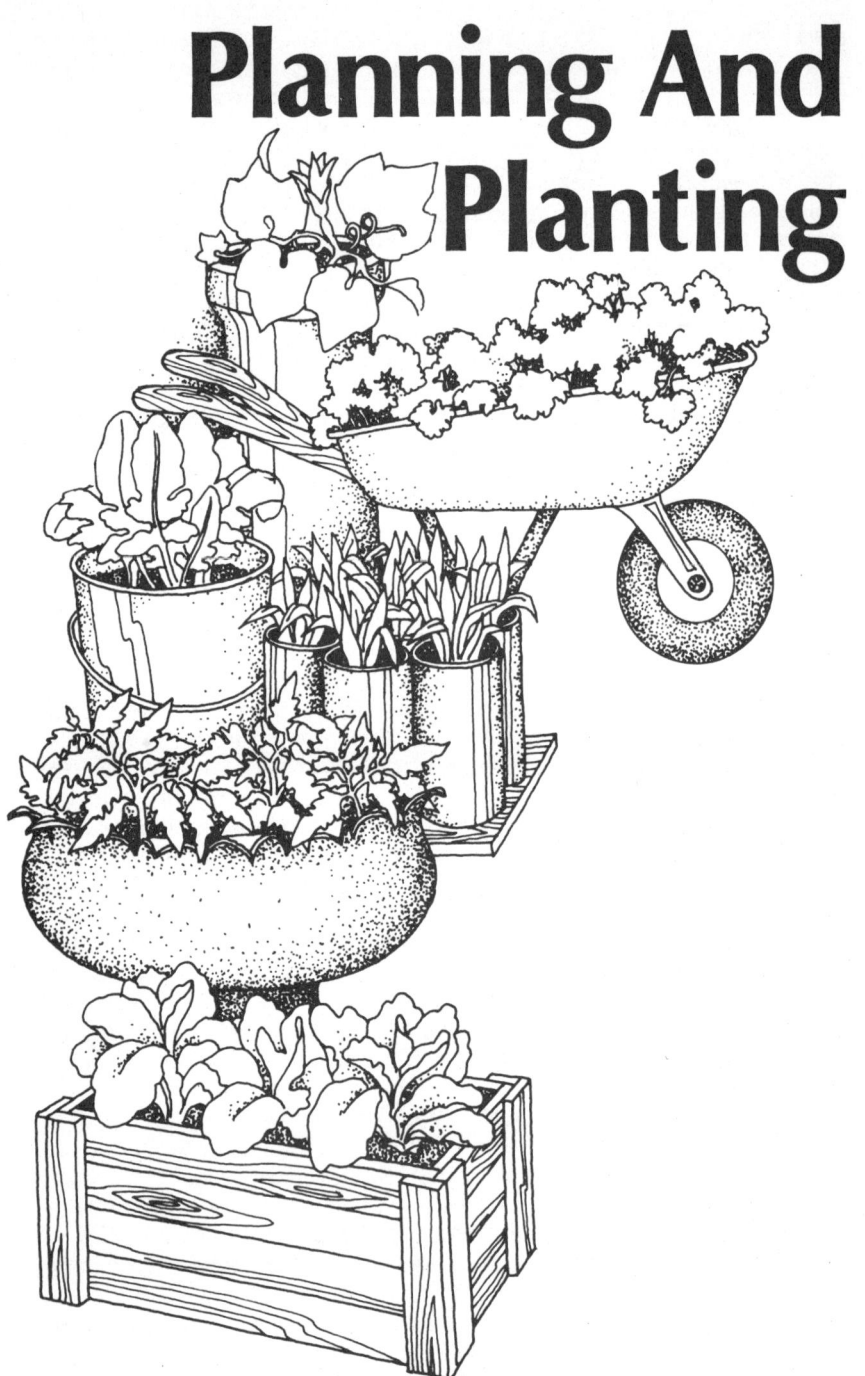

Planning

Successful gardening begins with good planning. Planning on paper may not seem as exciting as getting outdoors on a balmy spring day to work in the soil. But if you put off planning until that balmy spring day, you may well spend the rest of the growing season struggling to correct the mistakes you made at the start. It is a whole lot easier to erase a line on a piece of paper than to move a garden bed. Besides, from the more positive point of view, good planning can help you make more efficient use of your time and gardening area and result in bigger, better harvests.

Start by taking an inventory. What you like to eat is probably most important, so make out a list of your favorite eatables and then check out how many of them you can grow given the space you have available and the length of your growing season. Sometimes by persistence and craft you can squeeze in more plants or use places that are not quite prime. Sun will be a vital consideration since light is necessary for most things to grow. A spot that receives six or more hours of sun each day is to be cherished. Your garden should be conveniently located, too. A small spot in the backyard or on the roof may be much more productive than an acre several miles away that has no water spigot. In fact, unless you are a confirmed gardening addict, it is better to start small, have a fun time and great success, and leave everyone wanting more. Build up your gardening skills by degrees.

This section will give you the overall picture of the what, when, where, why and how of planning and planting. See the sections in this book entitled "Catalog of Eatables" and "Favorite Crops Step by Step" for guidance on the specific cultural requirements of a wide variety of popular eatables. The section "Rating the Eatables" will also be of help as you make your decisions about what to plant.

When to Plant

Learning to pace yourself is a vital part of growing eatables. Generally, you plan in the winter, plant in the spring, protect or replant in the summer, and pick, eat or preserve in the fall. The outdoor growing season runs from the last freeze in the spring to the first freeze in the fall. Of course, in some parts of the country there never is a frost and it is possible to keep your garden growing all year long. If you live in a frost-free area you may either have to use the dry season as your rest period, or use your better judgment and take a vacation.

Those who live in less moderate climates will have to wait until the soil is thawed and dry to start their planting. Tough plants can survive the cold, but they will not grow until the weather warms up.

Personal Gardening Calendar

SAMPLE GARDENING CALENDAR (Use this calendar as a guide when filling out blank calendar.)	MARCH	APRIL	MAY	JUNE	JULY	AUGUST	SEPTEMBER	OCTOBER	NOVEMBER	DECEMBER	JANUARY	FEBRUARY
Start of growing season (average date of last spring freeze)			5/15									
End of growing season (average date of first fall freeze)								10/15				
Length of growing season			←———	———	154 days	———	———	→				
Start hardy plants indoors (7 weeks before date to set out)	3/6											
Start tender plants indoors (7 weeks before date to set out)		4/3										
Plant hardy plants and seeds outdoors (2 weeks before average date of last spring freeze)			5/1									
Plant tender plants and seeds outdoors (2 weeks after average date of last spring freeze)			5/29									
Clean up garden									↕			
Plan next year's garden, order seeds	←									↓	↑	
Leave garden for vacation												

Nothing is gained by getting out and working in the cold, except an excessive show of moral fiber. If you plant while the soil is wet it will be as hard as a brick when it dries; very few young plants have the strength of character to push their way through brick.

The date to sow seeds depends on the hardiness of the plants, the date of the last spring freeze, your willingness to modify your environment, and your gambling instinct. Gamblers can take a chance and plant two to three weeks ahead of the date of the last killing frost, or plant so that the plants will mature after the first frost expected in the fall. You may beat the odds, but remember that if you plant 14 days before the average date of the last spring freeze you stand a 90 percent chance of being frozen out. If you plant 14 days after that date there is only a 10 percent chance — and the planting weather is much more pleasant. When seeds are put in the cold, cold ground they often sulk, rot or get eaten by hungry birds.

With a little planning you can pace yourself so that you can work indoors until planting outdoors will produce results. The first step is to get all the facts for your particular situation. Remember there are a number of ways that a climate can be modified — even in one's own yard. Why not do your homework now for once and for all, save time for years to come — and get better odds on your returns?

As a permanent aid to planting, fill out the blank year-round planning calendar at the back of this book. The completed calendar here will show you how. Get the average dates of the last spring freeze and the first fall freeze from your local library or weather bureau. The number of days between these two dates will give you the average length of the growing season in your area. The season for hardy crops starts approximately two weeks before the last spring freeze and ends two weeks after the first fall freeze; the season for tender crops begins two weeks after the last spring freeze and ends two weeks before the first fall freeze. For more specific information about when to plant different crops in your area, see "Planting Dates for 68 Eatables".

Deciding when to plant involves more than avoiding killing frosts. It also means pacing your planting so that you get maximum yields from limited space. You can harvest some crops gradually, enjoying them for a long period of time; others mature all at once. This takes careful planning. You'll have to have a good idea of how long it will take your eatables to mature and how long the harvest will last. It will also take some self-control. The temptation to plant full rows of everything at once is great.

A simple way to pace your harvest is to plant only short rows or partial rows. Planting short rows is probably easier; we often feel more comfortable with a complete row, even if it is short. Still, you'll have to use your judgment to decide what is short. A 10-foot row looks short, but 10 feet of radishes ready to eat at the same time is more than most folks want. Ten feet of parsley or garlic may be more than enough for

EARLY SPRING PLANTING		LATER SPRING OR EARLY SUMMER PLANTING		LATE SUMMER OR FALL PLANTING
Very hardy: plant 4 to 6 weeks before average frost-free date.	**Hardy:** plant 2 to 4 weeks before average frost-free date.	**Not cold-hardy:** plant on frost-free date.	**Tender:** needs hot weather	**Heat tolerant**	**Hardy**
Asparagus	Artichoke, Jerusalem	Artichoke, Globe	Bean, Four-Angled	Bean, Snap	Beet
Broccoli	Beet	Basil	Bean, Lima	Cabbage, Chinese	Collard
Broad Bean	Carrot	Bean, Mung	Cucumber	Chard	Kale
Brussels Sprout	Cauliflower	Bean, Snap	Eggplant	Corn	Lettuce
Cabbage	Celeriac	Chayote	Muskmelon	Spinach, New Zealand	Mustard
Chive	Celery	Corn	Pepper	Squash	Spinach
Collard	Chard	Marjoram	Potato, Sweet		Turnip
Endive	Chicory	Okra	Watermelon		
Garlic	* Corn	Pea, Black-Eyed			
Grape	Cress	Peanut			
Horseradish	Dill	Pumpkin			
Kale	Fennel	Soybean			
Kohlrabi	Mustard	Spinach, New Zealand			
Leek	Parsnip	Squash			
Lettuce	Potato, White	Tomato			
Onion	Radish				
Parsley	Rosemary				
Pea, Sweet					
Rhubarb					
Rutabaga					
Sage					
Salsify					
Spinach					
Strawberry					
Tarragon					
Thyme					
Tree Fruit					

*Not completely hardy; some early plantings may be hurt by frost.

the whole neighborhood. You can freeze parsley and dry the garlic, but what can you do with all those radishes: Unwanted excesses of crops can be avoided if you divide up your seeds before going out to plant. Put them in "budget" envelopes to be planted on definite dates later on in the season but before the early crops are harvested. This way you can have eatables all season, rather than glut followed by famine.

With careful planning you may be able to get two or three harvests from the same spot. This is called succession cropping. After early-maturing crops are harvested, their portion of the bed is cleared and replanted with a new crop. Companion cropping is another way to double up on growing eatables. You can do this by planting short-term crops between plants that will take a longer time to mature. The short-term plants are harvested by the time the longer-season crops need the extra room.

Where to Plant

Since many of us do not have much choice, we have to make the best of any potential garden plot. Often the best spot is where the grass is thriving. Eatables can be grown in the backyard, in the front yard, and even in the parkway between the sidewalk and the street. (Parkway planting works best when you are on good terms with your neighbors and your neighbors' dogs.)

As you are deciding where to plant, sun will be a vital consideration since light is necessary for the growth of good eatables. A spot that receives six or more hours of sun each day is to be cherished. In the city and on small lots, try to avoid the shade from buildings and large trees. Besides blocking out sun from your garden bed, large trees will compete for the available soil nutrients and moisture. Remember that a tree's root system can often reach beyond the span of its branches.

Once you have found your spot in the sun, get it down on paper. Take measurements in all directions and make sure you indicate the non-growing areas — the trees and shrubs, sidewalks, garages, swing sets, and any obvious foot-traffic patterns. After you have eliminated all those non-growing areas and have an idea of the sunlight conditions, you can start fiddling with the shape of the beds. Beds do not have to be rectangular; they can be any shape at all. Gardening is easier, however, if the beds have a definite edge so you can tell where the eatables stop and the weeds begin.

If you can manage it, position the tall-growing plants on the north and northeast side of the garden so that as they grow they will not shade the rest of the bed. Rows are important if you are going to use a tractor, a plow or a people-pushed cultivator. But if the space is small you can often eliminate the rows and grow eatables in solid four- to five-foot wide blocks. The width should be determined by the distance you can comfortably reach as long as you can get to it from all sides.

Soil is important to the growing of eatables, but good drainage is crucial. Measures must be taken to ensure that moisture neither drains away too quickly nor stands in the bed too long. In this respect, living on a cement slab or on a rock ledge presents a real challenge to the gardener; it may be easier to grow eatables in raised beds or containers since shallow beds do not drain properly and plants may either dry up or drown. In a small space, they look good and are easier to tend, perhaps because when they start to look ratty it is harder to walk by and ignore them, so they get more attention.

In a very small, easy-to-care-for space, container-grown lettuces, tomatoes, and radishes can add a creative touch to your landscape as well as your salads — and feed your ego, too. In small spaces you can also use handy 2x2-foot or 3x3-foot modules. In a 3x3-foot space you can grow one of the following groups:

- 1 tomato with an edging of herbs, lettuces or radishes
- 4 eggplants
- 9 heads of lettuce
- 15 leaf lettuces
- 64 beets
- 144 radishes

Any creative combination of plants with similar growing requirements or seasons is possible.

What to Plant — Seeds or Transplants

Whether you start plants from seeds yourself or adopt plants already started by someone else is often a matter of personal choice. To help you make this decision, here are some of the advantages and disadvantages of each method.

SEEDS	TRANSPLANTS
Less expensive.	More expensive.
Greater number of varieties available.	Fewer varieties available.
May be less adapted to your area.	Suited to your area.
More kinds of vegetables.	Fewer kinds.
Take longer to grow.	Instant garden, earlier harvest.
More plants than you can use.	Get the exact number you need.
Sometimes they do not come up, or they die young.	You know what you have.

Indoors, seeds can be messy and difficult.

Indoors, less mess and better results, especially if space is small and light and cultural conditions are not good. (Playing Bach will not compensate for not enough light and too much heat.)

In addition to the above pros and cons for starting eatables from plants or seeds, the flexibility of the plant itself should be considered. Some plants easily survive transplanting. Beets, broccoli, Brussels sprouts, cabbage, cauliflower, chard, lettuce, and tomatoes are among those plants which make the adjustment without much difficulty. Carrots, celery, eggplant, onions, and peppers are among the less tolerant. They require care in transplanting. Some other eatables, especially those with large seeds, do much better when planted where they are to grow after the soil has warmed up. Among these are beans, corn, cucumbers and peas. They are not successfully transplanted by the usual methods. If you start them indoors, use individual containers that can be planted along with them so their roots systems will not be disturbed.

Starting from Seeds

Many eatables are started from seeds directly where they are going to grow. Others are bought as transplants or started in a "nursery" outdoors and then transplanted. In this way the plants can get more careful attention when they are young. Another way is to grow the plants indoors in containers or flats.

Many people find growing their own transplants can be a satisfying, challenging activity that can save money and provide kinds and varieties that are unavailable at the local garden centers or nurseries. On the other hand, people who want just a few plants, are just starting out in the gardening business, have limited growing space or cannot provide a good environment for growth will prefer to have someone else do the preliminary growing for those plants that should have a head start because of the shortness of the growing season.

Getting Started

Timing is very important. Seeds should not be started too early. This is as true indoors as outdoors. Started too early, plants will get long and stringy and do poorly when they are finally planted outdoors.

Decide when your eatables should be planted out and then set your indoor planting date no more than six to eight weeks ahead of that date. This will give those plants that are going to be transplanted outdoors a long enough head start.

When the right time for planting your seeds rolls around, here's how you go about it.

1. Small numbers of seeds can be started in pots, flats (the low-sided plastic or wooden boxes that greenhouses use), styrofoam cups, or cut-off milk cartons. If you are starting plants that are fussy about transplanting, start them in individual containers from the very beginning. Use styrofoam cups, peat pots or expanded peat pellets. Containers used for starting seedlings should have drainage holes to keep the soil from getting soggy and to allow watering from below once the seeds are planted. Clean your containers thoroughly to reduce the odds of attack by pests and diseases. A good scrubbing should be followed by a disinfecting session. A couple of days in strong sun will do it. Or you can wet or submerge the clean-scrubbed container in a solution of three tablespoons bleach to one quart of water. Leave the bleach liquid on for five minutes and then rinse with clean water.

2. Fill the container with potting mix. Because of the problems with diseases killing off young sprouts (damping off), an artificial mix is the best choice for starting seeds. These mixes are light, easy to handle, and sterile. Some of them come pre-fertilized so that young plants can continue in them for quite some time.

3. Press the potting medium down firmly and water thoroughly. Let the excess water drain away before seeding.

4. To plant seeds in a flat, mark the rows and then distribute the seeds along the rows as evenly as possible. If you are using a separate container for each kind of seed, you can just sprinkle them evenly on the surface.

5. Before you go on to the next variety of seed, you will save yourself a lot of work in the long run if you label each row or container with the plant name and date. Good labels can be made from the plastic trays that produce and meat are packed in. If you press hard enough, the pencil or marking pen won't fade.

6. Unless the seed is very tiny, cover it lightly with sifted sphagnum moss. Mist gently and cover the container with a sheet of plastic wrap. If the wrap is pulled flat across, the "rain" of condensation will fall more evenly on the seed bed. Watch carefully that the system does not become too wet. If it looks too moist, punch a few more holes in the bottom of the container and lift the plastic up from time to time.

7. Since most seeds germinate best at a temperature that is higher than their growing temperature, place the containers in a warm spot. Give bright but not direct sunlight until seedlings get growing.

Different seeds do not germinate in the same amount of time. If

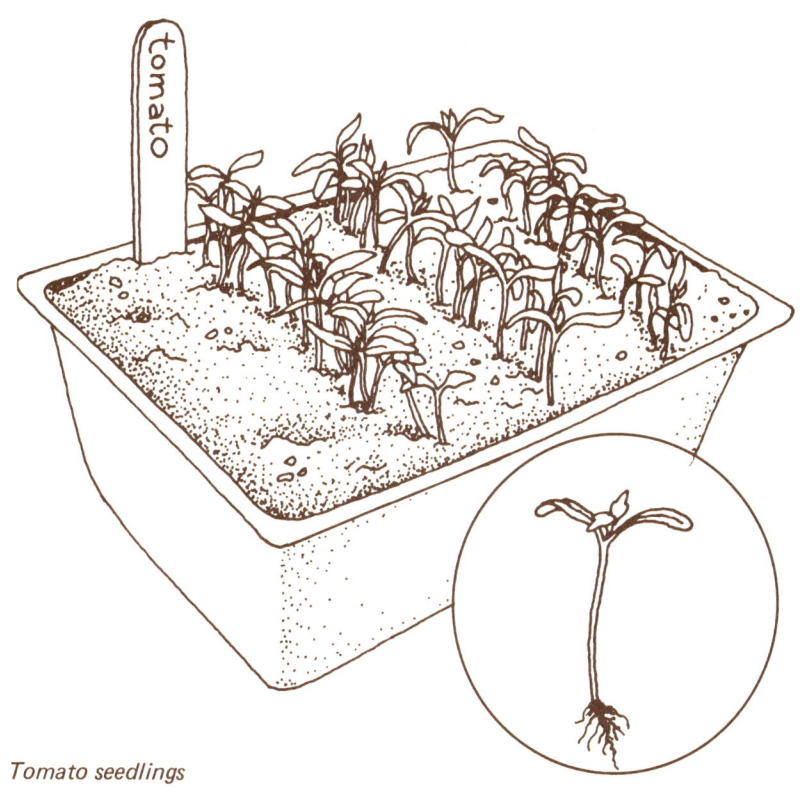

Tomato seedlings

you are planning to start several different kinds of seed together in one flat, it is easier if they all have about the same germination time. Once the plants germinate, it will not be long before they have used up all the energy stored in their seeds and they will have to start growing on their own. This is a very important stage in an eatable's life and what you do in these few critical days can make a big difference in the final product. It is of primary importance that the seedlings do not dry out. Also, once they've gotten started, many will grow better if the temperature is decreased from germinating temperature and the light is improved.

First Transplanting

Seedlings will be ready for their first transplanting when they have developed a couple of true leaves. The true leaves are not the first leaves, but the ones which come a little later and look different from the first leaves. But don't let the seedlings go too long before trans-

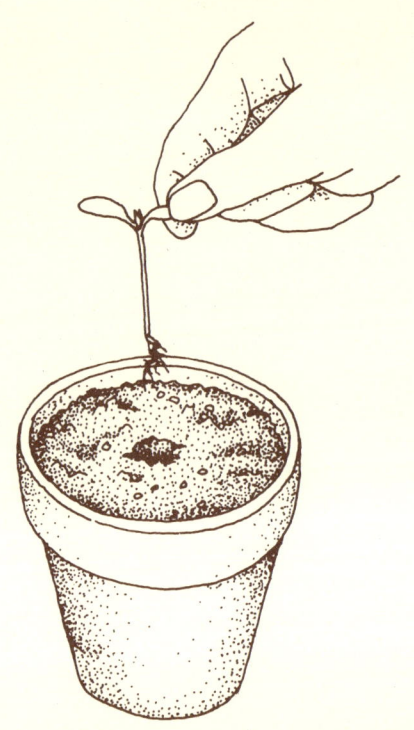

First transplant

planting them. They do better and get over the shock faster if they are transplanted when small.

At this transplanting, seedlings can be moved into individual pots or flats filled with potting mix or soil, depending on your preference. Unless you have room for all kinds of stuff, it is easier to keep using the mix. Prepare the containers as you did for seeding. Then gently lift the fattest, most charismatic seedlings out of the seedbed. Lift them from the bottom with a knife, spatula or stick. Control the selection and placement by holding the seedlings by their leaves. This avoids permanent damage to the stems. Poke a hole in the new potting material deep enough to accept the roots without crowding. Drop the seedling's roots into the hole and press the soil around them. Water the newly planted seedlings carefully to get rid of air pockets and to ensure that the roots will not dry out. Then label the seedlings carefully. This labeling may seem like a bother but cabbage, cauliflower, collards, and kohlrabi look alike when they are young and hot peppers and sweet peppers look a lot alike until they start to bloom.

Planting

Now that you have your plot, your plan and your plants, what next? Mark the rough boundaries of the space you are going to plant. If you can, dig up all the soil for eight to 12 inches, removing all the stones, trash, and hidden treasure. This is a good time to dig in organic matter if needed. Organic matter makes a better bed by improving the drainage, moisture retention, aeration — in short, it makes it easier for the plants to grow.

If the soil has been tested and is very acid, add lime, but do not over do it since eatables prefer growing in a slightly acid soil. Manures or slow release fertilizers can be worked into the top few inches of the soil. Fast release fertilizers should be applied a week or two before planting or applied carefully around the plants after they have been planted to avoid injury. Rake the area smooth, getting rid of the big lumps, small rocks, and miscellaneous roots. Level it off with the back of your rake.

If you are going to have rows, keep them straight. To mark them use a heavy string. Tie it to one end of a stake. Plant the stake in the ground, pull the string tight to the other end of the plot, and wrap it tightly around another stake. Then take a stick, your finger or the handle of your rake or hoe and draw a line on the soil under the string. If you have long rows you can "pin the line" with a rake or tools at

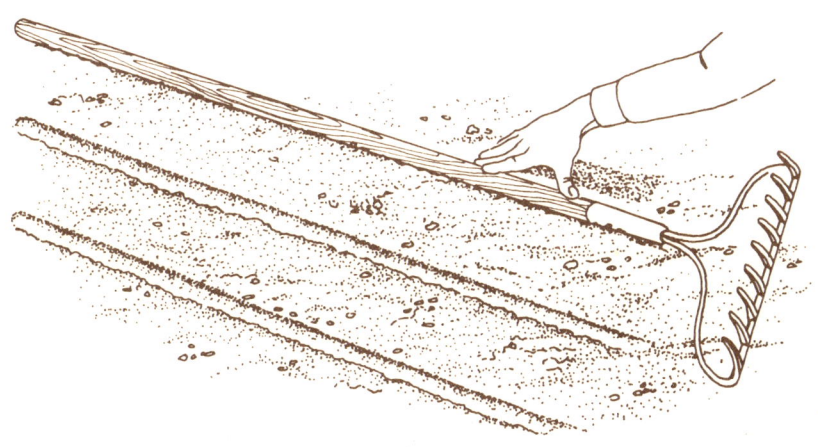

Lay a rake on cultivated soil to mark rows

several points along its length to keep it from curving out. If you are making short rows you can sometimes just use the handle of the rake or hoe and lay it down in the soft soil to mark the row.

Planting Seeds Outdoors

In planting seeds, use whatever arrangement is most convenient for you and your plants. Seeds can be planted in single file (rows), in groups or bands (broadcast), or in circles (hills). Hills are often used with vine crops to keep their roots in one place for cultivation and watering while giving the plants plenty of room to spread out.

Do not bury the seeds. They need only enough soil to cover them and supply even moisture for germination. They can be planted deeper if the weather is uncertain or if the plant will need a firm anchorage when starting out. In small areas, sprinkle the seeds with soil so they are covered up to four times their smallest diameter and then keep the ground moist but not wet. Fine seed can just be pressed into the soil's surface.

Planting Transplants

When the plants are ready to go out into the world it is considered crude to just take them out of the house and plant them in the ground. Hardening is the ritual of getting the plants used to the outdoors by stages. Not only is it more polite, but it helps produce stronger, sturdier plants. This can be done two ways. First by taking the plants out during the day and bringing them back in at night (keep them in their containers, though), or by putting them outside in a protected place, like a cold frame or a large box, and covered with a rug or blanket at

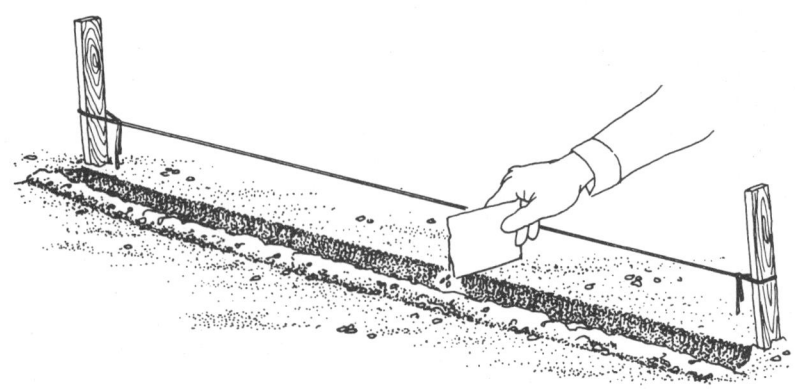

Keep rows straight by tying a heavy string between stakes

Boards can protect young plants from hot sunshine

Remove both ends from a 2 lb. coffee can to create a cold weather protector

night. If you are buying your transplants from a greenhouse ask them if they have been hardened to the rigors of outdoor life. If they haven't, follow the same procedure with them.

When the time has come for them to go outdoors permanently, arrange transplants on the bed's surface so you can see the way they will look. Then dig a hole under each one of them as they are planted. Plants growing in clay or plastic pots should be slipped carefully out of their containers. If they do not pop out easily, take a knife and slide it carefully around the inside. Remove the plant as gently as you would a cake. Be careful not to bruise the stem since that can result in permanent damage. Some people think it's safer to always handle transplants by their leaves. If you are going to be using stakes, consider planting them with the plant they will support since you do not want to stab the darling's best roots later on.

Spacing

Although the distance between rows can be compressed, in a small garden squeezing plants too close together may mean very poor crops or no crops at all. Beets and carrots need enough room for their hips, and cabbages and head lettuce need room for their heads.

When you are thinning the seedlings or planting transplants, space them far enough apart to get the results you want — plus a little extra to cut down on the claustrophobia. The description in this book of each individual eatable will give you an idea of how closely you can squeeze the plants together, but check the descriptions in seed catalogs for the particular variety that you plant.

Some perennial eatables can stay in the same spot year after year, so give them a permanent location and reserve the space for them.

After Planting

The weather and other circumstances can frustrate even the most carefully calculated planning and planting programs. It is important to keep your cool and your sense of humor and just do what you can to help your eatables through the tough times.

If the sun is hot, provide the young plants with shade — a board, a basket or even a paper hat. If the nights are cold, cover each plant with a gallon plastic jug with the bottom removed, or a two pound coffee can minus its top and bottom. The jugs should be removed during the day, but the cans can stay until the weather improves. Protection against birds and other pests can be provided by nets or by screens stapled to frames or stakes. Until the plants are established, watering is crucial because their roots are not ready to find water on their own.

Bottomless plastic jugs make good insulators against cold night temperatures

Record Keeping

If you are serious about gardening, record keeping is a must. Planning your records should be part of planning your garden. The better the planning, the more efficient the use of your time, and the more time you will have for enjoying the eatables you grow. Build your records the same way you build your garden: profit from past mistakes and incorporate new priorities and plants.

Start out with a ledger that has sewn-in pages. Do not write notes on slips of paper and expect to be able to find the one you want when you want it. Do not use a 3-ring notebook because if you can take a page out you will — and then you may not be able to find it again. Your first entry in your record of eatables probably should be the garden you plotted out when you ordered the seeds. Mark this page with a paper clip so you can easily find it.

After the garden plot, you can keep a daily record of preparing the soil, planting, weeding, fertilizing, growing results (or lack of results), whether the harvest of each item was sufficient, too much, or not enough, and problems with weeds, bugs, and lack of rain. What you will have at the end of the growing season is a record of what you did (and a record can be good for the morale). Your record will list the plants that did well in your garden or did not do well and you will have the basis for planning next year's garden. Include in your ledger comments about the weather, varieties of plants that were productive or flopped, and notes about why you think some plants made it and others did not.

27

Extending Your Garden

Extending Garden Space

Where garden space is limited or where there is no garden space at all, eatables can be grown in almost anything that will hold soil and drain adequately. Of course plant stores, garden centers and large mail-order houses offer large assortments of ready-to-plant containers. But you probably have around the house all kinds of things that can be recycled into planting containers. Tin cans, old washtubs, plastic bottles, peach baskets (though these rot out very quickly), old tires, sewer pipe, plastic bags, poultry wire, pantyhose, and even little red wagons are a few of the possibilities.

Perhaps the easiest container you can make is the plastic bag of potting soil, just as you buy it, poked with a few holes for drainage and then hung or placed in a good location. These containers are especially attractive to those people who have portraits of large tomato soup cans in their living rooms. Water the soil well before you put in the eatables.

Old dresser drawers, champagne cases and boxes you make yourself are great. A container that is three by four feet wide and eight to ten inches deep will grow most leaf and root crops, especially if you select the smaller varieties. You can make a large, 4x4-foot planter out of one sheet of A-D half-inch exterior plywood. Have the lumber yard cut it for you and then all you have to do when you get home is nail it together. Just provide enough drainage. Recycled nylons work well as screening to let the water escape while keeping the soil from leaking out.

Hanging containers can add another dimension to growing eatables, both indoors and out. Commercial containers have built-in saucers to catch the water run-off and prevent drips and splashes on your floor or patio. If you are creating your own container, be sure to double pot (put one pot inside another) or add your own saucer to catch the run-off at watering time.

Whether you buy or make your container, be sure to consider where it will go. Is the floor, stand, bracket, or hook going to be able to hold the container when it is filled with soil, plants, and water? A cubic foot of water weighs about 64 pounds, or approximately eight pounds per gallon. It is an unconfined mess when the hanging garden comes crashing down all over the floor the first time you water it. If the container is going to sit outdoors somewhere, be sure that it is heavy enough not to blow over in the wind and large enough not to dry out too fast. It is wise to put large, standing containers on casters to make it easier to move the plants into the sun and pull them out into the open. Planting or placing smaller containers in wagons or wheelbarrows accomplishes the same purpose.

Retired tire planter ©1973
Virginia L. Beatty

Tire Planter

When a tired tire stops rolling, it can end its days in beauty. It can be recycled into a container that is inexpensive, works well, and looks good. Placed on soil, pavement, or a balcony, it can protect plants from mowers, bicycles, and small animals. It neither rusts nor wears out, and the insulatory properties of the rubber keep roots cooler in summer and warmer in winter. Here's how to convert a tire on a wheel into a planter.

Mark O's four inches apart around the outer edge and then mark X's halfway between the O's along the inner edge. Draw cutting lines in a zigzag pattern between the O's and X's all the way around the tire. Using a sharp knife, cut along the lines. Then turn the tire over and punch down the center of the tire to turn it inside out. Cover the large hole in the wheel. Use old pantyhose if you want the water to run out; use plastic if you do not. Fill in the bottom of the container with stones,

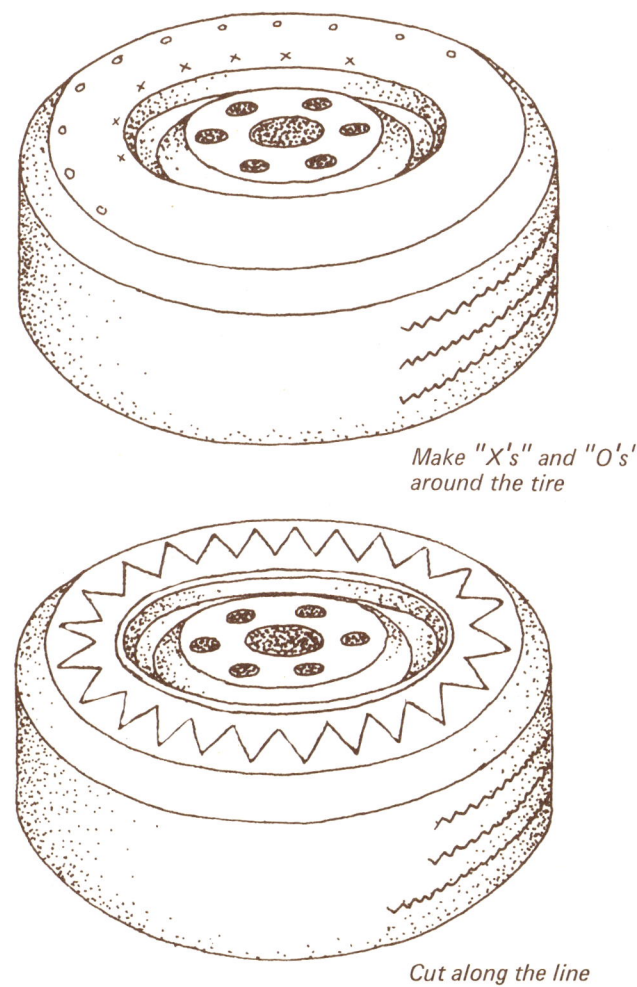

Make "X's" and "O's" around the tire

Cut along the line

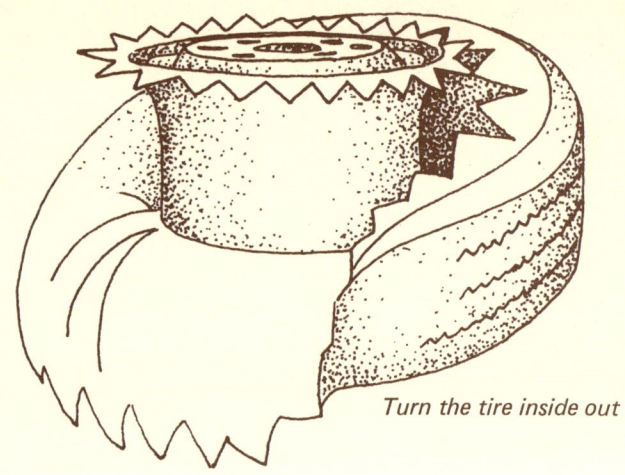
Turn the tire inside out

broken pottery, old nylons or other drainage material. Fill in with soil and plant your eatables.

The same procedure can be used with a tire that is not on a wheel. You will get a planter without a bottom, but you will have an extra decorative piece that can be placed beneath the planter or used as a bumper on a garage wall.

High-Rise Horticulture

On top of a very tall building in one of our country's largest cities, the observant eye looking down from an even taller building can see a small red barn surrounded with green indoor-outdoor carpeting. On three sides of the "lawn" (or putting green), flowers and vegetables are growing in raised beds.

From a pot on a windowsill to a farm in the sky there are a number of ways city people can grow eatables with a flair.

Just like gardening on the ground, gardening on a terrace, balcony, or roof will be more successful if you study your site and plan before you plant. Spend some time on your property. Assess its advantages and its challenges. Containers filled with soil, plants, and water can get pretty heavy. Make sure that your structure can take the stress. How much sunlight do you get? Eatables should get five or six hours of direct sunlight a day. Does the building across the way cut the sun or wind? Or does it reflect or deflect them? Check the wind velocity and direction. On the fifteenth floor you may have to water twice as often as you would on the second floor because of the increased breezes. And while you are looking around, don't forget to look up. If there is a balcony right above, you might consider painting the underside with a light color to create better reflection. A pale blue with white clouds might be nice.

When you have finished studying your site, make a diagram of your property showing your planting plans. Plant to accent the positive, conceal the negative, provide a view, and most important, leave some room for you. Think tall. Use your vertical space, training plants to stand up straight — they may need some support — or hanging them up in containers.

Enjoy yourself but remember that pressures on plants and people are much greater in the city. Make provisions for keeping the water from dripping on the people below. There is a division of opinion about flying saucers, but most everyone objects to flying pots. So make sure your containers are heavy enough not to blow over in the wind, or fasten them to your garden area somehow to keep them where they belong.

After you have your plans and your containers lined up, you'll be ready to get down to the business of planting. Natural soil is hard to find in the middle of town, and most suppliers of "good black dirt" are more used to thinking in truckloads than carloads. Since soil is delivered loose, toting it up fifteen floors can be a real problem. Easier to get and lighter to carry, potting mix comes in convenient packages. It also has the added advantage of not packing as hard as some soils. But why not mix your own? Peat moss and perlite or vermiculite mixed in equal amounts do quite well, particularly if it is fertilized with every watering. Use a complete fertilizer and follow all directions, except dilute it to one-fourth or one-half the strength recommended on the package.

Starting from plants is good for your morale and avoids the frustrations of trying to start them from seed in cramped, inadequate space. Even if you do have a good place for growing plants, ask yourself if you want to use it for messing around with little pots. Since you only need a few plants of each kind, you can have a greater variety if you buy plants. Other advantages to starting with plants are that you don't have to commit yourself so early to what you want to grow and that they instantly give you a garden that satisfies the eye from the very beginning. In addition, more and more seed houses and plant stores are working on eatables scaled for small spaces. These smaller plants require less soil, take up less room, mature faster and are easier to work with in a confined area.

After your garden is planted, be prepared to help nature out. If you do not have insects at your altitude, you may have to pollinate some plants by hand. Use a clean, fat, watercolor brush to transfer pollen. You can help pollinate squash, cucumbers, tomatoes, and peppers by shaking the plants to make the pollen fly.

Extending the Growing Season

Extending the growing season usually means protecting plants from cold. But it can also mean cooling them in very hot weather by shading them or by spraying them with water. Light is another aspect of the growing season that can be extended or altered. Occasionally production can be increased by growing plants under artificial light or by covering the plants with boxes to shorten the day length.

With very little effort you can sometimes add 10 to 15 days to each end of the growing season. Hotcaps, jars, plastic jugs, cardboard boxes, plastic sheeting, old blankets, or newspapers can be used to protect early plantings from the cold and give them a headstart. Used at the end of the season, the same protectors can extend the harvest.

Cold Frames and Hot Frames

If you have the space for it, a cold frame can add an extra dimension to your growing pleasure. It is an ideal place to start hardy annuals and perennials. It is also a good place to put plants in the spring to harden them for the rigors of outdoor life. When you have started eatables, especially the cold-tolerant ones, inside you can move them to a cold frame and give them the benefit of much more light in a protected place. The hardy herbs, radishes, lettuces and other greens can be grown in a cold frame during a good part of the year, even in the North.

Often called a "poor man's greenhouse," a cold frame can be made from scrap lumber and old storm windows. It should not be too deep from front to back or you will have trouble getting plants in and out. Cold frames capture solar heat and if they slant to the south they can take advantage of the greatest amount of sun.

On the days that the sun is bright you may have to give some shading to keep the plants from sunburning or lift the cold frame windows to keep plants from steaming. The temperature inside a cold frame can get 85°F to 95°F when the temperature outside is only 15°F if the sun is bright enough. But on cold nights when the temperature drops below freezing, a cold frame will need some extra protection. An old quilt or blanket under a tarp is a good cover. If you have nothing else, newspapers will do although they are a bit harder to handle.

If a cold frame sounds like something you'd like to try, look around for some turn-of-the-century garden books. These provide excellent step-by-step instructions for building and using cold frames and offer suggestions on how to do all kinds of serious cold-frame growing.

Hot frames are a bit more challenging than cold frames and the opportunities for frustration are multiplied. In hot frames, heat is provided either by manure (the classic system) or by electricity (the modern way). Decomposing cow, horse and mule manure do not work the same way and the heat of decomposition depends on the age, the kinds and amount of litter present. When using manure there are no thermostats or controls, except the gardener's know-how. Electricity is much easier than manure, but a lot more expensive than manure and there is still work for the gardener to do.

If you have a basement window facing south with some space outside you can incorporate it into your hot or cold frame and multiply your gardening fun. It also will provide a basic course in the management of a greenhouse — the next step in gardening addiction.

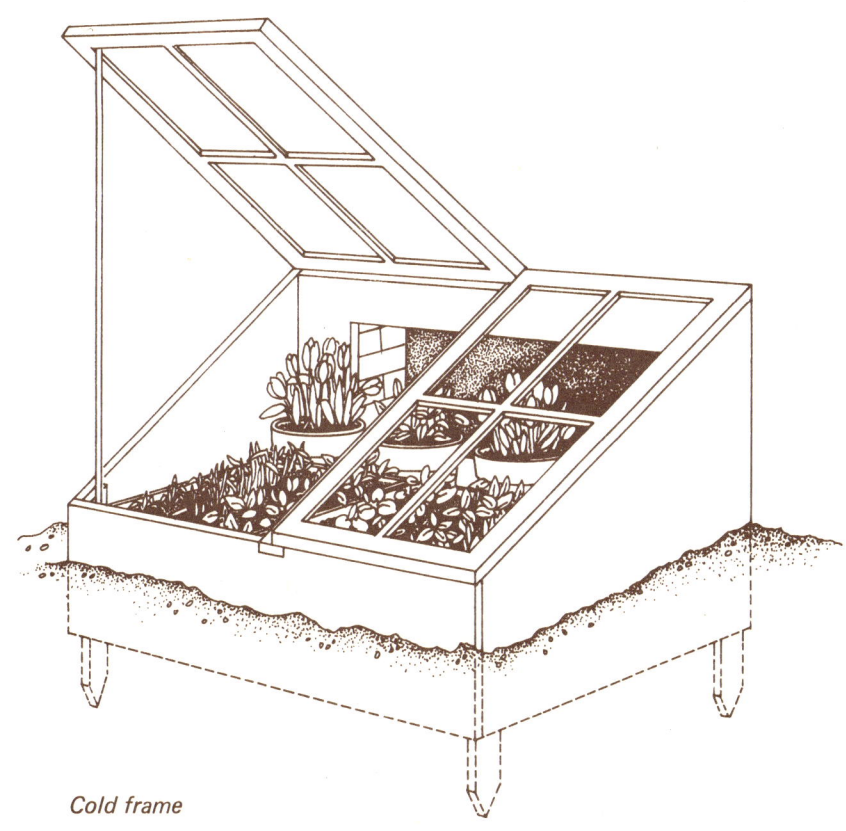

Cold frame

Extending Your Garden Indoors

A number of eatables can be grown successfully indoors. In a bright window that is not too warm, leafy eatables such as lettuce, parsley, and chives will do nicely. Fruiting plants are worth a try but they take a lot more light at a higher intensity. Unless the window available is very bright, the plants may grow but not produce. Cherry tomatoes in hanging baskets will sometimes grow in very bright windows. Sometimes plants can be brought in from outdoors and grown on for several months. Herbs are often rewarding indoor-garden-grown eatables. They go a long way in adding your personal touch to everyday eating. If you have sources for buying herb plants in the wintertime, the project will be easier than if you start from seed. By adopting plants you avoid the trauma of their early weeks.

Under Lights

If you have lights or if you have a place for putting lights, you can have fun growing eatables indoors without any sun at all. Lettuce does beautifully in the basement or the attic when grown under fluorescent light. Usually these spots are not as warm as the rest of the house. Lettuce can also be grown in an apartment if you can find a spot where the heating is not as efficient or if you do not mind wearing a sweater. Get a four-foot fixture with four or eight tubes and hang it with chains so that its height can be adjusted. The lights should be four to six inches above the plants. The cool-white 40W tubes do fine with lettuce and are less expensive than some of the special plant lights.

If you are planning to grow lettuce to eating size, the plants will need root space and, although they will grow in six- or eight-inch pots, it is more efficient to use boxes or plastic dishpans (with drainage holes) that are at least six to eight inches deep. For "soil" you can use potting mix, perlite or vermiculite. In the latter case you have a hydroponic situation in which you have to use diluted fertilizer in every watering. When you use soil or enriched soil mix, feeding will not be necessary. If possible water the soil mix from the bottom to make sure it gets thoroughly soaked. Water is important to lettuce. Sometimes it can use two waterings a day. The lights can be kept on around the clock, making your lights last longer since they will not be turned on and off every day. When the lettuce starts getting full, cut off the outside leaves, enjoy and encourage the plant to grow more.

Cucumbers will grow beautifully under artificial light. But just as

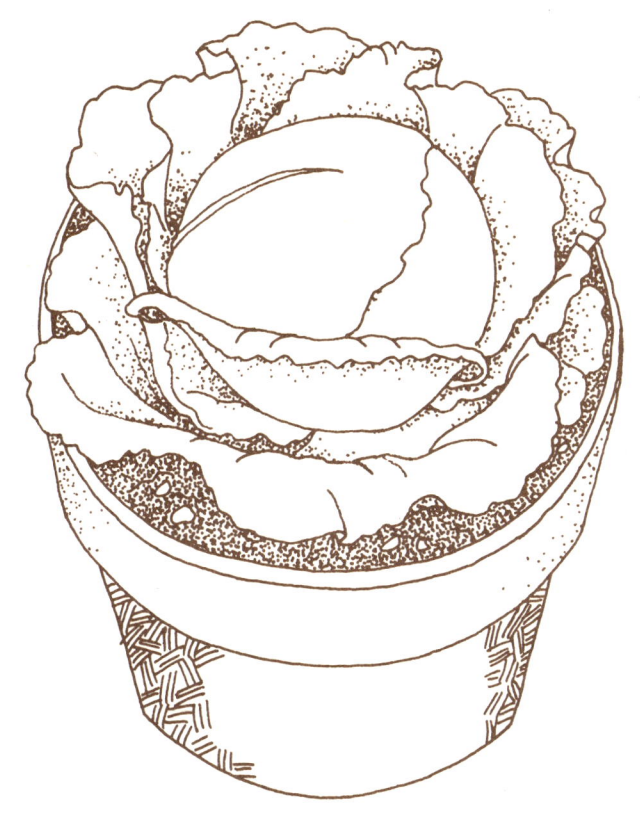

Grow cabbage in a flower pot

long day length will prevent flowering, so will long periods under artificial light. The best thing to do is experiment and find what does well with you. A timer can be useful in giving certain plants a dark resting period.

Given lots of water, water cress works almost as well as lettuce under the lights. Instead of seeds you can start with cuttings (the bottoms of some of those stems of fresh water cress you bought to indulge yourself).

It is fun to tell people in the dead of winter, "I grew this." Also, it costs less and is more practical than any other status activity. For more information on indoor light gardening, talk with a member of the Indoor Light Gardening Society of America, Inc. For information on the closest chapter, write Mrs. James Martin, 423 Powell Drive, Bay Village, Ohio 44140.

In the Dark

Seeds can use their stored-up energy and produce something fresh to eat in a few days. Sprouts are probably the fastest and easiest of all eatables to grow. They are also inexpensive, high in vitamins, trace elements, and protein, low in calories (less than 20 calories per cup).

Seeds for sprouting are available from health food stores, Oriental shops, supermarkets, or by mail. However, do not use seeds that were intended for planting outdoors since often they have been treated with chemicals and may be poisonous when eaten as sprouts.

Mung beans, which provide the bean sprouts for Chinese dishes, are simple to grow. You can also sprout alfalfa, lentils, barley, wheat, rye, pumpkins and soybeans. Generally, the larger the seed the longer the sprouting takes but that is not always the case. Rye and wheat will sprout in two to three days, mung beans take four to five days and alfalfa, which has a tiny seed, takes six to seven days.

In producing sprouts, the most important factors are the viability of the seeds, a moist environment with a temperature between 70°F and 80°F to break dormancy, air, and darkness to keep the sprouts tender and to prevent them from turning green. Once you have found ways to account for these factors, here's how you can turn one-fourth cup dry mung beans into two cups of sprouts:

1. Wash the seeds removing any fluff, rocks or broken bits.
2. Pour a pint of warm water over the dry beans, and let them soak overnight or for 8 to 12 hours.
3. Pour off the water. (Use it in soup; it is full of vitamins and minerals.)
4. Put the seeds in a container where they will stay moist without getting soggy. There are commercial "sprouters," but you can use a clean eight- to ten-inch clay pot, a crock, or a glass quart jar.
5. For the commercial sprouter, follow the instructions that came in the box. For the flowerpot, cover the hole in the bottom with nylon net or a piece of plastic screen. Pour in the seeds, run warm water from the tap through them for 30 seconds, wrap the pot in a damp, clean dish towel, and then put the bundle in a dark place. With a crock or a wide-mouthed glass jar, follow the same procedure, except cover the opening with a piece of net. The net can be held in place by a rubber band.
6. Rinse the sprouts two to three times a day (when the towel dries out) by pouring water through the sprouting seeds. In the flowerpot, the water will go out the bottom. In the crock and jar, the water will have to be poured out the top. Do not let the sprouts sit in water.
7. When they are large enough to eat, enjoy. If you do not care for blond sprouts, bring them out into the light and they will turn green. If there are too many, put the rest in a plastic bag and keep them in the refrigerator. They will last almost a week.

Growing Essentials

Light

Sunlight or some other kind of light provides the energy that turns water and carbon dioxide into the sugar that plants use for food. Green plants use sugars to form new cells, thicken existing cell walls, and develop flowers and fruit. The green plant has to have an excess of stored energy beyond what it needs to grow stems and leaves if it is going to oblige you with flowers and fruit. There may never be any flowers or fruit on a plant if light is limited, even though the plant looks full and green. This can be a problem with tomatoes where you eat the fruit, but it is not a problem with lettuce where you are only interested in the leaves. Still most vegetables are sun lovers and without enough light all the watering, weeding and wishing in the world will not make a bit of difference in the results.

Light Intensity

As you consider your future garden, ask yourself how intensely the sun shines on the garden. The more intense the light, the more effective it is. Light intensity undiminished by obstructions is greater in the summer than in the winter, and greater in areas where days are sunny and bright rather than cloudy, hazy, or foggy. This means that even if your growing space is completely open to the sky, two or three hours of fog each day can cut down on the light intensity. As a general rule, the greater the light intensity the greater the production of sugars by the plants — provided that it is neither too hot nor too cold and the plants have the right amount of water.

If you have a choice of growing spots for your eatables, do not plant them in the shade of buildings, trees or shrubs. Trees and shrubs, in addition to the shade they provide, also have roots that extend for a considerable distance beyond the stretch of their branches. These roots compete for the water and nourishment available. In other words, trees and shrubs can be resident weeds, from your garden's point of view.

Day Length

Many plants including tomatoes and most weeds are indifferent to the day's length, and if the part eaten is not affected by the length of day, do not fret about it. But for many plants the length of day is very important. Generally, more sugar is made on long days than short days, but there are some plants whose flower and fruit production takes place only during short days.

Plants such as radishes and spinach need long days to bloom. This is the main reason that spinach and radishes go to seed so fast in the middle of the summer. If you want to grow radishes or spinach in midsummer and you have been having trouble with them going to seed quickly, try covering the plants with a light-proof box about 4:00 p.m. every afternoon.

Some other plants such as soybeans and corn are short-day plants, and Jerusalem artichokes, which produce flowers on long days, do not start producing tubers until the days become shorter. Many varieties of short-day plants have been bred to resist the effects long days have on them; but most of them will still flower more quickly when they have shorter days.

Partial Shade, Partial Crop

Vegetables grown for their fruits need at least six hours of direct sun each day — sometimes as much as eight to ten hours. Less than full sun often means less than a full crop. Trying to grow tomatoes, peppers or eggplant in the shade is very frustrating. They will often produce a good green plant without giving you anything to eat. However, in partial or light shade you can produce satisfactory crops of eatables that are grown for their roots and leaves. Root crops such as beets, carrots, radishes and turnips are plants that store up energy before producing flowers and they do rather well in partial shade — especially if you do not compare them with a crop growing in full sun. Plants grown for their leaves are the most tolerant of light shade and in fact, where the sun is very hot and bright, such plants as lettuce and spinach may need some shade for protection. A few eatables, such as bean sprouts can be produced without light.

Finding Light

A vegetable garden does not have to be grown in one large block. The sun lovers can be separated and grown in the sun-drenched spots they crave. They can be mixed in a flower border, grown in the front yard or even grown as a decorative element in the parkway. If the sunny spots move about during the day, eatables can be grown in containers on wheels that can be trundled about to follow the sun. The sun can be deflected or reflected by means of mirrors or aluminum foil arranged to catch and concentrate as much of the sun's energy as possible. Artificial light can be used in small areas outside and indoors to extend day length. Indoors plants can be grown completely under artificial light.

Available light can sometimes be increased by thinning out the branches of trees and shrubs. This can present a hard choice when you also want that same tree to provide cooling shade for the house. One way that tree lovers can solve this dilemma is to grow the eatables on the roof. If you consider the top level method, check first to make sure that your roof is sturdy enough to support the containers, the soil, the plants, the water and you. Also, the project is much more successful if you do not have to clutch a bucket of water while trying to climb up a ladder and through a trapdoor. In these situations, the plants will have enough light but will die of thirst because the water carrier is in traction. A real plus to roof gardening is the general absence of rabbits, raccoons and other vegetable-loving transients. Pigeons and people are still problems — both are always delighted to find eatables in an unexpected location. "Is this really a tomato?" people will say as they break it off the vine for a closer examination. Or, "You really are growing radishes here," they exclaim while pulling up a few to make sure they all have the proper parts.

Temperature

Temperatures, both high and low, can be very important in growing eatables. They affect growth, flowering, pollination, and the development of fruit. If the temperatures are not right, plants may flower prematurely or go to seed without providing you with something to eat. Generally between 40°F and 85°F the rate of growth is proportionate to temperature with growth increasing at warmer temperatures and slowing down or stopping altogether when temperatures are low. In addition, the temperatures required for seed germination are usually warmer than those for growing.

Eatables have different temperature preferences and tolerances and are usually grouped as cool-season crops and warm-season crops. Cool-season crops are those which must have time to mature before the weather gets too warm or they will wilt and fret. They can be started in warm weather only if there will be a long enough stretch of cool weather in the fall to allow the crop to mature before freezing. Warm-season crops are those which will not tolerate frost. As a matter of fact, if the weather gets too cool they may decide to sulk and not produce. These plants are often larger than cool-season ones. They also have deeper root systems which means they can often go longer between drinks. But even though it is convenient to think of plants as being cool-season or warm-season, there can be considerable differences within each group. Certain cool-season crops, for example, need not only cool temperatures but freezing temperatures and dormancy before they will produce a satisfactory harvest.

Cool-Season Crops		Warm-Season Crops
Apple	Grape	Basil
Artichoke, Globe	Horseradish	Bean, Four-Angled
Artichoke, Jerusalem	Kale	Bean, Lima
Asparagus	Kohlrabi	Bean, Mung
Beet	Leek	Bean, Snap
Broad Bean	Lettuce	Chayote
Broccoli	Mustard	Corn
Brussels Sprout	Onion	Cucumber
Cabbage	Parsley	Eggplant
Cabbage, Chinese	Parsnip	Marjoram
Carrot	Pea, Sweet	Muskmelon
Cauliflower	Potato, White	Okra
Celeriac	Radish	Pea, Black-Eyed
Celery	Rhubarb	Peanut
Chard	Rosemary	Pepper
Chicory	Rutabaga	Potato, Sweet
Chive	Sage	Pumpkin
Collard	Salsify	Soybean
Cress	Spinach	Spinach, New Zaland
Dill	Strawberry	Squash, Summer
Endive	Tarragon	Squash, Winter
Fennel	Thyme	Tomato
Garlic	Tree Fruit	Watermelon
	Turnip	

Water

Some plants are up to 95 percent water. Water is vital for sprouting seeds; plants need water for cell division, cell enlargement and even for holding themselves up. If the cells do not have enough water in them, they collapse like a three-day-old balloon and the result is a wilted plant. Water is essential, along with light and carbon dioxide, to produce the sugars that provide the plant with its energy for growth. It also dissolves fertilizers and carries nutrients to the different parts of the plant.

How Often to Water

Ideally, water for plants comes from rain or other precipitation and from underground sources. In reality supplemental watering from a bucket, watering can or hose is often necessary. (If you have too much rain about all you can do is pray.) How often you water depends on how often it rains, the water-holding capacity of your soil, and how fast water evaporates in your climate. Clay soils hold water very well — sometimes too well. Sandy soils are like a sieve that lets the water run right through. Both kinds of soil can be improved with the addition of organic matter. Organic matter gives clay soils lightness and air, and gives sandy soils something to hold the water. Here are some other factors which may affect how often you need to water your garden:

1. More water evaporates when the temperature is high than when low. Plants can rot if they get too much water in cool weather.

2. More water evaporates when the relative humidity is low.

3. Plants need more water when the days are bright.

4. Wind and air movement will increase the loss of water into the atmosphere.

5. A smooth surface will not retain water as well as one that is well cultivated.

6. Water needs vary with the kind and maturity of the plant. Some vegetable seeds are tolerant of low soil moisture and will sprout in relatively dry soils. These include Brussels sprouts, cabbages, cauliflower, collards, corn, kale, kohlrabi, muskmelon, peppers, radishes, squash (winter and summer), turnips and watermelon. On the other hand, beets, celery and lettuce seeds need very moist soil. Herbs generally do better with less water. Lettuces need lots of water. A large plant that has a lot of leaves and is actively growing uses more water than a young plant or one with small leaves.

7. Sometimes water is not what a wilting plant needs. When plants are growing fast, the leaves sometimes get ahead of the roots' ability to provide them with water. If the day is hot and the plants wilt in the afternoon, do not worry about them. The plants will regain their balance overnight. But, if the plants are drooping early in the morning, water them right away.

8. Mulches cool the roots and cut down on the amount of water needed, increasing the time that plants can go between watering. When the soil dries out, plants slow their growth — or stop growing altogether. A swift, steady growth is important for the best tasting fruits and vegetables. Mulches keep the soil evenly moist so the plants do not stop growing.

How to Water

Rule number one for watering is: Always soak the soil thoroughly. A light sprinkling can often do more harm than no water at all; it stimulates the roots to come to the surface and then they are killed when the sun bakes down on them. Rule number two is: Never water from

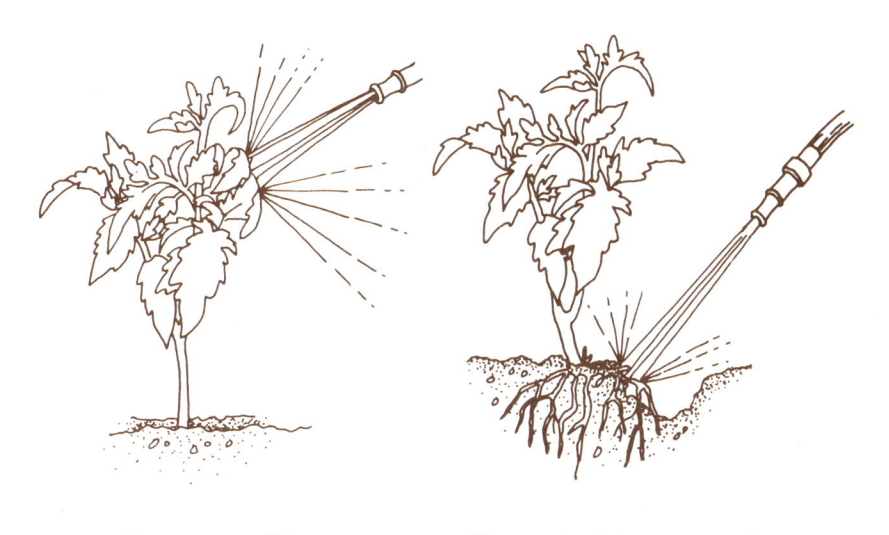

Keep water off leaves

Sharp water jet exposes roots

above. Overhead watering with a sprinkling can or a hose is easy, feels right and looks great "Look Ma, I'm watering!". But overhead watering wastes water, makes a mess and sometimes bounces the water away from the plant so the roots do not get any at all. Furthermore, many diseases are encouraged by wet leaves. So water should be directed at the soil, but do it gently so the soil will not be washed away or the roots exposed.

Carrying water in a can or a bucket can be exhausting and extremely boring, especially if the water slops over the top into your shoes. Watering cans are easier to carry than buckets, but often are harder to fill. They are good to use for gently moistening the soil after planting seeds and for settling dust. If you unscrew the watering can's sprinkler head and replace it with an old sock, it will be easier to concentrate the water at the base of the plant where it is needed. The

A sock on the hose breaks the force of the water

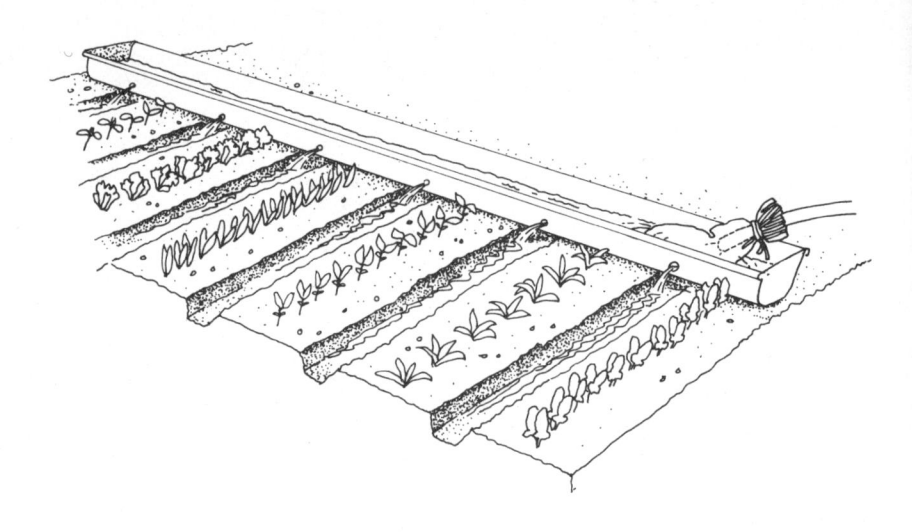

Capped gutter waters several rows at once

sock will break the force of the water and will not disturb the soil around the roots.

A well-placed faucet and hose can save a lot of energy. If you have a large garden, a "Y" connector for the faucet makes it possible to attach two hoses at one time. Hose strategy includes having enough hose to reach all points in the garden and arranging it in such a way that it does not decapitate plants when you move it around.

If there is a lot of watering to do, a 5/8-inch hose will carry twice as much water in the same amount of time as a 1/2-inch hose. Spreading the water about can be sped up by using basins to catch the water, and by digging furrows or trenches between the plants. A length of gutter with capped ends (placed on the higher side of the garden) can be punctured at the trench intervals. Then, when water is slowly added to the gutter it flows down all the trenches at the same time. If you want to change the placement of the holes, the unneeded ones can either be soldered up or filled by putting a metal screw in the hole — if the holes are not too large.

Lawn sprinklers are gentle, but they waste water by covering the whole area indiscriminately, spraying water into the air where it evaporates and blows about. In addition to wetting the leaves, sprinklers can often turn the whole area into a mud hole. Canvas soil-soakers and plastic hose sprinklers carry water gently to the soil around the roots. A wand and water breaker can make it much easier to put water where you want it and they are especially useful in watering hanging baskets and patio containers. A water timer that mea-

Concentrated soaking with bottomless coffee can

Concentrated soaking with earth wall around hill planting

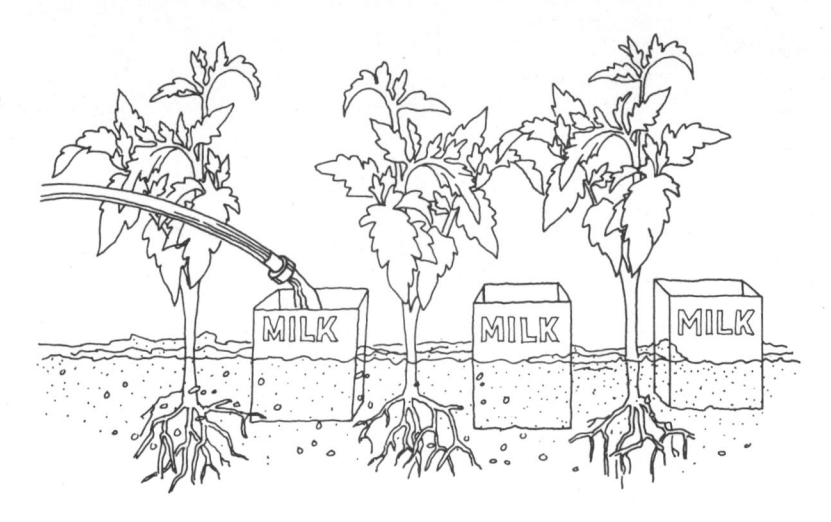

Concentrated soaking with bottomless milk cartons

sures the flow of water and shuts off automatically when that amount has been delivered is an excellent device for the forgetful and can free you to do other things.

Soils and Mixes

Soil is that thin blanket between sterile rock and the sky. Precious stuff, the soil supports all life and is, in part, the product of living things. With all of that, we often treat it like dirt under our feet, because for such a long time soil has been dirt cheap. A good soil is getting harder to find. Some conservationists are even thinking of putting soil on the endangered list, encouraging people to cherish the soil we have and to work hard to create more good soil.

A good garden soil is not found merely lying about in a backyard after the developers leave. Often, if there was any soil originally on the lot, it was either carefully removed before construction started or was buried under the excavation for the foundation. Although the study of soil, like the study of vintage wines, can be a lifetime work, most people just want enough information to get going with growing. Except for farmers and commercial growers, most people pick the spot that is convenient for their garden and they try to make the best of what they have.

Ideal Soil

Fortunately for the growers of eatables, many plants will survive even in poor soil or in artificial potting mixes. Nevertheless, really fine soil is a goal worth shooting for. Good soil is slightly lumpy. If it is worked too fine it will pack hard in rains or blow away. On the other hand, it must be fine enough to pack firmly, providing good contact with the roots and supporting the plant. Good soil holds moisture but lets excess water drain away, leaving room for air, too. Every gardener's dream soil efficiently stabilizes water retention and permits good aeration and root penetration. An ideal soil for supporting eatables is neutral or just slightly acid and contains nutrients in proper balance. It is high in organic matter to feed the millions of microorganisms that improve soil texture.

Kinds of Soil

Soil is a collective word for many kinds of soils around the earth — just as vegetation means all kinds of plants. There can be several different soils in one 50 x 100-foot plot. That is why, if you are making a soil test, it is important to take several samples from different spots and mix them for a composite sample. Each natural soil is made up of fine rock particles, organic matter and microorganisms. The voids are even more important than the solids in a soil. A good soil is 50 percent solids and 50 percent porous space that provides room for water, air and roots. The solids are 80 to 90 percent inorganic matter and 10 to 20 percent organic materials. The porous space should be divided about half and half between water and air. Soil texture depends on the different proportions of various-sized rock particles.

A clay soil is made up mostly of particles that are less than 1/31,750 of an inch (1/200 mm) in diameter. The minute particles pack closer together than large particles and a clay soil's total surface can hold more water than other soils. Clay soil often drains poorly but can be improved by the addition of organic matter and sand (builder's or #4 sand) to aggregate the clay particles and improve drainage. Working with a clay soil when it is wet compresses the particles even more closely together; it then dries to something like baked brick or concrete. Still, properly managed clay soils are the most productive.

A sandy soil is made up mostly of particles that are over 1/3,175 of an inch (1/20 mm) in diameter. These particles are irregular in shape and do not pack as closely together as clay particles. These larger particles have less total surface so they hold less water than smaller particles and are much more porous. Sandy soil drains like a sieve, but it can be improved by adding organic matter to help retain moisture. Clay also can be added to improve water retention and provide minerals.

A silt soil has particles intermediate in size between clay and sand and may act like a clay soil or a very fine sandy soil, depending on the size of its particles. A loam is a mixture of clay, silt and sand particles. A good garden loam is something to cherish, particularly if it also includes a healthy supply of humus (decayed vegetation, recycled organic matter).

Drainage and Moisture Retention

The production of eatables depends as much on the physical condition, of the soil as on its fertility. A root zone that has been cleared of rocks, tin cans and other debris 18 to 24 inches down will help give the plants a good start. Since plants need more water than any other substance in the soil for their growth, whatever affects the soil's ability to provide water will affect the growth of the plant.

Good soil permits water to enter it easily. Water should not stand on the surface or run off, causing erosion. Much of the water that moves into the soil drains right on out, but some is held in the soil by capillary action and it is this water that contains dissolved minerals and gases. This is also the water that is available to the plants. The drier the soil becomes, the greater the soil's ability to hang on to moisture and the harder it is for the plants to tear moisture away from the soil. Some materials, such as peat moss and calcined clay, really like to hold on to water. It is very important not to let peat or calcined clay dry out because they will soak up and hold on to any moisture — even if they have to take it from the plants.

Soilless Mixes

For container growing, soilless mixes offer many advantages over soil. They are lighter, easier to handle, more readily available. They also do not compact as hard as soil. One disadvantage, however, is that you will have to fertilize more frequently. A liquid fertilizer, diluted to one-eighth to one-fourth its recommended strength, can be applied with every watering.

A simple soilless mix you can make yourself contains one part (by volume) peat moss and one part perlite or vermiculite. But if you want to whip up a big batch of soilless potting mix, here are three highly recommended recipes. Each makes one cubic yard.

UNIVERSITY OF CALIFORNIA MIX
- 11 bushels each shredded peat moss and clean sand
- 7½ pounds dolomite lime
- 2½ pounds calcium carbonate lime
- 4 ounces potassium nitrate
- 4 ounces potassium sulfate

Mix well. You can store this mix for some time, but if you are going to use it within a week, you can add 2½ pounds of horn and hoof meal or dried blood (13 percent nitrogen).

CORNELL PEAT-LITE MIXES
MIX A
- 11 bushes shredded German or Canadian sphagnum peat moss
- 11 bushels horticultural grade vermiculite (#2 or #4)
- 5 pounds ground limestone, preferably dolomite
- 1 pound superphosphate (20 percent, preferably powdered)
- 2 to 12 pounds of 5-10-5 fertilizer

MIX B
Same ingredients as A except substitute perlite for vermiculite.

Of course if good soil is available you can still make your own mix by combining equal parts (by volume) of garden loam, clean sand, and peat moss. If greater drainage is needed, add more sand. But before you mix them together, be sure that all parts are pasteurized to prevent diseases.

Whether you choose to use soil or soilless mix for container plantings, prepare it a day ahead of time. Enough water should be added to the mix so that the moisture is evenly distributed and the mix does not crumble when picked up.

Growing Aids

Fertilizers

A fertilizer can be either a substance or the person who applies it. Since 95 percent of a plant's food comes from water and air, you can be fairly sure you will get something to eat even if you do not fertilize at all providing that the plants get enough water and plenty of sun. Many times the mechanical condition of the soil has a greater effect on how well plants do than any fertilizer you add.

Growing plants need 10 basic elements: carbon, hydrogen and oxygen, which they get from water and air; iron, calcium, sulfur and magnesium, which are usually available in the soil; and nitrogen, phosphorus, and potassium, which are also present in the soil but not always in usable amounts. Most natural soils contain reserve amounts of plant nutrients. When growing eatables, remember that less fertilizer is better than more. Too much fertilizer can burn plants (pull water out of the roots and leaves) and you might kill them with your kindness.

Natural or Synthetic

In most people's minds fertilizers are either natural, or organic, and synthetic. And to people there's a big difference. However, since plants can only absorb nutrients after they have been broken down and dissolved in water, it doesn't make much difference to them whether the nutrients come from organic or synthetic sources. Still, the differences between organic and synthetic fertilizers are worth the conscientious gardener's consideration.

Organic fertilizers are complex substances that are insoluble in water and have to be broken down by soil microorganisms over a long period of time before plants can use them. This requires temperatures above 40°F, probably about 60°F, before the nutrients are available. Synthetic fertilizers, on the other hand, are water soluble and provide instantly available nutrients because they are not dependent on soil organisms to break them down. Because they are insoluble in water and act more slowly, natural fertilizers will not damage germinating seeds and young plants as synthetic fertilizers can. In fact, a heavy dose of synthetic fertilizer can knock a plant out once and for all.

Synthetic fertilizers may be manufactured from a variety of sources including chemicals, natural minerals, and by-products of industry, and are generally less expensive than organic fertilizers. Organic fertilizers come from plants and animals. Guano (undiluted bird droppings), dried blood, kelp, bone meal, horn and hoof meal, and cottonseed meal are all organic fertilizers.

Organic Fertilizers	Percentage of N-P-K
Blood	13-1.5-0
Fish Scrap	9-7-0
Guano, Bat	6-9-3
Guano, Bird	13-11-2
Kelp	1-0.5-9
Bone Meal, Raw	4-22-0
Cottonseed Meal	6-2.5-2
Hoof & Bone Meal, Steamed	14-0-0
Cattle Manure	0.5-0.3-0.5
Horse Manure	0.6-0.3-0.5
Sheep Manure	0.9-0.5-0.8
Chicken Manure	0.9-0.5-0.8
Sewage Sludge	2-1-1 (Be sure sludge contains no toxic substances.)

Although manures are bulkier and contain lower percentages of nutrients than other fertilizers, they do provide many of the trace elements which other types may lack. In addition, organic manures increase organic material in the soil and a well-rotted manure makes a great mulch. Farm manures are diluted with straw and other bedding materials. Connoisseurs expect different things from horse, cow, and pig manure. However, to the average vegetable gardener the most important difference between manures is that chicken and duck manures are twice as high in nitrogen and potassium as the manures of larger animals.

Sewage sludge is sometimes used as an organic fertilizer. It can contain up to 8 percent nitrogen, but it is often very low in nitrogen and phosphorus and when it comes from industrial areas it may contain so much lead, copper, and zinc it will poison plants, or so much cadmium it will poison people.

Nitrogen, Phosphorus, Potassium

Commercial fertilizers are always labeled to show the percentage by weight of the nitrogen (N), phosphorus (P), and potassium (K, from the German word *Kalium*). N is always first, P second and K third. A zero anywhere in that sequence means that that element is not present in the formula. A fertilizer containing all three elements is termed a complete fertilizer.

Nitrogen builds stems and leaves and is also important in the growth of the fruit. However, if there is too much of it, the plant may never go into production. It will just keep growing and growing. Nitrogen needs to be used with care; too much can damage the plants or sprouting seeds. In those cases where soil pH is critical to healthy plant growth, certain nitrogen fertilizers can help. Ammonium sulfate, ammonium nitrate, and ammonium phosphate are fertilizers that can lower the pH of neutral or alkaline soils while they supply added nitrogen. On neutral or acid soils, an alkaline fertilizer such as sodium nitrate, calcium nitrate, or potassium nitrate can be used to raise soil pH. The organic fertilizers, including guano, cottonseed meal, dried blood, and tankage are neutral in their effect on soil reaction.

Phosphorus is essential for fruit and seed production. If it is not available, the fruit will be stunted or fail to set. This is especially true if there is also a lot of nitrogen available, or if lawn fertilizer is used on the vegetable garden. Phosphate rocks and bones are the chief sources of phosphate fertilizers. Phosphate has to be applied in high concentrations because it locks into the soil very quickly and becomes unavailable to the plants. For that reason, apply phosphate fertilizers around the roots of plants when they are being transplanted.

Potassium builds roots and stems, help provide disease resistance, and aids in cell formation. Wood ash is a good source of potash. Most natural soils usually contain enough potassium. Root crops and celery often need added potassium.

Compost Piles

Composting is a creative activity. There are almost as many different methods of composting as there are gardeners. And, like a good stew, the proof is in the final product.

Composting takes advantage of natural processes to convert plant and other organic wastes into loose peatlike humus which provides some nutrients to plants and increases the soil's ability to control water. Composting can save money that would otherwise be spent on soil conditioners and fertilizers. It can save time because you have a place to put leaves and grass clippings that you may want to use as a mulch. It you cannot get around to mulching the composted leaves and clippings, they will transform themselves into high-class soil.

How the Composting Process Works

Organic wastes are broken down by microorganisms. Most soil organisms are inactive when soil temperatures are below 40°F. They do not begin working in earnest until the temperature goes above 60°F. Most of them do not work well in a very acid element. Since they are extremely small, microorganisms work faster when not overwhelmed with large chunks of material. If a lot of woody material is put in the compost pile, microorganisms will need added nutrients to break down the wood's sugar and starches. These microorganisms do not create food, they just break down the complex materials into simple ones that plants can use.

There are two basic kinds of microorganisms — those that need air to work and those that do not. It is possible to compost in an airtight container, thanks to the microorganisms that do not need air. A tightly-covered plastic trash can in the kitchen can convert an enormous amount of kitchen waste into compost in a winter's time. The classic outdoor compost pile should be turned regularly to provide air for the microorganisms that need it.

What to Use

Use all garden waste except diseased and pest ladened materials. Use grass clippings, leaves, weeds, sod, kitchen leftovers — vegetables and fruit peels, vegetable tops, coffee grounds, tea leaves and eggshells. The finer they are chopped up and the deeper they are buried, the quicker they will be converted and the less chance that they will be dug up by a curious four-legged visitor. You can also use hay, straw, hulls, nut shells and tree trimmings. But, unless they are shredded, they will take a long time to decompose.

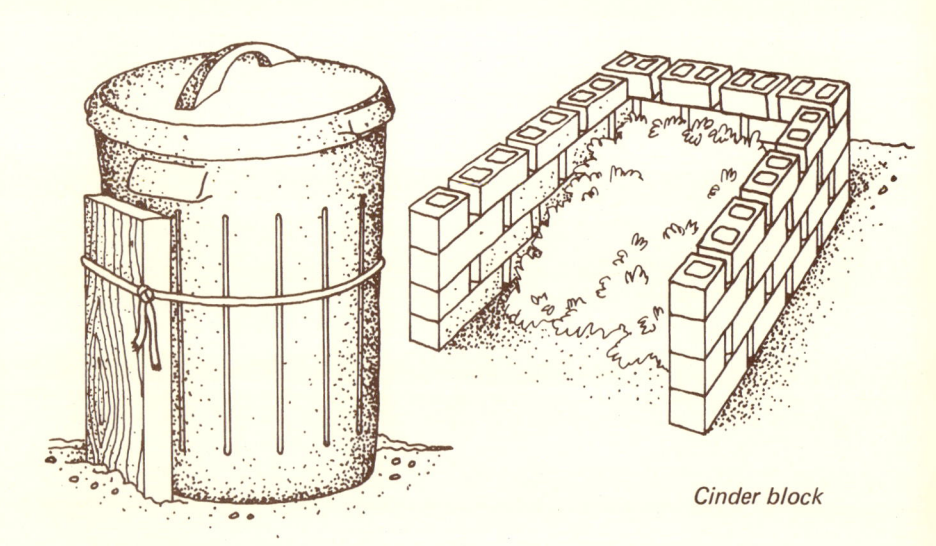

Cinder block

Plastic garbage can

How to Build a Pile

If there is room, put the compost pile in one end of the garden. It can be square, rectangular or round, and four to five feet across. A pile can be as long as the space available. You can use fencing or cinder blocks to keep it under control — it will look neater and will not blow away.

If space is at a premium (or if a compost pile does not go with the decor), put it behind some bushes or the garage. If the space available is extremely small, composting can be done in a large heavy-duty plastic bag or plastic garbage can. If there is not enough room for a pile, composting can also be done by using the waste material as a mulch and working it into the soil.

Start out with one to two feet of leaves, if you have them, or six to twelve inches of more compact stuff such as grass clippings or sawdust. Over this put a layer of fertilizer (manure, blood, bone, cottonseed meal, or commercial fertilizer) and some finely-ground limestone (most microorganisms like their environment sweet). Then add some soil to hold water and provide a starter colony. Water the compost carefully. Add a second layer of leaves or other garden waste and repeat the layers. If you have enough material or enough room, put on a third layer. The pile should be kept moist — like a squeezed, not sopping, sponge.

There are a number of things you can do to speed up the process.

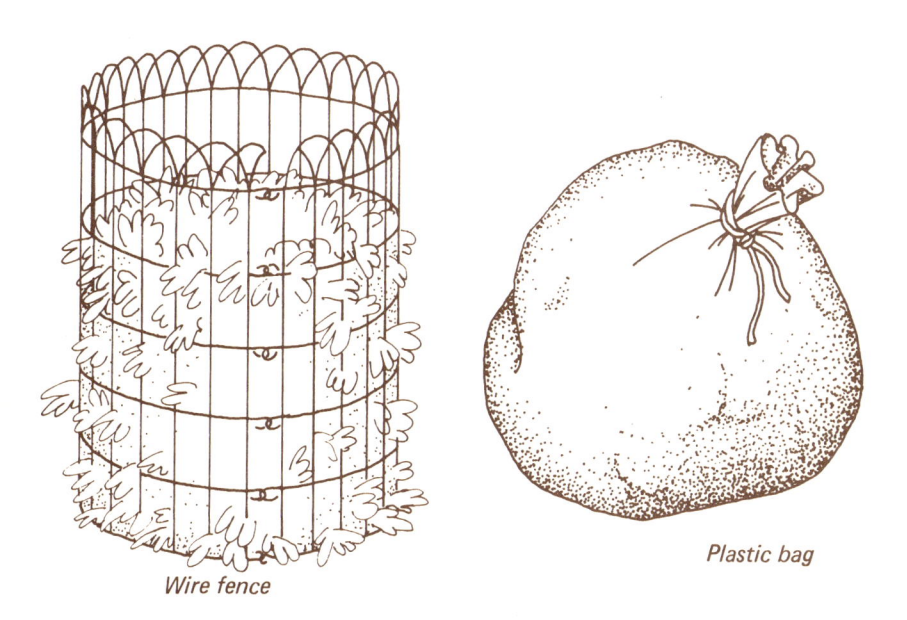

Wire fence

Plastic bag

Soil
Fertilizer

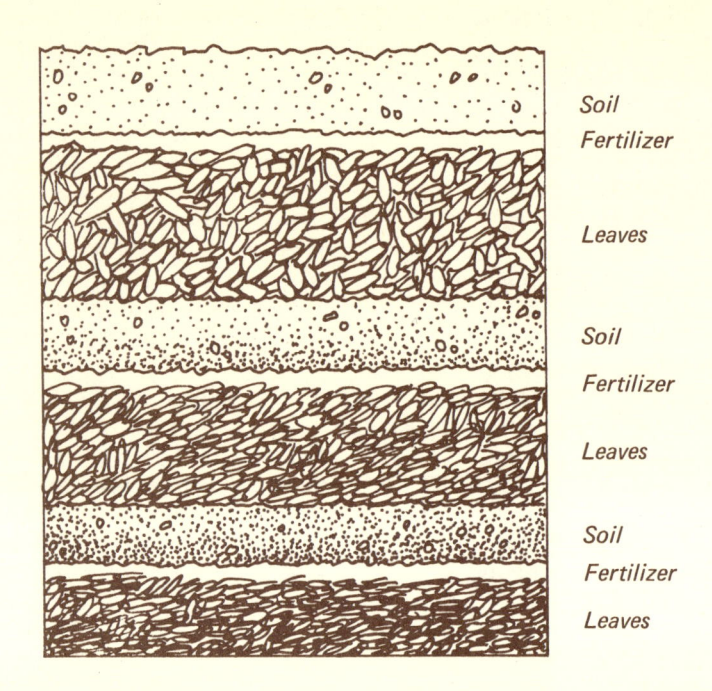

Leaves

Soil
Fertilizer

Leaves

Soil
Fertilizer

Leaves

Pile is compressed towards bottom

First, you can grind or shred all materials to be composted to give the microorganisms a head start. Make sure the pile does not dry out and provide enough fertilizer to encourage rapid growth of the bacteria. You can also use a starter culture, either from an ongoing compost pile or a commercial starter culture. The composting process works faster when the temperature is around 60°F.

Mulches

Mulches are either natural organic or inorganic and processed materials placed on the soil around plants. They can cut down soil erosion; and by breaking the force of heavy rains, they can reduce soil compaction and increase the amount of water the soil can absorb. They also keep the mud off the plants and conserve soil moisture by reducing evaporation. Mulches are insulators, making it possible to keep the soil warmer during cool weather and cooler during warm weather. If they are put on before the soil has warmed up, the ground will be kept cool and root development will be slowed down.

Mulches do not get rid of weeds. Nor do they eliminate plant disease, reduce insect attacks or add flavor and vitamins. They can, however, help keep weeds down if the area is weed free to begin with. If the mulch is thick enough or dense enough, the weeds cannot push through and the darkness can frustrate their germination. Persistent perennial broadleaved weeds can push their way through most mulches — except polyethylene film and heavyweight aluminum foil.

Sometimes mulches can improve the looks of an area by giving it a neater, more finished appearance and sometimes they can give the area a look that only the vegetables can appreciate.

Organic Mulches

Organic mulches are organic materials which, when laid on the soil, decompose to feed the microorganisms and improve the quality of the soil. If you use mulches that decompose quickly, nitrogen should be added to make up for nitrogen used by the bacteria. Some mulches can carry weed seeds and others can harbor undesirable organisms or pests, but both diseases and pests can usually be controlled by keeping the mulch stirred up.

For organic mulches, spread a two- to six-inch layer (depending on the material used) on the surface around the plants after they are four inches tall and after the soil has warmed up. Be careful not to suffocate the eatables while frustrating the weeds.

The following are materials often used as organic mulches.

Buckwheat hulls. These hulls last a long time and have a neutral color. They are lightweight and can blow away. Sometimes buckwheat hulls smell when the weather is hot and wet.

Chunk bark. Redwood and fir barks are available in several sizes. They last a long time. Bark makes good-looking paths and helps finish an area, but it is not very good around vegetables — too chunky. And it sometimes floats away in the rain or when watered.

Compost. Partly-decomposed compost makes a great mulch and soil conditioner. It looks a little rough, but other gardeners will know you are giving your garden the very best.

Crushed corncobs. Crushed cobs make an excellent and usually inexpensive mulch. The cobs need additional nitrogen, unless they are partially decomposed. Sometimes crushed corncobs have kernels mixed in which will give you some extra weeding to do.

Lawn clippings. Do not use lawn clippings if the lawn has been treated with an herbicide or weed killer — they can kill the eatables you are trying to grow. Let untreated clippings dry before putting them around your garden since fresh grass mats down and really smells

while it is decomposing.
Leaves. They are cheap and usually easy to find but hard to keep in place. They will stay where you want them better if they are ground up or partially decomposed. Nitrogen should be added to a leaf mulch.
Manure. Vintage, partially-decomposed manure makes an excellent mulch. It has a high bouquet and is not for everyone. Manures which have been treated with odor-reducing chemicals should not be used because they contain substances such as boron which are unhealthy for plants.
Mushroom compost (leftover, used). Where it is available, used mushroom compost is usually inexpensive and the rich color blends in well.
Peat moss. Expensive when large areas have to be covered, peat moss should be kept moist or it will act like a blotter and pull moisture out of the soil and away from the plants. Once it dries, peat tends to shed water rather than letting it soak in. The fine grades of peat also have a tendency to blow away.
Poultry litter. This is potent stuff since poultry manure is about twice as strong as cow manure. No need to add nitrogen! Proceed with caution — a good, weathered, four-year-old poultry litter can give you mulch, plus compost, plus high-nitrogen fertilizer.
Sawdust. Often available for the asking, sawdust needs added nitrogen to prevent microorganisms from depleting the soil's nitrogen.
Straw. Straw is very messy and hard to apply in a small place. Matches or cigarettes can result in short order cooking.
Wood chips or shavings. There are more chips and shavings available since they are no longer being burned as a waste product. They decompose slowly and need added nitrogen. Beware of maple chips which may carry verticillium wilt in to your garden.

Inorganic Mulches

The following materials are used as mulches.
Aluminum foil. Foil reflects light, keeps plants clean and confuses bugs. They see the sky reflected and they cannot tell which end is up.
Backless indoor-outdoor carpet. Ideal for the small garden. Indoor-outdoor carpeting makes it easy for the fastidious gardener to keep the place vacuumed. Water goes through it easily and the weeds are kept down.
Newspapers. Apply newspapers thickly. They need not have been read. Keep them in place with rocks or soil. They will decompose slowly and can be turned under as a soil modifier.
Rag rugs. An old rag rug holds water and keeps the soil moist. It will be less contemporary looking than backless carpeting, but the nostalgia look is "in" — very nice for the informal touch.

Plastic Mulches

Both clear and black polyethylene are used by commercial growers as inorganic mulches. Clear plastic is not recommended for small gardens because it encourages weeds; weeds just love the cozy greenhouse effect it creates. Black plastic is sometimes used in small gardens for plants that are grown spaced apart, such as eggplants, peppers, strawberries, and tomatoes, or plants that are grown in a group or hill, such as cucumbers, squash or pumpkins.
There are some advantages to growing with a plastic mulch.
1. Black plastic reduces the loss of soil moisture.
2. The soil temperature is increased. (Gardeners in Alaska use a lot of black plastic mulch.)
3. Crop maturity is sped up.
4. There is a reduced weed growth because the black plastic cuts out their light supply.
5. You will not have to cultivate as much. That means less root damage.
6. Plants and fruits are kept cleaner.
7. When a new garden is being made in an area where there was a lot of grass (a lawn was dug up, for instance), the use of black plastic can keep the grass from coming back and choking the eatable.

There are some disadvantages to keep in mind as well.
1. You may need to water more frequently. Because of the greater growth, the plants lose more water through transpiration, especially on well-drained, sandy soils. However, you will need to water less if the black plastic is used on soil that holds water or drains poorly.
2. If the soil moisture is kept at too high a level and there is not enough air in the soil, the plants can wilt and rot.
3. Black plastic should not be used for crops that need a cool growing season — cabbage or cauliflower, for instance. It cannot be used for cool season crops unless it is covered with a thin layer of light-reflecting material, such as sawdust.
 Black plastic can be bought from many garden centers and can be ordered by mail from seed and garden equipment catalogs. It should be at least 1-1/2 mil thick and about three to four feet wide. If you have a piece of wider or thicker black plastic, use it. The wider plastic is somewhat harder to handle. Thick black plastic is more expensive.
 Black plastic should be applied before the plants are set out. Try to pick a calm day. If there is a wind, it can whip the plastic about and make laying it down hard work. Take a hoe and make a three-inch deep trench the length of the row. Lay one edge of the plastic in the

trench and cover the edge with soil. Smooth the plastic over the bed and repeat the process on the other side. Be sure it is anchored securely or the wind will get under it and pull the plastic up. When you are ready to plant cut holes about three inches across for the plants or seeds. After planting, anchor the edge down with stones or soil to keep the wind from blowing off the plastic. Water the plants through the holes in the mulch. After a rain check to see if there are any spots where water is standing. If there is, punch a hole through the plastic so the water can run through.

After the plants are harvested the plastic can be swept off, rolled up and stored for use the next year.

Soil Analysis

Soil testing can be very useful, though it certainly is not an obligatory step for home gardening. In many states soil test results are provided by Cooperative Extension Services, and all states can give you information on firms in your area that do tests for a fee. Testing identifies deficiencies that sometimes cause poor growth; on the other hand

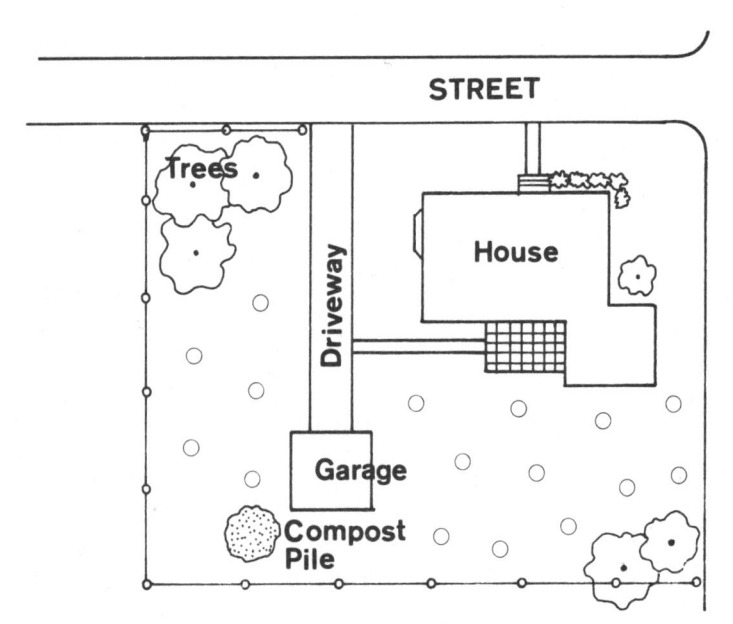

Take samples from 15 or 20 spots in the planting area

Take a soil sample 8" straight down

testing can eliminate lack of proper nutrition as the reason plants are not growing well. Once you have eliminated a nutrient deficiency as the reason for your fruits and vegetables doing poorly, you are left with the physical condition of the soil, insects, diseases and air pollution (including herbicides) as the possible culprits.

Taking a Sample

Soil samples can be taken any time of the year that the ground is not frozen hard. Use a plastic bucket (do not use metal, especially if the soil sample is to be used for testing micronutrients), a digging tool, such as a spade or a trowel, and a clean container — a carefully washed-out one-pint milk carton or the container provided by the testing service. All equipment should be perfectly clean.

If there is any grass on the spot you are sampling, remove it and then take a slice of soil 1/2 inch thick and about 8 inches straight down from 15 to 20 scattered locations. If you are sampling a large area, 20 samples mixed together will do as fine a job as 40 or 100. Place each sample in the plastic bucket and when all samples are in, mix them thoroughly. If the soil is very wet, wait and let it air dry before mixing. (DO NOT HEAT IT IN THE OVEN OR ON A RADIATOR. Heat will kill the microorganisms and cause nitrogen and other elements to change form, making the test inaccurate.) If there are a lot of lumps, crush them with a wooden spoon or use a rolling pin on a wooden surface. After the soil is thoroughly mixed, fill your container and follow the laboratory's instructions for sending them the sample.

If you are asking for recommendations, send in as much information as you can about what you are planning to grow, how you plan to water and whether you anticipate special problems or conditions.

Soil pH Factor

The Danish chemist Sørenson first defined pH as the p (power of) H (hydrogen) ions. (If you want to impress your friends, tell them that after a change in sign, pH is the power of ten needed to express the negative log of the hydrogen ion concentration in moles per liter.) On a scale of 14, 7 is neutral and each unit in either direction from neutral represents a ten-fold increase in acidity or alkalinity. A pH of 6 is 10 times more acid than a pH of 7, and a pH of 5 is 10 times more acid than a pH of 6. One is the most strongly acid (sour) and 14 is the most alkaline (sweet). For growing plants, any soil below 4.5 is considered extremely acid and any soil over 9 is very strongly alkaline. Most eatables grow best in a pH that ranges between 5.5 and 7.5, with most doing best on the acid side of neutral.

There are soil testing kits available for testing pH, or if you are a confirmed do-it-yourselfer, you can buy litmus paper from a drug store and do it all by yourself. If you are using a kit, follow the instructions very carefully. Keep your color chart clean and out of bright light (so it will not fade) and start with a representative sample from 15 to 20 spots in your garden. If you are going to use litmus paper, get the red (pink) and the blue from your drugstore. Take your soil sample and select a representative measure of water. Shake well and let the soil settle. Dip in a piece of litmus paper. If the red paper turns blue or the blue paper stays blue, the soil is alkaline. If the red paper stays red or the blue paper turns red, the soil is acid. If both the red and the blue papers turn purple, the soil is neutral. You can keep reusing the litmus papers by dipping them in an acid or alkaline solution.

Tools

Tools are not really essential for growing eatables. In fact, most seeds and plants grow by themselves. For thousands of years eatables just grew and people picked them, and then for thousands of years more, all that people used were their fingers and toes. The first implement salesman was probably the person who found that fire-hardening a stick would save on the fingernails. Hands are still the number one tool in a garden. The number of attachments for your hands are almost infinite. Some are quaint, others are interesting, and a few make the job easier.

There is a greater variety of gardening tools than there are golf clubs. What you use is a matter of personal comfort preference. There are some growers of eatables who do everything with a machete and others who manage well with only a small spade. When buying tools, do not go overboard. Check with the pros and see what they use. If possible, try a tool before you buy it. One tool can often do a number of jobs, and a comfortable well-balanced tool that fits your needs is better than a whole shed full of specialized instruments — especially if you are not well supplied with tool-toters and tool-pickeruppers. The first test for a tool is how it feels in your hand. Is it well balanced? Can you lift it full as well as empty? People and tools come in different sizes and weights. Since you will be spending time together, you and your gardening tools should be compatible.

Buy the best tools you can find and then take good care of them. Good tools work better, last longer, and in the long run are a lot less expensive than the cheap ones that just go to pieces when you put them to work. Clean your tools before putting them away. It is a bore, but it is even more boring to try to clean them up before using them the next time. Have a regular place for every tool; it looks impressive and simplifies finding the ones you need. It also can save time when cleaning up. A tool shed or tool board is also safer than throwing them on the floor. Safety also means laying rakes and hoes on the ground with the working side down — if you do not, you can easily puncture your foot while bopping yourself on the head.

Here is a list of common gardening tools and some of their uses.

Hands. Used for planting seeds and plants, hands are also

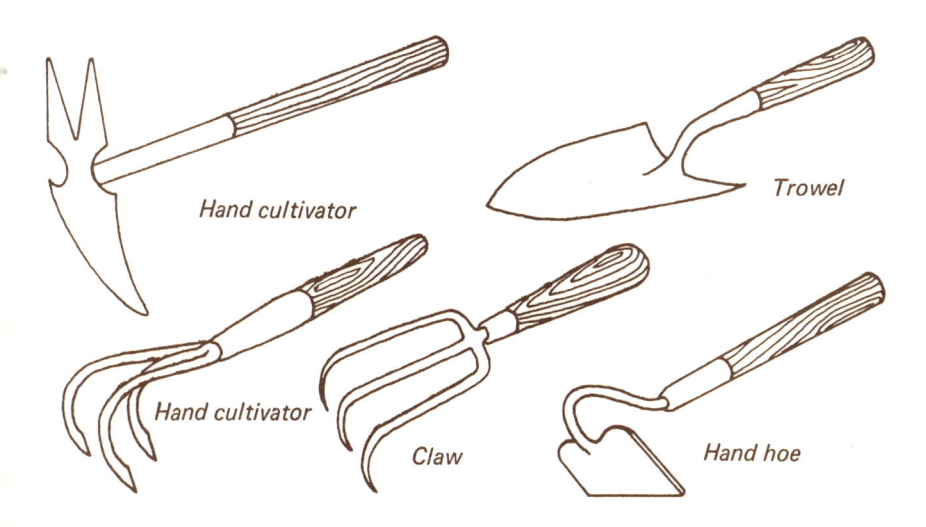

Hand cultivator

Trowel

Hand cultivator

Claw

Hand hoe

65

Sharpening a hoe

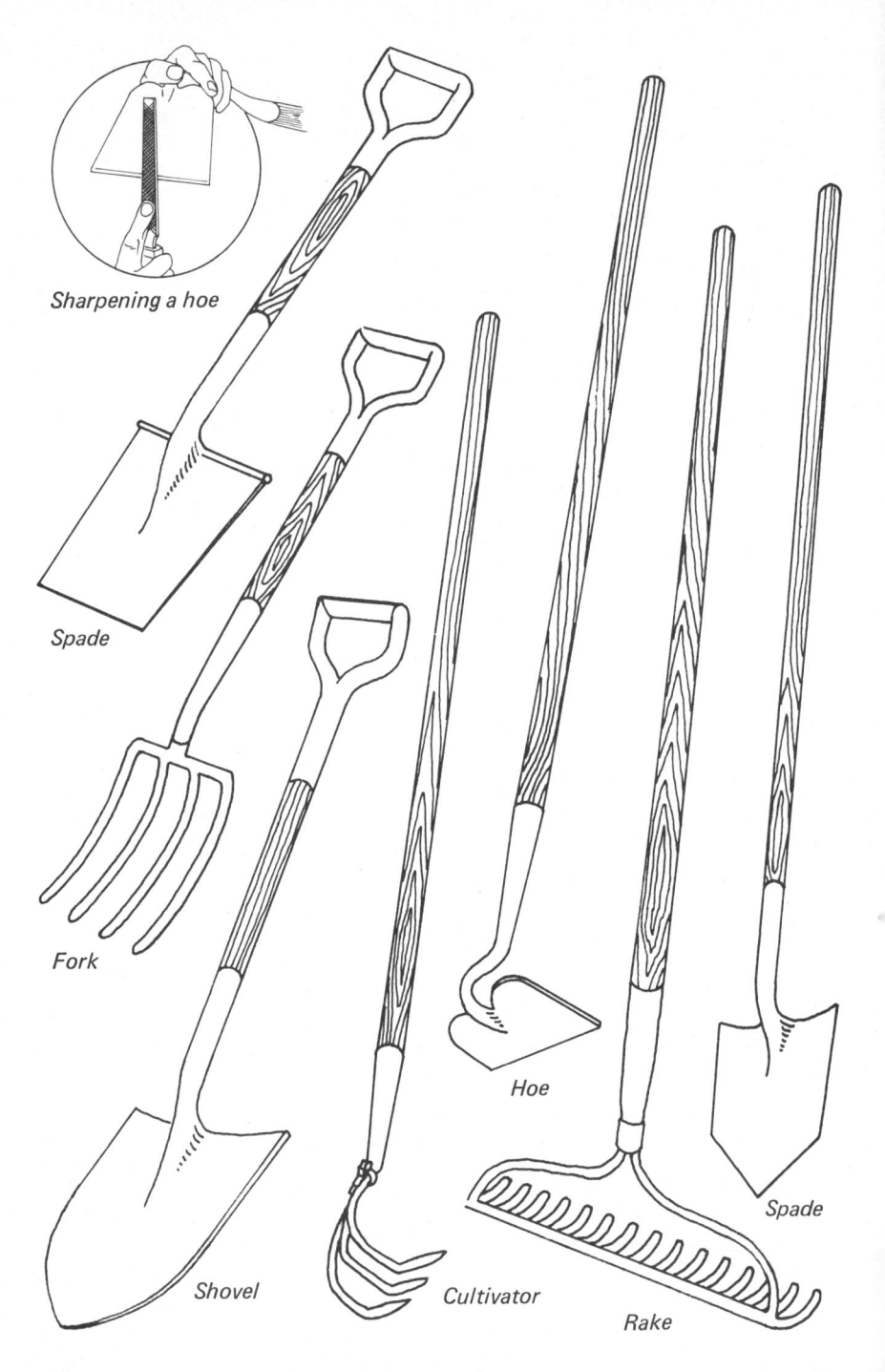

Spade

Fork

Shovel

Cultivator

Hoe

Rake

Spade

66

superior instruments for thinning plants, pulling weeds, manipulating a spade, knife, rake and hose. They also perform a useful role in frustrating pests, harvesting and testing (destructive testing is the whole point of growing eatables, of course).

Shovel. A tool with a handle and somewhat flattened scoop, a shovel is used for picking up, lifting and moving soil. Many times shovels and spades can be used interchangeably.

Spade. Spades are sturdy tools with thick handles and heavy blades that can be pressed into the ground with a foot. Spades are for digging; they should be light and strong. The blade should be finished off at the top so it will not cut your foot. They can also be used to edge a bed (flower or vegetable), divide clumps of plants or support your sweater while you work in the garden. A floral shovel or floral spade makes an excellent all-round tool in a small garden.

Trowel. If the eatables are being grown in an even smaller space, or you like to get close to your work, then use a trowel. A trowel is a small implement with pointed scoop-shaped blade that can be used as a hand shovel or spade.

Forks. Forks are tools with two or more prongs used for digging and breaking up compacted soils, lifting up root crops and digging out weeds.

Hoe. A tool with a flat blade attached at right angles to a long handle, a hoe is used for frustrating and beheading weeds, stirring up the soil, mounding the soil and making rows.

Rakes. Rakes with iron fingers are used for leveling and grading soil, removing rocks, roots and soil lumps and for stirring up the soil surface. Rakes with flexible fingers are used for gentle cultivating, cleaning up and collecting trash from between plants.

Hand Forks, Claws and Cultivators are used in the same way as the larger farm models and often are all that you need in a very small garden.

Gloves. Some people use them to protect their hands, other people think that they dull the "feel" of gardening. It is a good idea to have a heavy pair of gloves for rough work, when the weather gets cold, or just to show that you have them.

Strong, Sharp Pocket Knife. A knife can either be a sixth finger or a second thumb. Once you get used to using one they save wear and tear on the fingers and nails.

Thermometers. Outdoor thermometers can take a lot of the guesswork out of day and night temperatures (especially thermometers that record the maximum and minimum temperatures). For the serious gardener there are special soil thermometers.

File. Use a file for sharpening spades and hoes.

Paint. If you use bright colors to mark your tools they will be easier to find, especially at dusk or after dark. Also, marked tools are more likely to be returned by friends and neighbors.

Where to Get Seeds

If you are going to seed-plant your eatables, start with good, fresh, viable seed. Buy your seed from a reputable source. If there is a seed store in your community, that is usually a good place to start since the people in it are generally very knowledgeable about their wares and local conditions. If you plan to pick their brains, get an early start so you are not in the store trying to ask questions when everyone else is in there too. Seed and bulb stores are special places — they are not the seed rack in the hardware store or the seasonal spot in the produce section of the grocery store. Seeds from racks or produce sections can be good, or good and dead, depending on how they have been kept. If they have been kept too hot, too moist or too long they can only produce disappointment. Also, the pretty packages often contain fewer seeds for the money spent and the picture on the outside often does not look too much like the plants whose seeds are inside. Another satisfactory way to buy seed is by mail from a seed catalog. There are many catalogs offering a great variety of seeds. A good catalog will tell all — or almost all — about the varieties it lists.

It takes great self-discipline and a bit of studying to figure out what kinds of eatables you want and which variety will fill your needs. When reading a seed catalog or a seed packet, concentrate on the nouns and the verbs and try to ignore all the adjectives and adverbs as you make your choice. Different varieties have different growth habits. Depending on where your eatables are going to be grown, you may want to choose plants that are upright representatives of their kind or you may want the kinds that tend to sprawl. If you are living in an apartment or have a very small growing space, concentrate on the dwarf or small varieties. Whenever possible, concentrate on varieties that have built-in resistance to diseases common in your area. Your local extension service can provide you with a list of varieties best suited to your part of the country.

If you are interested in shopping for your fruit, vegetable, and herb seeds by mail, here are some catalog sources you might want to look into.

W.F. Allen Co.
Salisbury, MD 21801

Burgess Seed and Plant Co.
P.O. Box 3000
Galesburg, MI 49053

W. Atlee Burpee
(good herb selection)
3 locations:
Riverside, CA 92502 or
Warminster, PA 18974 or
Clinton, IA 52732

D.V. Burrell Seed Growers Co.
Box 150
Rocky Ford, CO 81067

Comstock, Ferre & Co.
Wethersfield, CT 06109

DeGiorgi Co., Inc.
Council Bluffs, IA 51501

Farmer Seed and Nursery Co.
Faribault, MN 55021

Henry Field Seed & Nursery Co.
407 Sycamore St.
Shenandoah, IA 51601

Gurney Seed & Nursery Co.
1448 Page St.
Yankton, SD 57078

Joseph Harris Co., Inc.
Moreton Farm
Rochester, NY 14624

Chas. C. Hart Seed Co.
Main & Hart Streets
Wethersfield, Ct 06109

H.C. Hastings
P.O. Box 4088
Atlanta, GA 30302

Hilltop Herb Farm
Box 866
Cleveland, TX 77327

Howe-Hill Herbs
Camden, ME 04843

J.L. Hudson
P.O. Box 1058
Redwood City, CA 94604

J.W. Jung Seeds and Nursery
Randolph, WI 53956

D. Landreth Seed Co.
2700 Wilmarco Ave.
Baltimore, MD 21223

Earl May Seed and Nursery Co.
6032 Elm St.
Shenandoah, IA 51601

Meyer Seed Co.
600 S. Carolina St.
Baltimore, MD 21231

Nichols Garden Nursery
(good herb selection)
1190 N. Pacific Hwy.
Albany, OR 97321

L.L. Olds Seed Co.
Box 1069
Madison, WI 53701

Geo. W. Park Seed Co., Inc.
(good herb selection)
Greenwood, SC 29646

Seedway
Hall, NY 14463

R.H. Shumway Seedsman
628 Cedar St.
Rockford, IL 61101

Stokes Seeds Inc.
Box 548 Main Post Office
Buffalo, NY 14240

Thompson & Morgan, Inc.
Box 24
Somerdale, NJ 08083

Otis S. Twilley Seed Co.
Salisbury, MD 21801

Wyatt-Quarles Seed Co.
P.O. Box 2131
Raleigh, NC 27602

In addition to buying seed from a retailer or through a catalog, you can also get them free, straight from a plant. Growing plants from seed that you have collected yourself can often give you the warm feeling of being a plant grandparent. With some plants the results are as satisfactory as using purchased seed. However, if the parent plant providing the seed is a hybrid, the results may be very disappointing since the offspring will not take after their parents.

Seeds should be collected when they are about ready to fall out of the dry flower head. Seeds from different plants should be put into separate, labeled envelopes. Then the envelopes should be put into a glass jar with a tight-fitting lid and stored in the refrigerator. Seeds will stay viable longer if they are kept cool and dry. As long as they are dry they will even survive freezing. Properly stored, onion and sweet corn seeds will last about a year. Okra and parsley seeds will last about two years. Asparagus, bean, carrot, pea, pepper and tomato seeds will last about three years. Beet, Brussels sprout, cabbage, cauliflower, kale, pumpkin, radish, rutabaga, squash and turnip seeds will last four years. And seeds from celery, cucumber, eggplant, endive, lettuce, muskmelon, and watermelon will last at least five years.

When you are in doubt about the viability of your seeds you can run a seed germination test. The "rag doll" test is the easiest. Count out five or ten seeds of each kind and put them in marked squares, so you can keep track of which is which, on a damp paper towel. Roll up the towel, slip it inside a clear plastic bag, and keep it at about 70°F for a week or so. At the end of that period, open the bag, unroll the damp towel, and count how many seeds have sprouted. If most have sprouted and look strong, your germination rate should be high. If only a few seeds have sprouted or if the seedlings look weak, you'll know you should sow your seeds more thickly and adjust your expectations.

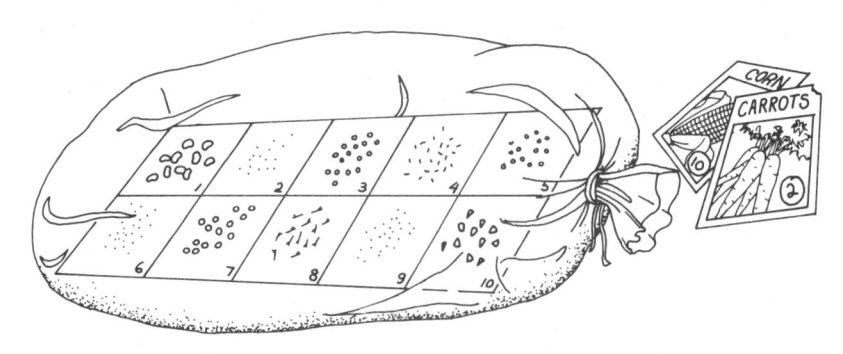

Germinate seeds on damp paper towel laid flat or rolled into a "rag doll"

Cooperative Extension Service

Experienced and inexperienced gardeners alike sometimes run into problems they cannot solve by themselves, even with the help of the local garden center and friendly neighbors. At these times one of the most valuable bits of information any gardener can have on hand is how to get in touch with the local Cooperative Extension Service.

The Cooperative Extension Service was created by the Smith-Lever Act (1914) as an organizational entity of the United States Department of Agriculture and the state land-grant colleges and universities. Its purpose is to disseminate information from experts in various areas to the public through publications, correspondence, and other educational activities of an informal, non-resident, problem-oriented nature. These activities are carried out primarily by the extension staffs at the county and state levels.

Extension people can supply the specialized information you need to make planning and planting decisions such as which plants to grow, which varieties of plants and seeds to choose, when to plant, what improvements you might need to make in your soil. And as the growing season proceeds, they can help you with other problems you encounter.

Although the Cooperative Extension Service is a bountiful source of information, there is a catch: you have to find them. This isn't so hard at the state level. You simply write to the Cooperative Extension Service at your state land-grant institution's College of Agriculture (you'll find the address at the end of this chapter). But at the local level, this service goes by different names in different places, or may be listed differently in local phone books. A good place to start tracking down your local extension service is under the name of your land-grant educational institution and then under Cooperative Extension Service or College of Agriculture. Or you can look under the name of your county and then for titles such as extension agent, extension advisor, county agent, or farm advisor. If you can't find these people — they are not lost, they know where they are — write your state land-grant institution.

Once you've found where to write for extension service information, knowing who to write will speed the response to your written requests. For information about cultural problems in general and recommended varieties of plants, consult your *extension horticulturist*. The *extension entomologist* is the person to write about bugs and other undesirable garden livestock. Questions about plant diseases should be directed to the *extension plant pathologist*. These experts are often available at both the county and state levels.

Sometimes getting a satisfactory answer to your questions will require sending a specimen of your plant or pest to an extension expert. Popping the material naked into an envelope usually results in the stuff being squished beyond recognition when it goes through the postal system. So here are some suggestions that will make consultation by mail worth the effort and the postage.

First, write a letter to send with the specimen. This letter should include all of the following information (if it applies) plus any other information you think might be pertinent:

- Date specimen was collected
- Kind of plant, if you know
- Description of problem and severity
- Description of recent watering and fertilizing schedules, including when, what kind and how much fertilizer you used
- Description of recent pest or disease control measures you have used
- Your name and address (People who fail to include this information don't get a reply)

Next, gather together the mailing materials you will need. These will consist of a dry paper towel, waxed paper, aluminum foil, or a plastic bag in which to wrap the specimen and a crushproof box or mailing tube large enough to hold the wrapped specimen.

After all this is done, collect the specimen. How much of a specimen you enclose depends on your question. If it concerns plant identification, send at least one whole leaf and part of a stem. If the question is about a pest or disease, the specimen should show the entire range of symptoms. Wrap your specimen and seal it tightly. DO NOT ADD MOISTURE. Place the sealed specimen in the mailing container and send it off at once. The freshness of the specimen is extremely important. Try to make sure it arrives at the extension early in the week, rather than late Friday afternoon.

State Extension Service Addresses

Listed here are the names and addresses of the land-grant colleges and universities which serve as state headquarters for the Cooperative Extension Service. For general information regarding the overall services available in your state, or to find out the address of your local extension service, direct your correspondence to the Extension Director of your state's land-grant institution. For more specific questions, write to the extension expert in the appropriate field: Extension Horticulturist (cultural problems, recommended plant varieties, availability); Extension Entomologist (bugs and insects); or Extension Plant Pathologist (diseases).

    Example: Appropriate Title
             College of Agriculture
             State Land-Grant Institution
             City, State, Zip

ALABAMA: Auburn University, Box 95151, Auburn, AL 36830
ALASKA: University of Alaska, Fairbanks, AK 99701
ARIZONA: University of Arizona, Tucson, AZ 85721
ARKANSAS: University of Arkansas, Fayetteville, AR 72701
CALIFORNIA: University of California, Berkeley, CA 94720
COLORADO: Colorado State University, Fort Collins, CO 80521
CONNECTICUT: University of Connecticut, Storrs, CT 06268
DELAWARE: University of Delaware, Newark, DE 19711
DISTRICT OF COLUMBIA: Federal City College, Washington, DC 20001
FLORIDA: University of Florida, Gainesville, FL 32601
GEORGIA: University of Georgia, Athens, GA 30601
HAWAII: University of Hawaii, Honolulu, HI 96822
IDAHO: University of Idaho, Moscow, ID 83843
ILLINOIS: University of Illinois, Urbana, IL 61801
INDIANA: Purdue University, W. Lafayette, IN 47907
IOWA: Iowa State University, Ames, IA 50010
KANSAS: Kansas State University, Manhattan, KS 66502
KENTUCKY: University of Kentucky, Lexington, KY 40506
LOUISIANA: Louisiana State University, Baton Rouge, LA 70803
MAINE: University of Maine, Orono, ME 04473
MARYLAND: University of Maryland, College Park, MD 20742
MASSACHUSETTS: University of Massachusetts, Amherst, MA 01002
MICHIGAN: Michigan State University, East Lansing, MI 48823
MINNESOTA: University of Minnesota, St. Paul, MN 55101
MISSISSIPPI: Mississippi State University, Mississippi State, MS 39762
MISSOURI: University of Missouri, Columbia, MO 65201
MONTANA: Montana State University, Bozeman, MT 59715
NEBRASKA: University of Nebraska, Lincoln, NB 68503
NEVADA: University of Nevada, Reno, NV 89507
NEW HAMPSHIRE: University of New Hampshire, Durham, NH 03824
NEW JERSEY: Rutgers, The State University, New Brunswick, NJ 08903
NEW MEXICO: New Mexico State University, Las Cruces, NM 88003
NEW YORK: Cornell University, Ithaca, NY 14850

NORTH CAROLINA: North Carolina State University, Raleigh, NC 27607
NORTH DAKOTA: North Dakota State University, Fargo, ND 58103
OHIO: The Ohio State University, Columbus, OH 43210
OKLAHOMA: Oklahoma State University, Stillwater, OK 74074
OREGON: Oregon State University, Corvallis, OR 97331
PENNSYLVANIA: Pennsylvania State University, University Park, PA 16802
PUERTO RICO: University of Puerto Rico, Rio Piedras, PR 00927
RHODE ISLAND: University of Rhode Island, Kingston, RI 02881
SOUTH CAROLINA: Clemson University, Clemson, SC 29631
SOUTH DAKOTA: South Dakota State University, Brookings, SD 57007
TENNESSEE: University of Tennessee, P.O. Box 1071, Knoxville, TN 37901
TEXAS: Texas A & M University, College Station, TX 77843
UTAH: Utah State University, Logan, UT 84321
VERMONT: University of Vermont, Burlington, VT 05401
VIRGIN ISLANDS: Virgin Islands Agriculture Project, Kingshill, St. Croix, VI 00801
VIRGINIA: Virginia Polytechnic Institute and State University, Blacksburg, VA 24061
WASHINGTON: Washington State University, Pullman, WA 99163
WEST VIRGINIA: West Virginia University, Morgantown, WV 26506
WISCONSIN: University of Wisconsin, Madison, WI 53706
WYOMING: University of Wyoming, Laramie, WY 82070

Growing Challenges

Weeds

Weeds are pushy plants that take light, water, and food from more cultivated plants. They shelter insects and diseases. For example, cabbage aphids will often visit with mustard weeds until a more succulent member of the same plant family comes along. Grass, clover, mustard, violets and mint can be decorative and delightful in one location and a real pest in another. The same mustard plant that provides the golden highlights for so many picnics can take over whole fields in California with monster plants 12 feet high. And mint, the perfect foil for lamb, the very essence of a mint julep, can wear out its welcome in a garden.

Not all weeds are outsiders. Vegetables planted too close together, or young plants that have not been thinned out, can also choke each other. And although in its proper place a green lawn soothes the eye and feeds the pride of its keeper, grass can murder tender little plants if it makes its way into the garden.

To be a successful weeder you have to recognize the gatecrasher early. When unwanted plants are small, they can be pulled out, cut off, or disposed of by regular cultivation. Waiting and hoping that they will be smothered out by the vegetable is wishful thinking. Weeds are usually tougher than vegetables — that is one reason why there are so many of them. Weeds lack breeding and do not act in a civilized manner. Get them out before they take control. Once they are gone you can use a mulch to discourage their return.

A few weeds are poisonous, and some will trigger an allergy or hay fever, but most of the weeds that are problems in a vegetable garden are the so-called common weeds — the little pests. Personal introductions by an experienced plant person are the best way to identify weeds in their seedling stage since some are pleasant to look at, delightful to smell, and have a vague resemblance to something else. Keep in mind that many of these out-of-place plants are eatables, and you can think of your weeding as a harvesting for either the pot or the compost.

Weed Glossary

Bindweed *(Convolvulus spp.)*. A climbing plant with small delicate morning-glory-like flowers, the bindweed will start climbing up plants (and if there is nothing else, will climb up itself) and soon choke everything in reach. This pest is very difficult to get rid of since every piece of broken root seems capable of starting a new plant.

Burdock *(Arctium spp.)*. This plant looks like a coarse rhubarb. Many people have given it garden room only to find, late in the summer, that their only harvest will be burrs. The flower stalk, harvested while the flowers are still in bud, and the roots (be sure you use a spade) can be peeled, cut in pieces, and boiled in salted water with a pinch of baking soda. Discard the first water, boil again, drain, and serve buttered or in a cream sauce. With all this work you will not have to worry about its feelings being hurt.

Chickweed *(Stellaria media)*. A lacy plant, the chickweed spreads out over the ground like a doily. It has tiny daisylike flowers and it should be destroyed when quite young. Think of it as an early eatable. Cook chickweed quickly in salted water and serve it as spinach. If you do not have enough to cook, chop it up in a salad.

Dandelion *(Taraxacum officinale)*. Dandelion is a cheerful plant, rich in minerals and more vitamin A and C than almost any other garden product. Sometimes it is an unwelcome guest. The leaves, when young, are tasty in German potato salad, wilted, or even boiled. The roots, roasted and ground, make a coffeelike drink.

Grass (Lawn rather than Mary Jane). Any out-of-place plants with jointed stems and sheathing leaves should be plucked early and fed to the rabbits or put on the compost pile.

Seedling

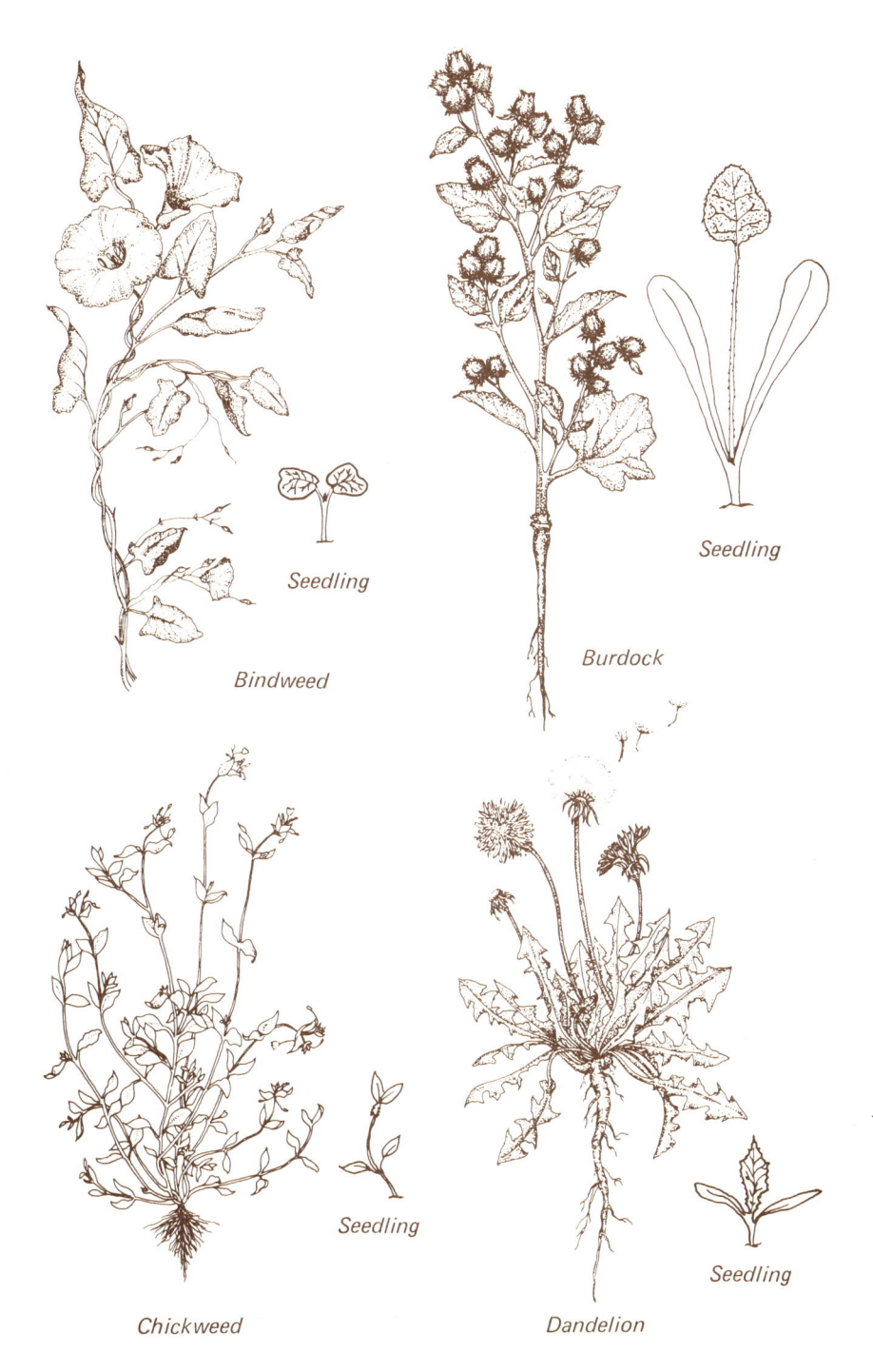

Bindweed

Seedling

Burdock

Seedling

Chickweed

Seedling

Dandelion

Grass *Lamb's quarters* *Seedling*

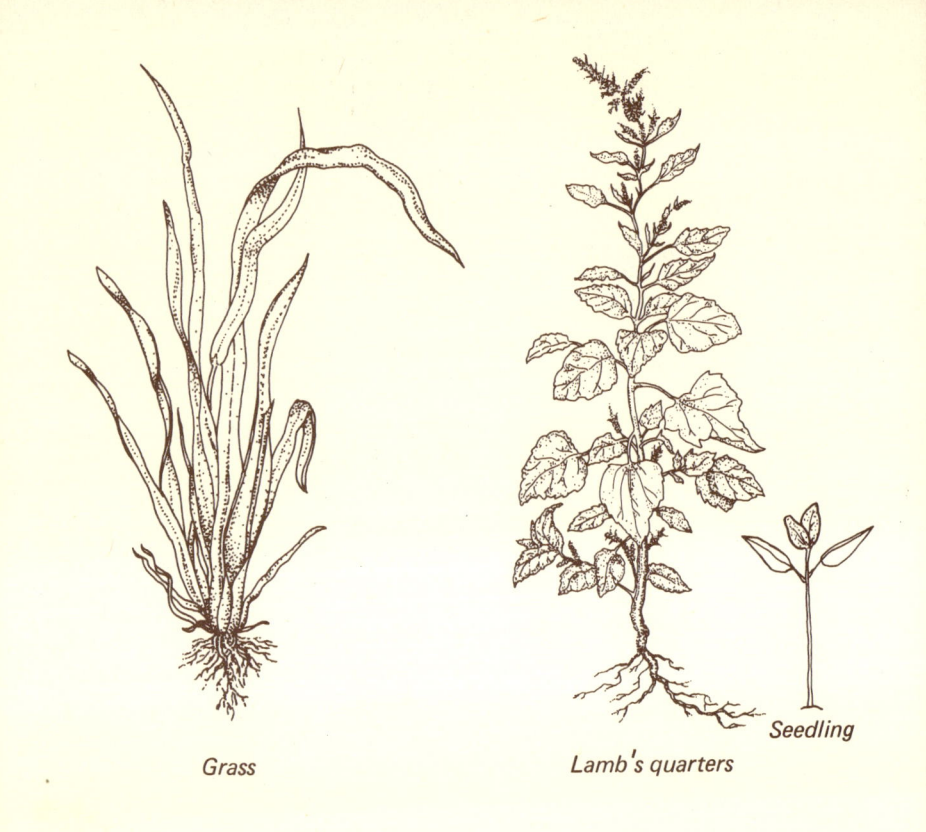

Lamb's Quarters or Goosefoot *(Chenopodium album).* Lamb's quarters contains more iron and protein than cabbage or spinach. It was pushed off the table in the 16th century when spinach appeared. Its ritzier relatives in the family Chenopodiaceae include beets, spinach, and chard. Perhaps it will come into fashion again, like Good King Henry *(Chenopodium bonus henricus)* which is now being sold in herb seed catalogs. The young seedlings are good cut up in salad and the leaves can be cooked like spinach or popped into soup or stew. Why not be the first on your block to serve lamb's quarters souffle?

Mustard *(Brassica nigra).* The black mustard grown for its seeds is a good example of a useful plant that escaped from a proper garden and went wild. In some parts of California mustard plants 12 feet high have taken over whole fields and become real pests. The leaves have a distinct mustard flavor and are good in salads or soups. If you have time, chopped mustard sandwiches are very refined — the strong flavor perks up tired palates.

Pigweed *(Amaranthus retroflexus).* Pigweed is known as red root, wild beet or rough green amaranth. It is a rough plant that can get

Seedling

Seedling

Mustard

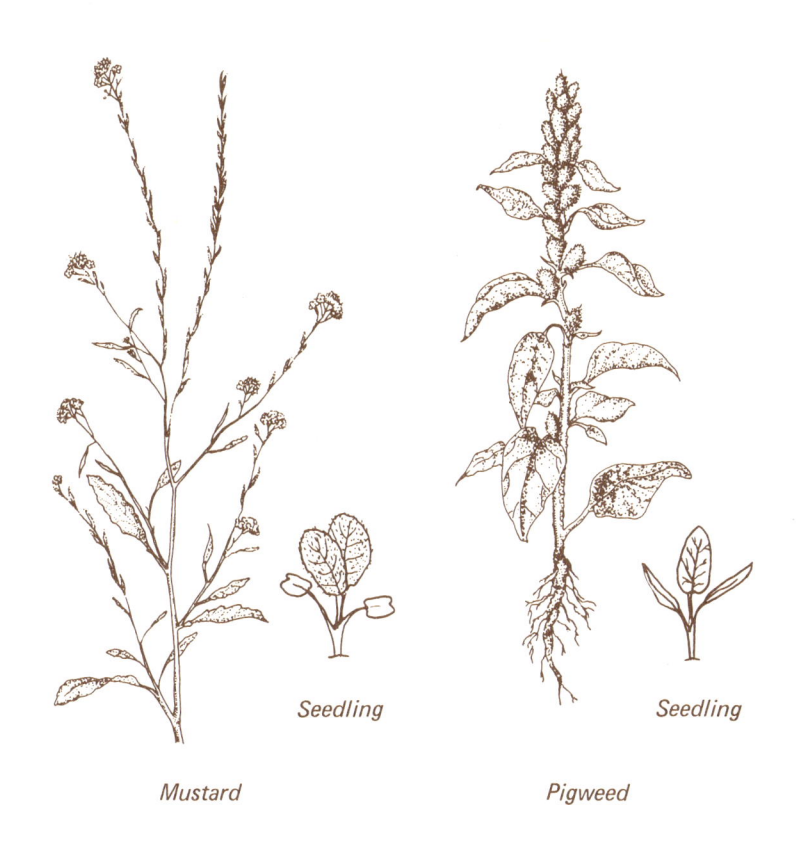

Pigweed

over six feet tall in good ground. It is eatable, but it does not have much flavor. Pigweed can be used as an extender for other garden greens and it is great on the compost pile.

Plantain *(Plantago major* and *Plantago lanceolata).* These are two plantains, common plantain and buckhorn — also called English plantain or white man's footsteps. Both plants grow in rosettes, and are rather similar to the plantain lily *(Hosta).* They have thick clumps of roots that make them hard to pull out, except when the soil is very moist and soft. They can be served in salads or cooked in soups when they are young. When they are older, the fibers in the leaves are suitable for repairing tears in your moccasins.

Purslane *(Portulaca oleracea).* Also called pusley or pigweed, purslane grows flat on the ground and has thick leaves and thick juicy stems. It adores rich, freshly-worked soil. It is good in green salads, as a garnish on a meat dish, cooked in soups or stews, or boiled in very little salted water and served with either butter or oil and vinegar dressing. Remove the flowers when preparing it — they are tough. Strewn about your bed, it is reputedly good for keeping away evil spirits.

Smartweed *(Polygonum spp.).* Tough-rooted plants, with smooth stems and swollen joints, smartweed has long narrow leaves. The water pepper *(Polygonum hydropiper)* has peppery-tasting leaves; pull up the smartweeds and pepperweeds and toss them on the compost pile.

Sour Grass *(Oxalis stricta).* Sour grass is yellow wood sorrel, a delicate plant with shamrocklike three-part leaves and delicate yellow flowers. Its seed capsules are capable of shooting seeds yards

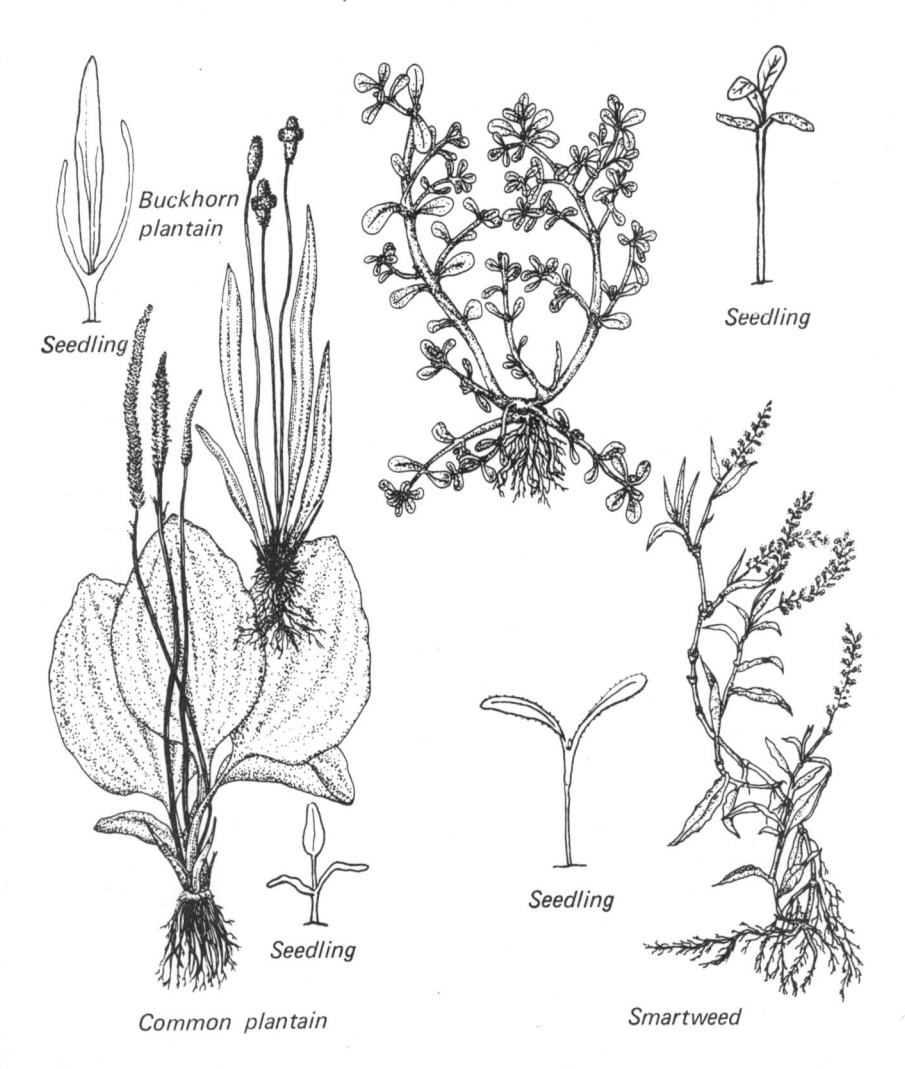

Seedling *Sour grass* *Violet*

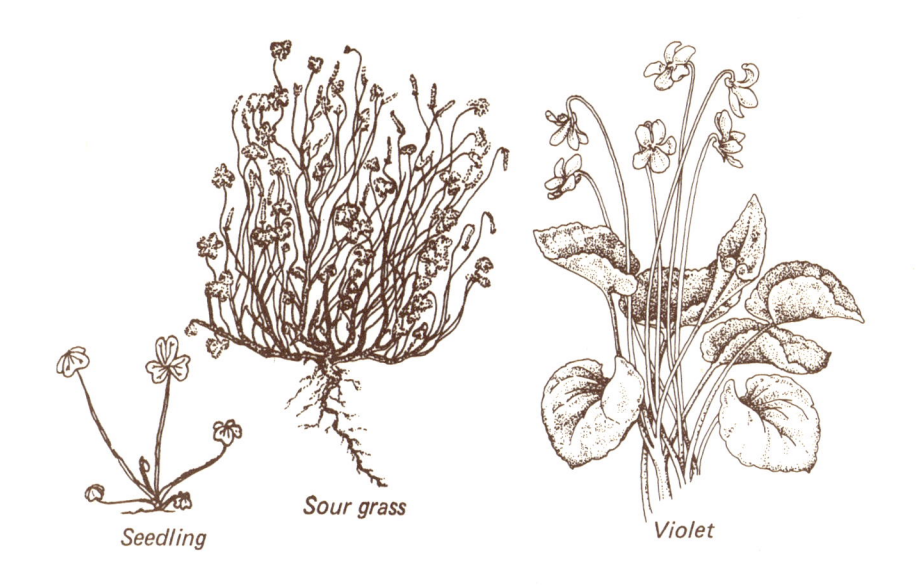

away when they ripen. It also has an underground root system that can reproduce without any seeds at all. In the time of the first Queen Elizabeth it was highly thought of as an ingredient in salads and soup. A green sauce made from its sour leaf, so rich in vitamin C, was a special delicacy with fish.

Violet *(Viola spp.).* An innocent flowering plant, the violet has heart-shaped leaves high in vitamin C. A few leaves a day will fill your minimum daily requirement of vitamin C. The flowers can be candied and used on petits fours. This is a lot of work, but have you tried buying candied violets lately? Do not encourage it, unless you want to make a lot of candied violets.

Getting Rid of Weeds

Many times a good, sharp knife is the best defense against weeds. The knife can cut the weed out selectively, without damaging the nearby eatables, and while you have it in your hand you can decide if the weed is for soup or compost. Another way to discourage weeds is to introduce them to soft living. Well-cultivated, fertile soil will often make them so precocious and prolific that they will either wear themselves out or will dawdle instead of reproducing and you can cut them off in their prime.

Herbicides, which are selective, and soil sterilants, which kill everything, can be very useful under certain conditions which are hardly ever found in the small garden. If you have a problem that cannot be solved by weeding and cultivating, contact your Cooperative Extension Service or a reliable landscaper.

Here are the facts and rules about using herbicides.
1. Herbicides do not kill all weeds.
2. Herbicides can kill vegetables.
3. Read all of the label, every bit of the fine print.
4. Do not use a herbicide unless it is labeled for a specific crop (read the whole label).
5. Be sure that the herbicide will not leave a toxic residue on the eatable parts of the plant.
6. Herbicides work best when conditions favor rapid growth.
7. Herbicides that are safe to use in a certain area can drift quite a distance and cause damage to sensitive plants, such as grapes.
8. No vegetable is entirely resistant to herbicides, so follow the instructions exactly as they appear on the label.
9. Clean spray equipment carefully right after each use.
10. Mark your herbicide application equipment and keep it separated from that used for fertilizers and insecticides. Use herbicide equipment only for herbicides.

Pests

Pests of many descriptions compete for eatables in your garden. Kids, grown-ups, pets, wildlife and crawly critters are all common garden pests. Sometimes by just adjusting our point of view we can relieve the situation. Is it bad when children eat strawberries or peas in the garden and good when they eat them inside on a plate? Should we be distressed with the birds that eat the seeds and small seedlings when we have been feeding them all winter? Did you put out a sign in Bird saying "Do not eat the ones planted in rows?" They probably thought your planting was just another indication of your thoughtfulness.

People, raccoons, rabbits, birds and such can usually be kept in line by forceful language, a fence or a net.

Birds. Unless you are fluent in Bird and are used to getting up very early in the morning, it is easier to cover seedlings and seeded areas until the plants are established. Use a net over small fruits.

Cats. Cats are very good at keeping birds and small animals out of the garden, but they work limited hours, and they often enjoy digging in the loose earth and rolling on tomatoes and cucumbers to scratch their backs. Plastic mulches and cages (for the eatables, not the cat) are often a solution.

Dogs. Not one's own, of course, but other people's dogs can be a nuisance running about or stopping to scratch or test the quality of the soil. Dogs as well as cats occasionally are responsible for the deposit of too much fresh nitrogen.

Humans. They walk all around compacting the soil, feeling the fruit to see if it's ready and picking eatables to "help." They often suggest that everything you are doing should be done another way. Smile, spend a little time with them to explain the hows and whys of what you do and you soon will have a real helper.

Rabbits. The amount of damage rabbits do is in direct proportion to how hungry they are. Usually cats and a three-foot chicken-wire fence bent out at the bottom are enough to keep them away. Since rabbits are shy and do not like to run in the open, getting rid of cover and protective piles of stuff may discourage them.

Raccoon. Raccons are connoisseurs of fresh vegetables, especially sweet corn. A good fence and an active cat are about the best solutions. Some people report that a portable radio playing loud hard rock will keep them away, but it has the opposite effect on the neighbors.

Rats. In urban areas rats can be quite destructive. Cats will keep them away if the rats are not too large. Clearing out rubbish piles in the area also helps.

Squirrels. No matter how cute they are, don't ever encourage squirrels. They are hard to get rid of except by shooting or trapping. They are as fond of sweet corn and other goodies as raccoons.

Good Bugs, Bad Bugs, Non-Bugs

To many people, any crawling or flying thing in the garden smaller than a chipmunk or a sparrow is an insect, including a number of non-insect creatures — mites, slugs, snails, nematodes, sowbugs, symphylans and the like. Many people get very concerned when they find other creatures sharing their garden and some develop a real paranoia. Most insects are harmless in the garden. Indeed many times they are necessary for the development of fruits and vegetables. But there is something about insects that frustrates people and brings out killer instinct.

There are two schools of thought on getting rid of pests: dust or spray. Dusting or spraying can be effective if the pest is properly identified and the correct material is applied properly, according to all the directions and precautions. Pesticides do not distinguish between friend and foe and you may kill some friendly insects that are out there working for you. Also, you must check the time between spraying and harvesting. A residue of pesticide can be poisonous.

Many times a blast of water from the hose, plus help from the weather and insects, like ladybugs and praying mantids, that are on your side will help your vegetables survive the attack. Think of the pest problem this way: it is better to eat a hole than a pesticide. Of course, the pests may take your sharing as an invitation and the situation may go from bad to worse, especially when the insects involved are too small to pick off and are also transmitting diseases.

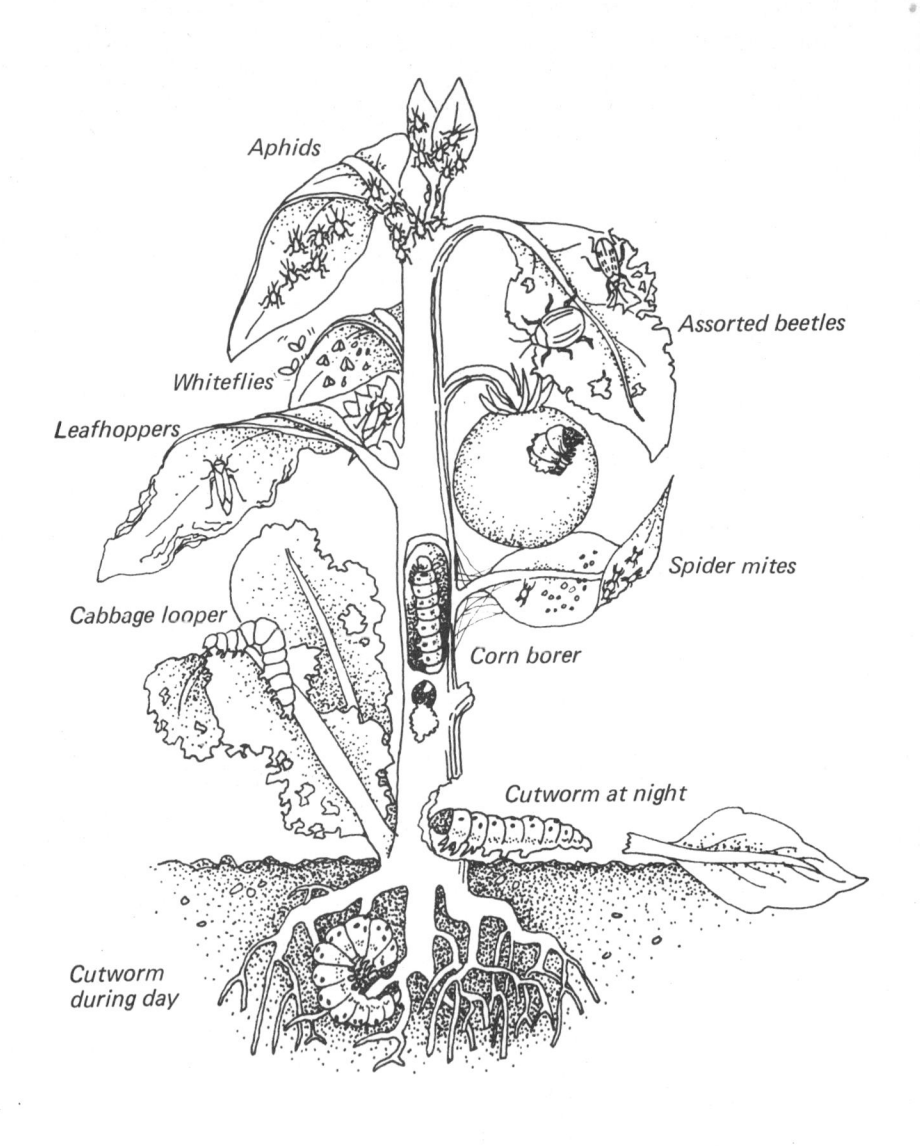

Whichever system of control (or combination of systems) you decide to use, it is important to know what the pest is. Get a knowledgeable neighbor to introduce you or check with your garden center or extension service. Cynthia Westcott's *The Gardener's Bug Book* (4th ed., New York, Doubleday) is an excellent book. Use the book as a reference, not as a shopping list. Remember that these pests are common because there are so many of them, but that often they don't show up at all.

Underground and Nocturnal Pests

Cutworms. These obese caterpillars of a hairless night-flying moth feed at night, often cutting off seedlings and transplants at ground level. They spend the day curled up just under the soil's surface. They can be controlled without chemicals by putting a collar around each plant when it is transplanted. Thin cardboard or a styrofoam cup with the bottom cut out will work. The collar should go down at least an inch into the soil and should stand away from the plant 1½ to 3 inches on all sides. Cutworms attack most eatables but they usually attack the early-season plantings.

Grubs. Grubs are the immature stage (larva) of beetles. They live just below the soil's surface and feed on roots. Usually grubs are not too much of a problem, but they indicate things to come.

Root Maggots. Maggots are fly larvae. They are yellowish-white, legless, wormlike creatures (¼ to 1⅓ inches long) that feast on roots and stems just under the soil's surface. The best control is to prevent the fly from laying eggs near the seedlings. Use plastic or tar paper (3x3 inches or 4x4 inches) around each plant when transplanting and do not cover the paper with soil when you cultivate. Root maggots attack beans, broccoli, Brussels sprouts, cabbage, carrots, cauliflower, corn, cucumbers, melons, mustard, onions, parsnips, peas, radishes, spinach, squash and turnips.

Wireworms. A slender, hard worm about one inch long, wireworms eat the seeds in the ground and feed on underground roots

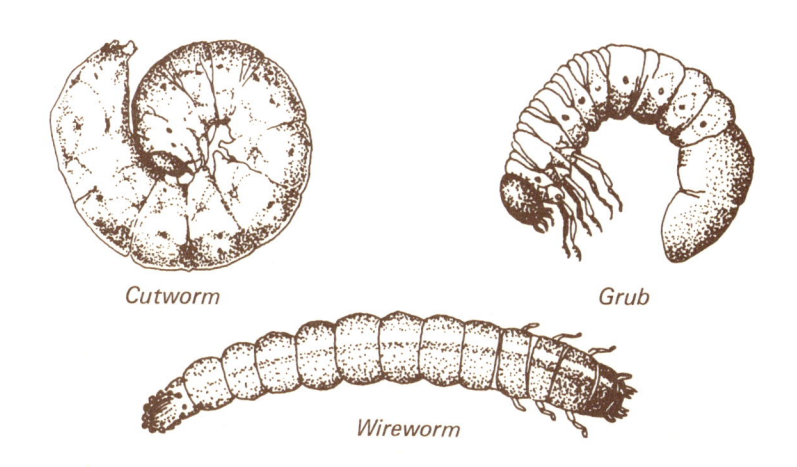

Cutworm

Grub

Wireworm

and stems. After doing their damage they grow up into click beetles. They attack beans, beets, carrots, celery, corn, lettuce, onions, potatoes (both white and sweet) and turnips.

Chewing Pests

Chewing pests are usually easy to find, especially when they have put in a good day's work. Many of them can be handpicked off the plant or knocked off with a blast from the hose. Try to choose a dry day to use the hose treatment so the leaves will not remain wet. Watch for chewing pests and kill them in the egg stage, if possible. If more drastic measures are needed, use pyrethrum or rotenone or Sevin. Check to make sure you have the guilty party and use pesticides according to directions. Start when the pest is first discovered and repeat the treatment as often as necessary.

Ants. Ants, except for the leaf cutting ones in the South and West, generally do not create much of a problem. They often have a sweet tooth so they protect aphids and scale insects in order to enjoy honeydew these insects secrete.

Beetles. Beetles come in many sizes and shapes. Some prefer one or two vegetables, some chew on whatever looks tender. Asparagus beetles dote on asparagus. Mexican bean beetles love beans. Blister beetles eat beans, beets, chard, corn, potatoes and tomatoes. Cucumber beetles (spotted and striped) are often found on melons, pumpkins, squash, and watermelons, as well as cucumbers. They do little damage but carry cucumber bacterial wilt. The flea beetle will eat most garden crops. They are small and hard to see, but you will know they are there when leaves suddenly appear full of small round holes. Potato beetles chew on eggplants, potatoes and tomatoes.

Borers (Squash Vine). Cucumbers, melons, pumpkins, squash and watermelons are attacked by borers. They grow inside the stem, eating it out and causing the vine to wilt. Slit the stem, remove the borer and cover the spot with earth to encourage root growth at that point. If the vine is too badly wilted, cut it off.

Cabbage Loopers and **Cabbage Worms.** These love all the members of the cabbage family, plus lettuce. If you do not want to share with them, indulge in biological warfare and spray with *Bacillus thuringiensis* which is available under a number of trade names.

Corn Earworms. Corn earworms eat beans, okra and tomatoes, but they prefer corn as does the European corn borer. Prepare for a regular schedule of dusting or spraying (get information from your garden center or extension service) and cut out the damaged part before you eat the vegetable.

Grasshoppers. They have great appetites and will eat anything and everything. They usually appear in late summer and are worse

Ants

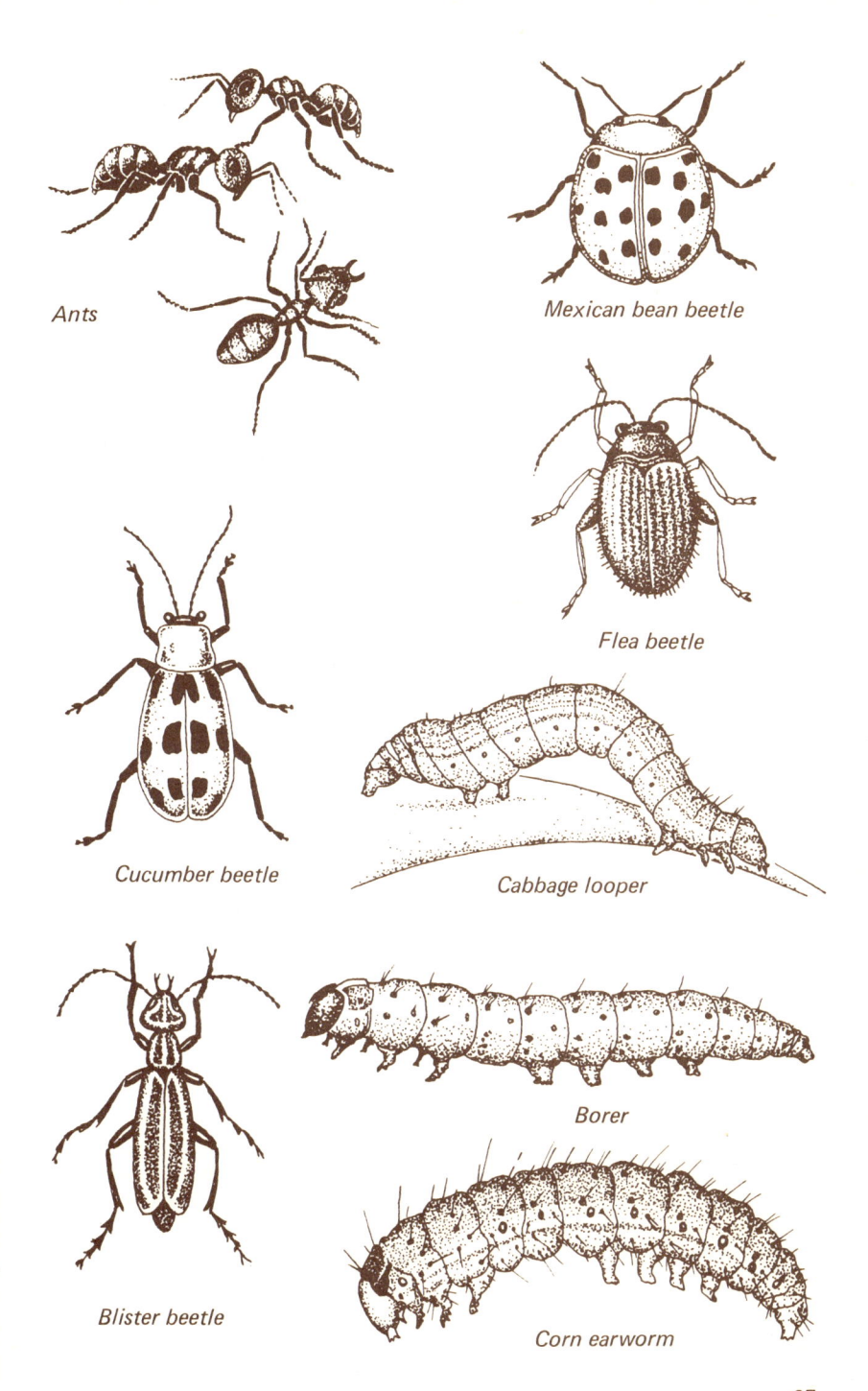

Mexican bean beetle

Flea beetle

Cucumber beetle

Cabbage looper

Borer

Blister beetle

Corn earworm

Hornworm

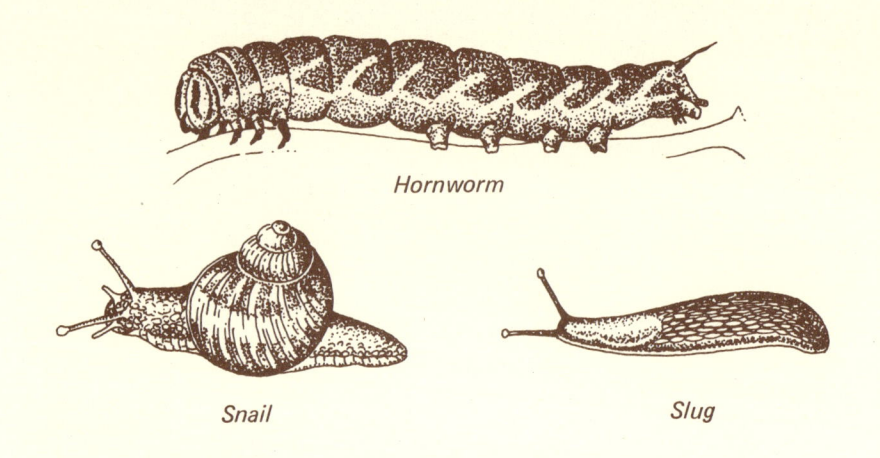

Snail *Slug*

where the winters are warm and the summers are hot. Try to get them while they are small. They begin life in untended spots near the garden.

Hornworms. Hornworms are large green caterpillars, three or four inches long with a hornlike growth on their rear end. You can tell the tomato hornworm from the tobacco hornworm, which also feeds on tomatoes, because it has eight rather than seven diagonal white stripes on its side. Handpick hornworms off the plant by grabbing them gently — but not too firmly — at the back of the neck and disposing of them. *Bacillus thuringiensis* (a bacterial preparation) is very effective in eliminating hornworms.

Parsley Caterpillars. These caterpillars feed on parsley, dill, fennel and other members of the parsley family. They are easy to remove and very interesting to watch grow. Put them in an insect cage and feed them (if you have to buy parsley be sure it's well washed) and they will eventually change into swallow-tail butterflies.

Slugs and Snails. Snails have the shell but slugs have none. Both are more closely related to oysters and clams than they are to insects. They do not like to be out in the heat of the day. You can detect their presence by the slimy trail they leave from the scene of their crime. They like cabbages and all their relatives, carrots, lettuce, strawberries, tomatoes and turnips. They like to eat and run and can be hard to control. Get rid of hiding places. Put scratchy sand or cinders around each plant. Pour beer in a saucer and hope they have one too many. This works for some gardeners, others report no effect. Arrange cool spots that they can crawl under so you can collect them in the morning. They are much easier to handle if called escargot.

Tomato Fruitworms. This is what you can call a corn earworm when you see it on tomatoes, eggplants or peppers.

Sucking Pests

Aphids, leafhoppers, mites and thrips are hard to see. By the time their damage is apparent it is often too late to do much. Watch for scraped and rusty-looking places on leaves, twisted and deformed leaves and tips, and stems that look unusually thick.

Aphids. Aphids feed by sucking the sap of the tender stems and leaves, causing a distortion. They also exude a sweet substance called honeydew which is attractive to ants and sooty molds. Aphids are sometimes carriers for mosaic and other diseases. Ladybugs and their larvae (if they are hungry) are aphid eaters. Some gardeners pinch out the infested ends. Rotenone and pyrethrum are safe to use on food crops. If you want something stronger check with your extension service. Aphids are pests on asparagus, Jerusalem artichokes, beans, broccoli, Brussels sprouts, cabbage, cauliflower, celery, chayote, collards, cucumbers, eggplant, melons, okra, peas, peppers, potatoes, spinach, strawberries, tomatoes and turnips.

Leafhoppers. These are jumping insects that feed on the undersides of leaves, sucking the sap and causing light-colored spotting on the upper side. They also spread plant diseases. They are the worst on beans, carrots, chayote, cucumbers, endive, lettuce, melons, and potatoes.

Spider Mites. If the leaves are losing color in spots and turning yellowish, light green or rusty, and if there are silvery webs on the

Aphids

Whiteflies

Leafhopper

Thrip

undersides, the culprits are probably spider mites. These are not insects; you should use a miticide recommended by your extension service for food crops. Spider mites can infest cucumbers, beans, melons, strawberries and tomatoes.

Spittlebugs. If you see something that looks as if somebody spit in the garden, it is probably a spittlebug in its protective bubbles. They are not very serious, but sometimes spittlebugs are quite noticeable in the spring around strawberries.

Thrips. Small, fast moving insects, thrips are almost invisible to the naked eye. They are very destructive. The damage shows up first as white blotches, then is a distortion of the leaf tips. If they attack onions, they dwarf and distort the bulbs. Thrips are found on beans, beets, carrots, cabbage, cauliflower, celery, cucumbers, melons, peas, squash, tomatoes and turnips.

Whiteflies. Whiteflies are minute sucking insects that look like tiny white moths. They live on the undersides of leaves and exist unnoticed until someone disturbs their plant — then they fly out in great clouds. They usually can be ignored.

Diseases

Several plant diseases are the results of unfavorable growing conditions. But many are caused by parasitic bacteria and fungi that live off the plant because they are unable to produce their own food. Bacteria and fungi lurk around, just waiting for a plant to weaken so they can take over. A strong healthy plant is always in better shape to resist disease than a weak or feeble one. Parasitic diseases can be spread by infected seeds and soil, by insects and by handling plants when wet.

There are about 80,000 different plant diseases and some are much more common than others. A good reference is Malcom C. Shurtleff's *How to Control Plant Diseases ... in Home and Garden* (2nd ed. 1966), Iowa State University Press, Ames, Iowa. This book covers the disease possibilities for over 1,000 different plants and offers suggestions for control.

Anthracnose. This name covers a number of diseases caused by different fungi. Anthracnose fungi occur more frequently in wet weather. Look for well-defined dead areas on the leaves and fruit; the dead areas are generally depressed with a slightly raised edge around them. Beans, cucumbers, melons, peppers, potatoes, pumpkins, squash, tomatoes and watermelons can all host anthracnose fungi.

Blights. The highly descriptive word "blight" is loosely applied to a wide variety of disasters that befall plants, including insect attacks. A blight is a disease condition where there is sudden and very noticeable damage to the plant, but it is neither a wilting disease nor a disease with sharply defined spots or blotches. During a blight, water-soaked spots spread and fuse into irregular blotches and rot sets in shortly after.

Blossom End Rot. Great variations in soil moisture, especially when wet weather is followed by dry weather, sometimes cause rot on the blossom ends of peppers, tomatoes and squash. A calcium deficiency, or soil condition that affects root growth (such as shallow soil, poor drainage, deep cultivation and too much nitrogen fertilizer) also invites blossom end rot.

Mildews. Powdery mildews grow on the surfaces of plants. They thrive when the weather is humid, but not during rainy weather. Mildews are encouraged by poor air circulation and crowded plants. Powdery mildew is common on cucumbers, melons, pumpkins, squash, peas, and beans. Downy mildews usually grow on the under surfaces of the leaves and inside the tissues of the plant. Downy mildews thrive in wet weather. Downy mildew grows on cucumbers, melons, pumpkins, squash, lima beans and onions, and may cause unusual growth of sweet corn.

Pesticide Damage. Pesticide dusts and sprays, including herbicides, can all harm eatables. Sprays containing copper (such as Bordeaux mix) can cause reddish-brown spots, leaf drop and stunting of cucumbers, melons and squash. This damage is aggravated by cool, damp weather. Damage from sprays containing copper can burn the tips and edges of the leaves if the temperature is 90°F or over. Weed killers are very potent and their mist can drift hundreds of feet. Tomatoes, beans and grapes are particularly sensitive to weed killers. Minute amounts left in a sprayer can distort plants badly when the sprayer is used for applying something else.

Rots. Your plant has a rot when part of it decays and dies. Rots affect various parts of plants — roots, stems, flowers and fruits. They also attack the leaves, but then they are called leaf spots or blights. Peas, tomatoes, beans, celery, lettuce, peppers and strawberries suffer rots.

Rusts. A reddish or rusty appearance on the leaves is often caused by different rust fungi. Assorted rusts grow on asparagus, beans, beets and chard.

Smuts. Masses of black spores indicate smut. Corn smut thrives in hot weather and the spores retain their vitality for a long time. Get rid of the infected corn; eliminate the whole plant and try not to plant corn in the same spot for the next few years. Onion smut generally affects onions that are grown from seeds. Onion smut is worse in cool summers, but only very young plants are attacked. The spores remain alive in the soil for years. To prevent onion smut, either use sets, grow the seeds in sterile soil and then transplant them, or choose only disease-resistant varieties.

Sunscald or Sunburn. Grapes, peppers and tomatoes and other fruits that are used to growing with a leaf cover can develop irregular whitish splotches that often rot when the leaves are pruned back too severely, or the leaves have been destroyed by insects or diseases.

Virus. Virus diseases are not too well understood. When foliage shows an even yellow discoloration and a loss of green, the disease is called virus yellows. If the foliage is evenly mottled with green and yellow, then it is called mosaic. There are also ring spot viruses and others that cause distortion and stunted growth.

Water. Too much and too little water can both produce stunting and poor growth. Blossom end rot of peppers and tomatoes and squash may be due to a period of dryness after a period of wetness.

Wilts. Plants often droop because of a lack of moisture in the leaves and soft stems. This may be the result of a fungus, bacteria or virus affecting the roots or the water-conducting tissues. Members of the cabbage family are affected by cabbage yellows or fusarium wilt. Celery is affected by celery yellows or fusarium wilt. The whole squash family is prone to cucurbit wilt. Wilts also attack peas, sweet potatoes and tomatoes. The best control is to plant resistant varieties, rotate crops and destroy infected plants.

Disease Prevention Tips

1. Make it easy for the plants to grow well. Plant the eatables in full sun, if possible. Strong sunlight is a great disinfectant and the energy plants draw from the sun gives them extra strength. Make sure the soil is well worked, has good drainage and is high in organic matter so that the soil moisture will remain even. Do not plant the vegetables when the soil and air are too cold. Place them far enough apart so they do not crowd each other and there is good air circulation, allowing the plants to dry after a rain.

2. Select resistant varieties of seeds and plants. Buy seeds that are certified as disease free, use seeds treated with fungicide, or start seeds in a sterile soil mix.

3. Do not grow the same plant family in the same spot year after year. Repetition of the same crop gives diseases a chance to build up strength.

4. Do not work in the garden when it is wet. When watering, do not splash water on the leaves, especially in hot, humid weather.

5. Keep insects and other small pests under control. If you control them by hosing them off, do it on a dry day, or during the driest part of the day, so the plants will dry quickly.

6. If you smoke and are going to be working with peppers,

eggplants, and tomatoes, wash your hands well with soap and hot running water before touching them. Smokers can give their plants a case of tobacco mosaic, causing them to mottle, streak, drop leaves and even die. While transplanting, pruning, and tying plants in the tomato family, smokers can cut down the risk of tobacco mosaic by dipping their hands in whole or skimmed milk every few minutes.
7. Keep the garden free of weeds, trash, and plants that have finished producing.

Pesticides

In the small garden pests and diseases can often be controlled by keeping the garden clean of grass, weeds and harvested plants, by selecting resistant varieties and disease-free seeds and plants, by proper fertilization, by the judicious use of the hose and handpicking. Knowing the life cycle of the enemy also makes it possible to frustrate them at their weak points. But if pests or diseases begin to seriously threaten your crop, you may want to use a pesticide — a pest killer. Here are some important points to remember.
1. Read the label and observe *all* the precautions.
2. Carefully note all application restrictions. Often pesticides must be applied at a certain point in the plant's development. There is usually a time period between application and harvesting that must be strictly observed.
3. Store material (undiluted) in its original container out of the reach of children, irresponsible adults and animals — preferably in a locked cabinet or storage area.
4. Avoid breathing sprays and dusts.
5. Dust so both sides of each leaf get an even, light coating. Dust only when the air is still, preferably not just before a rain. Be sure the dust is compatible with both the problem and with people.
6. Sprays usually have to be mixed before each use. The proportions on the label must be followed exactly (please, no creativity here) to give effective control without injuring plants or people. Be sure that the spray is not being used in a sprayer that was used for weed killer.
7. Wear rubber gloves when handling pesticide concentrates.
8. Do not smoke while handling pesticides.
9. After using a pesticide, your clothes and all exposed parts of the body should be thoroughly washed with soap and water.
10. Do not apply pesticides near fish ponds, dug wells, cisterns. Do not leave puddles of pesticides on solid surfaces.
11. Be careful when you dispose of the pesticide container. Do not leave it where it might be recycled for another use.
12. Wash all treated eatables carefully before eating them.

Common Vegetable Gardening Problems

PROBLEM	MAY BE CAUSED BY	WHAT YOU CAN DO (MAYBE)
Seeds do not come up	Not enough time for germination	Wait
	Too cold	Wait
	Too dry	Water
	Too wet, they rotted	Replant
	Being eaten by birds, insects	Replant
	Seed too old	Replant with fresh seed
Young plants die	Fungus (damping off)	Treat seed with fungicide
	Rotting	Do not overwater
	Fertilizer burn	Follow recommendations for use; be sure fertilizer is mixed thoroughly with soil
Leaves have holes	Insects, birds, rabbits	Identify culprit and take appropriate measures
	Heavy winds or hail	Plan for a better defense

Tortured, abnormal growth	Herbicide residue in sprayer, in grass clippings used as mulch, in drift from another location	Use separate sprayer for herbicides; spray only on still days; use another means of weed control
	Virus	Control insects that transmit disease; remove infected plants (do not put them on the compost pile)
Blossom ends of tomatoes and peppers rot	Dry weather following wet	Mulch to even out soil moisture
	Not enough calcium in soil	Add lime
	Compacted soil	Cultivate
	Too-deep cultivation	Avoid cultivating too deeply
There is no fruit	Weather too cold	Watch your planting time
	Weather too hot	Same as above
	Too much nitrogen	Fertilize only as often and as heavily as needed
	No pollination	Pollinate with a brush, or by shaking plant (depending on kind); do not kill all the insects
	Plants not mature enough	Wait

PROBLEM	MAY BE CAUSED BY	WHAT YOU CAN DO (MAYBE)
Plants wilt	Lack of water	Water
	Too much water	Stop watering, improve drainage, pray for less rain
	Disease	Use disease-resistant varieties
	Nematodes	Rotate plants, change soil, move garden; get recommendation from extension service
Leaves and stems are spotted	Fertilizer or chemical burn	Follow instructions, read all fine print, keep fertilizer off plant unless recommended
	Disease	Use disease-resistant varieties of seed; dust or spray; ignore
Plants weak and spindly	Not enough light	Remove cause of shade or move plants
	Too much water	Improve drainage, stop watering, pray for less rain
	Plants are crowded	Thin out
	Too much nitrogen	Reduce fertilizing

Leaves curl	Wilt	Destroy affected plants; rotate crops, grow disease-resistant varieties
	Virus	Control aphids; destroy plants
	Moisture imbalance	Mulch
Plants are stunted — yellow and peaked	Too much water	Reduce watering
	Poor drainage	Improve drainage; add more organic matter before next planting
	Compacted soil	Cultivate soil deeper
	Too much rubbish	Remove rubbish
	Acid soil	Test, add lime
	Not enough fertilizer	Test, add fertilizer (this should have been done before planting)
	Insects, diseases or nematodes	Identify and follow recommendations from your extension service
	Yellow or wilt disease, especially if yellowing attacks one side of the plant first	Spraying will not help; plant disease-resistant seed in clean soil

Rating Eatables

How do you rate your eatables? Part of that question is — do you like them? If you don't like spinach, then naturally your rating will be low. If you don't like spinach, but enjoy the excuse for working outdoors, meeting other people, and giving the stuff away, then your rating will be higher. If, however, you like the special flavor of fresh spinach, thrill when seeds germinate and grow into productive plants, or enjoy the feeling of satisfaction that comes from having done something yourself, meeting and overcoming challenges — then the rating would be very high.

The rating system which follows has been developed for people who have to make the most of small plots. However, if space is no consideration, then many of the space-eaters can be grown profitably and the ratings would change. No one else can know your specific conditions, your inclination to work, or your likes and dislikes, all of which are very important in your final decision as to what you will grow.

What kind of a product will satisfy you? This decision will be tempered by your geographic situation and your immediate growing conditions. If you have partial shade, you usually get partial crop. If you want to grow black-eyed peas in Lansing, Michigan, tomatoes in Seattle, Washington, or asparagus in Orlando, Florida, you will have to settle for a lot less than if you were growing these same crops in Mobile, Alabama, Lafayette, Indiana, or Madison, Wisconsin. It may be worth the extra effort, but you are the only person who can make that decision.

Length of Growing Season

The amount of time between the average date of the last spring freeze and the first fall frost can vary from year to year. For this reason, if the time needed to harvest the crop you are interested in is just the same length as the growing season, you will have trouble 90 percent of the time. The time to harvest listed in the catalog is actual but optimistic, and since harvesting often continues over a period of time, a good part of the potential harvest could be lost. If motivation is extremely great, plants can be protected and the season extended. This is often difficult at the end of the season when the plants are large and cold weather, even if it does not kill the plant, can slow down or stop production and decrease the flavor. For perennials, consider if there is enough warm weather to produce a crop. Concord grapes need a 160-day growing season to produce fruit.

Sun and Shade

Does your garden spot have unobstructed sun? How much sunshine do you get? Are many days cloudy and foggy? Without six hours of full sun a day, many eatables will not produce. The leafy and root crops do better than those where the fruit is harvested, but partial shade means partial crop. Some eatables can exist in full shade, but they will not produce anything but frustration. Shade from a tree can be corrected by removing or thinning branches, but it is difficult to get rid of the shadow of your house or your neighbor's. If you have full sun and the plant prefers partial shade, shade can always be provided. If you like constructing things, this is simple to do, but if you are not inclined in that direction, providing shade can be a bother.

Ease of Growing

Some plants almost grow themselves. A number of plants will reseed themselves year after year. All you have to do with these volunteers is keep them in their places. Some plants are hospitable to many pests and if you are bothered by lacy collards or chewed carrots, then you will have to work harder and expect less. Some plants need to be pruned, sprayed, tied or propped, provided with support, or picked every day. If you enjoy this kind of puttering, then this effort is a plus; if not, then it becomes a burden. How much work do you want to do with the produce after it is grown? For example, do you like washing spinach or grating horseradish? If these considerations do not fit comfortably into your growing season and personality, then it's a definite minus for that plant in your garden. Is the plant sensitive to temperature or daylength sequences? Asparagus does better with three months' cold weather, and Chinese cabbage has to be planted late in the season or it will go to seed during long days.

Pest Potential

Will the plant stay where it is put or disappear at the end of the season? If it does, that means more flexibility in your garden. If, on the other hand, it is persistent like asparagus or horseradish, you can never get rid of it. If it spreads like mint or sows itself all over the garden like mustard, then it can become a real pest.

Spread of Harvest

If the plant can be harvested over a period of time, it is usually preferable to one that matures all at once. Ten feet of radishes coming in the house all at one time is more than enough, but leaf lettuce or sprigs of herbs that can be picked for salad over a period of time can be a delight. When selecting varieties, read the descriptions carefully since many vegetables today are being bred to come to maturity all at one time. This is an advantage to the commercial grower who wants to harvest his whole crop at once, but can mean glut and famine for the home gardener.

Potential Yield

This is based on averaging experiences of gardeners in different parts of the country where the plants grow. It gives an idea of relative production possible from a small space. Keep in mind how much you can use. Herbs and onions, which are used primarily as flavorings, will go farther and grace more meals than tomatoes or sweet corn. The points you enter on part IV of the rating chart will come close to the subjective evaluation that an experienced gardener might arrive at automatically. However, this is not good enough for making a commitment to grow that eatable in a small garden.

Personal Preferences

Personal considerations are very important — perhaps most important — in small spaces since each plant is so special. If you are curious, want to grow it, or love the stuff, that will make a great difference. People can grow sweet potatoes and black-eyed peas in central Michigan, but it's more work than growing asparagus and cabbage. On the other hand, if you have a negative feeling about an eatable, or no one in the family will eat it, or you can't give it to anyone in the neighborhood, then it is a lost cause and should not be taking up space, even if it grows beautifully in your area and is loaded with vitamins A, B and C.

Using the Rating Chart

The tailored rating chart incorporates your personal interests and the constraints of your geographic area to help you arrive at a rating for each eatable you are interested in growing. As you fill out the chart, if you find an item does not apply to your situation or the eatable you are rating, go on to the next item. Bear in mind that this rating chart is set up for production in a single season. For some perennials you will have to accept the fact that there will be no crop the first year.

After you have rated an eatable, parts I and II of the chart will generally remain the same from year to year. There may be a few changes. A tree may grow or be cut down, your interest may increase or you may have less time. But generally once you have figured out I and II for each eatable, the points will remain rather constant for you in your area. On the other hand, part V can change radically. Your tastes may change, those neighbors who love rutabagas may move away, or after you have grown Brussels sprouts and know how they do it, you may no longer want to bother with them. Your personal input, then, should be re-evaluated every year since any change here can make a radical difference in the final analysis.

The analysis and final decision are yours, but generally if the eatable rates 5 or over, you will have a successful experience. If it is 3 or 4, give it a try. If it is 1 or 2, why grow it, since even you don't care for it that much.

Rating Chart for Eatables

Before you begin, get the average date of the last spring freeze and first fall freeze in your area from your public library or weather bureau.

Count the number of days between these two dates to find the length of your growing season. Then select the eatables you are interested in and then turn to the "Catalog of Eatables." Read the discussion and fill out the rating chart. Give points for only the factors which apply to your situation and the eatable you are rating.

RATING QUESTIONNAIRE	EATABLE	EATABLE	EATABLE	EATABLE

I. Characteristics of Place
   A. Time available
      1. Enter the length of your growing season here.
	—	—	—	—

2. Enter days to harvest for variety here.	—	—	—	—
3. Enter the difference between length of season and days to harvest here.	—	—	—	—

4. Your season is 56 days longer than days to harvest ....+1
      5. Your growing season is 28 days longer than days to harvest 0
      6. Your growing season is the same number of days as days to harvest ..−1
      7. Your growing season is shorter than days to harvest ....−2
   B. Light available
     Select from one group only for each eatable.
      1. Plant *needs* full sun.
        You have full sun ....+1
        You have partial shade ....−1
        You have shade ....−2
      2. Plant *prefers* full sun but will tolerate partial shade.
        You have sun ....+1
        You have partial shade 0				

RATING QUESTIONNAIRE	EATABLE	EATABLE	EATABLE	EATABLE

3. Plant *prefers* partial shade.
You have partial shade ....+1
You have sun but are industrious enough to provide shade when it's needed ..+1
You have sun but are lazy or can't be around to provide shade ....−1
II. Characteristics of Plant
  A. Ease of growing
    1. Plant grows by itself ....+1
    2. Plant needs tying, staking, pruning, frequent picking or other special care.
      If you enjoy doing it ....+1
      If you don't enjoy doing it ....−1
    3. Plant is vulnerable to many pests and diseases ....−1
    4. Plant is generally not bothered much by pests and diseases ....+1
    5. Plant is sensitive to temperature and temperature sequences or daylength and daylength sequences.
      Conditions occur naturally ....+1
      You must modify conditions ....−1
  B. Plant as potential pest
    1. Plant stays where it's planted without spreading or dies at the end of the season ....+1
    2. Plant spreads or seeds itself to the point of becoming a pest or is hard to move or dig up ....−1
  C. Spread of harvest
    1. Eatable parts can be harvested over a period of time ....+1				

RATING QUESTIONNAIRE	EATABLE	EATABLE	EATABLE	EATABLE

    2. Whole plant must be harvested all at once .... −1

III. Potential Yield

    Find the eatable you are rating in one of the groups below and enter points accordingly. Remember, this is only the plant's potential; it may not grow at all in your area.

    A. High potential yield

        1. Jerusalem artichoke, basil, celeriac, chard, chive, collard, cress, dill, fennel, garlic, grape, horseradish, marjoram, parsley, rosemary, sage, squash, tarragon, thyme, tomato .... +5

        2. Apple, beet, broccoli, cabbage, Chinese cabbage, celery, chayote, cucumber, kale, lettuce, mustard, parsnip, radish, rhubarb, rutabaga, salsify, turnip .... +4

    B. Average to low potential yield

        1. Asparagus, snap bean, Brussels sprout, carrot, chicory, eggplant, endive, kohlrabi, leek, onion, pepper, white potato +3

        2. Cauliflower, muskmelon, okra, sweet potato, pumpkin, New Zealand spinach, strawberry, watermelon .... +2

        3. Globe artichoke, broad bean, four-angled bean, lima bean, mung bean, corn, peanut, black-eyed pea, sweet pea, soybean, spinach .... +1

IV. Subtotal

    Add plus points and subtract minus points. Divide the remaining points by two and enter the results here.

RATING QUESTIONNAIRE	EATABLE	EATABLE	EATABLE	EATABLE
V. Personal Preferences 　Select only one point value. 　A. Positive factors 　　1. You are curious about growing it ....+1 　　2. You like eating it and want to try growing it ....+2 　　3. You love the stuff and will do whatever you can to grow it ....+3 　B. Negative factors 　　1. You are not particularly enthusiastic about either growing or eating it ....−1 　　2. No one in the family will eat it ......−2 　　3. No one in the neighborhood will eat it −3 VI. Analysis 　Total your points for parts IV and V to find the rating for your eatable as it could be grown in your area. If the rating is 5 or more, the eatable is a good prospect. If the rating is 3 or 4, you might give it a try. If the rating is 2 or less, why bother?	—	—	—	—

Catalog of Eatables

The best way to learn about plants is to observe the plants themselves. If you can watch or talk with experienced plant people you can find the information you need as you go along, without being burdened with a lot of information you do not need at the moment. The discussion of each eatable in this catalog should provide you with the basic information you need to begin growing your own.

Names and Origin

For each plant, the informal and formal introductions come first. The common name, or nickname, is the name everyone knows and uses. There are sometimes several common names and occasionally some confusions. For instance, those lumpy tubers called potatoes in the North are called Irish or white potatoes in the South, and what are called potatoes in the South are called sweet potatoes in the North. Sometimes an ordinary common name such as pumpkin can refer to three different species of plants. So although common names are handy for everyday use, botanical names are important to making sure that we are all talking about the same plant.

As you look at botanical names, you may discover relationships between plants that you were not aware of before. This information may make it easier for you to plan your garden since close relatives can often be treated alike. Many times the same pests and diseases that attack one member of the family will attack the rest with equal relish.

Many eatables are immigrants. Knowing the country of origin for each eatable you want to grow can give you some insight into its individual needs and at times can suggest possible solutions to challenges you encounter along the way.

Description

The information included for each eatable under "description" will help you get acquainted with each plant's individual characteristics and growing habits. If the description tells you a plant is hardy, you will know it won't mind the cold too much. If it tells you the plant is tender, you'll know it won't take frost. The description will also tell you if the plant is an annual that will grow only one year, a biennial that usually doesn't flower or fruit until the second season, or a perennial that may reward you with several years of eating.

Many plants have flowers that can fertilize themselves without any help from the gardener. Other plants have separate male and female flowers. These plants can fertilize themselves although sometimes the gardener has to play matchmaker. Other plants are self-unfertile, meaning that the flowers cannot be fertilized by their own pollen and that there must be at least one other plant somewhere nearby for pollination to take place.

Plant breeders have developed varieties to meet a number of different needs. For example, some varieties have been especially developed to resist disease, to ripen early, or to travel well. Varieties have been developed to be adaptable to a number of different climates and environments but may do splendidly in one area and poorly in another.

The varieties listed in this catalog are the ones that are most commonly available, not necessarily the ones that will grow best for you. For information on varieties that grow well in your area, check with your local Cooperative Extension Service. Since growing conditions can vary greatly even within a state, your local extension people will be able to give you the most accurate information about your specific conditions. Most state extension services put out a list of recommended varieties each year.

The choice of varieties for some plants is so dizzying that you might wind up playing eenie-meenie-minnie-mo to make your choice. With other plants there are very few varieties to choose from, perhaps only one. In these cases you'll have to take what is available.

Eatables may be grown from seeds, cuttings, transplants, or divisions. Sometimes you have a choice of stages to start with. If you have a choice, the catalog description will tell you what the choice is. But even if there are choices, your local garden center or favorite seed catalog may not carry them all. If you are starting with seeds, the catalog description tells you how many seeds there are in an ounce. This will help you decide how much seed to order and how steady your hand should be in seeding the rows.

In the descriptions, the times from planting to harvest and the yields from a ten-foot row are optimistic estimates based on ideal conditions. If things go well, that's how soon and how much you can expect to harvest. There are many factors that can make your eatables take more time from planting to harvesting: cold weather, too much heat, day length, too much rain, too little rain or water, or not enough light. And all of those factors plus pests and diseases can reduce the yield. So don't lose patience — or your sense of humor — if your experience doesn't match the figures here. In gardening the suspense is part of the fun.

Which parts are eaten can depend on the variety and maturity of the plant as well as the region in which it has been grown. If the catalog description suggests a part that you have never considered eating, try it — you may like it.

Growing Information

The requirements for each plant are stated as optimistically as possible. Under "space," you will find the minimum distance you should leave between plants. Under "light," you will find out if the plant can be grown in partial shade or if it needs at least six hours of full sun per day. Remember, when growing eatables in partial shade you usually get a partial crop — but sometimes half a crop is better than none.

Temperature, both high and low, can be very important in growing eatables. If the temperature is too low or too high, growth, flowering, pollination, or the setting and development of the fruit may be affected. The wrong temperature can also trigger premature flowering and bolting.

Water is one of the three essentials for growing plants. If there are special requirements at different times during the growing season they are mentioned.

The soil provides the support and nourishment for the plant. Most eatables do best with a soil pH between 5.5 and 7.5. If there is a question about the soil's fertility, it is better to make a test than to indiscriminately add fertilizer. Often poor growth is due to the physical condition of the soil — poor drainage or inability to retain moisture, for example — rather than lack of fertility.

The pests and diseases mentioned for each eatable are the ones most generally distributed over the country and most likely to pay a visit. They are possibilities, in some instances probabilities, but don't feel neglected if none of them show up. In an isolated garden that is kept clean, years may go by before any of them show up. On the other hand, don't feel put upon if some not mentioned show up instead.

The laws governing the sale and use of pesticides and herbicides are changing. You should check with your extension service or garden center to find out what, if anything, you should use. Often it is just as effective to hose or pick off the intruders or to pull out the diseased plants.

Cultural hints should help you anticipate special care or equipment that the eatable might need.

Harvesting, Eating, Storing

Harvesting, eating and storing suggestions are included to help you get the greatest use and enjoyment from your eatables. Unless you have a large garden, or are specifically planning to plant enough extra to can or freeze, you should always eat produce fresh rather than preserved. After all, the great joy of growing your own is eating fruits and vegetables fresh — even doing it right in the garden.

Favorite Crops Step by Step

Many of the catalog discussions which follow refer you to another section called "Favorite Crops Step by Step" for additional information. These step-by-step discussions give in-depth information about growing some of the most popular eatables listed in the catalog. Other step-by-step discussions, such as those for beans, herbs, and root crops, draw together several related crops to expand upon the basic growing instructions for the group as a whole.

Apple

Common name: apple
Botanical name: *Malus pumila*
Origin: Europe, Asia

DESCRIPTION

A hardy perennial tree with short-stemmed oval leaves. Normally it grows 30 feet tall or more; dwarf trees grow 6 or 8 feet tall. The flowers are delicate pink and white, and the fruit, which has a size and shape to fit comfortably in the hand, is usually red, yellow, green, or rusty (russet) in color when ripe. Although they are hardy, apples cannot survive where winter temperatures go below −20°F for any length of time and dwarf apples are not recommended in extremely cold areas of the northern plains states.

Varieties: In northern states choose Northern Spy, McIntosh, Rhode Island Greening, Wealthy. Grow Delicious, Golden Delicious, Stayman, Winesap, Jonathan, or Turley in middle and southern states. Lodi, Yellow Transparent, Early McIntosh, and Gravenstein can be grown nationwide. Since an apple tree is a long-term planting, and since there is such variety in the trees and fruit flavors, be sure to taste test before you buy.
Grown from: 1-year-old trees.
Time from planting to harvest: 2 to 3 years for dwarf trees.
Parts eaten: Fruit.
Yield: 1 dwarf tree can produce a bushel of apples per season.

GROWING APPLES

Space between plants: At least 10 feet apart if you are growing separate trees. Plant 1½ to 2 feet apart if you are training them on a fence.
Light: Full sun.
Temperature: Since apples need cold weather to produce good crops, they will not do well in areas with a warm climate. On the other hand, they will not do well in areas where the temperature falls below −20°F.
Water: Water during prolonged dry spells, especially during the tree's first year.
Soil: Well-drained soil.
Pests and diseases: Aphids, apple maggots, codling moths, mites, and scale are common apple pests. So are rabbits and mice. Diseases such as apple scab, black rot, powdery mildew, and rust also attack apple trees. Apples need to be sprayed regularly in defense against pests and diseases.
Cultural hints: When you plant dwarf apples, take care not to plant

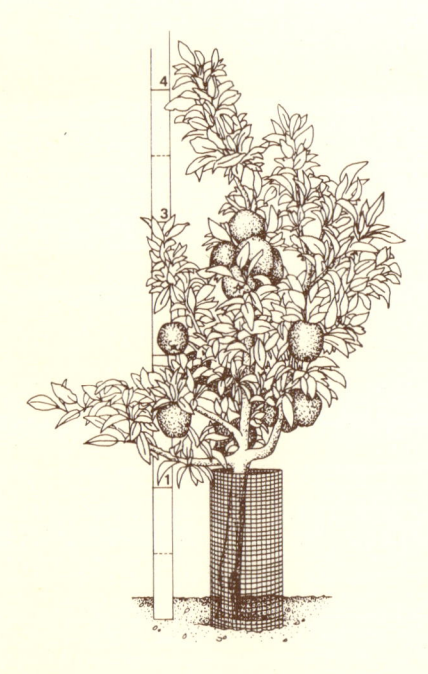

Dwarf apple tree

too deep or the graft union may get below the soil's surface. The tops may sprout new roots and the tree will grow to its full 30-foot height. Pack the soil firmly around the roots, but do not fertilize at planting time.

Cultivate or mulch to keep weeds 3 to 4 feet away from the trunk. Prune to shape tree as it grows. Keep the fruit thinned so that no more than 1 apple grows on every 5 or 6 inches of branch. Too much fruit can break the branch — even split the tree — and cut down on next year's flowering.

See the step-by-step discussion of tree fruit for more information about growing apple trees.

HARVESTING, EATING, STORING

The apple is ready to be picked when it separates easily from the branch as it is lifted up. Of course if you want green apples you can pick them sooner. Apple pie, apple fritters, apple dumplings, apple stuffing, stuffed apples — the cooking possibilities are endless. Can, freeze, or dry your excess crop.

BY THE WAY...

Apples are not what Adam ate in the Garden of Eden. The Serpent probably served apricots.

Artichoke, Globe

Common names: artichoke, globe artichoke
Botanical name: *Cynara scolymus*
Origin: Southern Europe, North Africa

DESCRIPTION

The artichoke is a thistlelike, tender perennial that grows 3 to 4 feet high and 3 to 4 feet across. It is grown for

Globe artichoke seedling

its flower buds which are eaten before they begin to open. Its elegant, architectural leaves make the artichoke very decorative, but since it is very tender and hates cold weather it is not for all gardens.
Varieties: Green Globe
Grown from: Offshoots, suckers, seeds (650 per ounce).
Time from planting to harvest: From suckers, 50 to 100 days. From seeds, at least 1 year for the first bud.
Parts eaten: Unopened flower buds.
Yield from a 10-foot row: 6 or more buds.

GROWING ARTICHOKES

Space between plants: 4 to 6 feet.
Light: Full sun filtered by fog.
Temperature: Not over 70°F by day with a drop to 55°F at night. In areas where the temperature goes below freezing they need special care and mulching.
Water: If it does not rain for a couple of weeks, give artichokes a slow, thorough soaking.
Soil: Rich, well-drained, moisture-holding soil.
Pests and diseases: Aphids, plume moths, and crown rot plague the artichoke. The plume moth is not very bad except in artichoke growing

Globe artichoke

or suckers of high-quality plants. There is tremendous variance in the quality of plants grown from seeds.

HARVESTING, EATING, STORING

Cut off the bud with 1 to 1½ inches of stem before the bud begins to open. The most common methods of cooking are boiling or steaming the buds until tender.

BY THE WAY...

Artichokes, an ancient Roman delicacy, were introduced to France by Catherine de Medici. Later they were taken to Louisiana by the French colonists.

Artichoke, Jerusalem

Common name: Jerusalem artichoke
Botanical name: *Helianthus tuberosus*
Origin: North America

DESCRIPTION

Jerusalem artichokes are large, upright, hardy perennials with small, yellow sunflowers 2 to 3 inches across. They grow 5 to 10 feet tall and have rough, hairy leaves 4 to 8 inches long. This plant was grown by the North American Indians for its tubers, which look like small potatoes. The tubers are low in starch and taste a bit like water chestnuts.

Varieties: Plant whatever kind you find. They grow wild by the side of the road. Sometimes commercial Jerusalem artichokes are sold in

areas. Crown rot is a challenge to combat where drainage is poor or where the plants have to be covered in winter.

Cultural hints: Artichokes have a definite preference for a long, frost-free season with damp weather. They grow best in the 4 central California counties and the southern Atlantic and Gulf coasts. In the North they need to be grown in a protected location. For the roots to survive the winter in cold areas, cut the plant back to about 10 inches, cover with a bushel basket, and then mulch with about 2 feet of leaves.

Artichokes bear best the second year and should be started anew every 3 or 4 years. The best plants are grown from the offshoots

is poor, the tubers can rot.
Cultural hints: Plant the tubers 2 to 6 inches deep. Be sure you know where you want them before you plant because they are hard to get rid of if you change your mind.

Cut off the flower stalks as soon as they appear to get the greatest tuber production. Seed production cuts down on tuber production. The

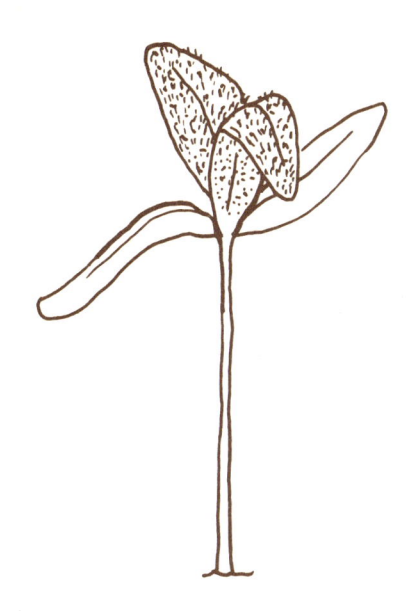

Jerusalem artichoke seedling

supermarkets and you can use those as starters.
Grown from: Tubers.
Time from planting to harvest: 120 to 150 days.
Parts eaten: Tubers.
Yield from a 10-foot row: 20 pounds.

GROWING JERUSALEM ARTICHOKES

Space between plants: 12 to 18 inches.
Light: Full sun.
Water: The plants can survive long dry spells, but the tubers will not develop without a regular supply of water.
Soil: Jerusalem artichokes will grow in almost any soil as long as it is warm and well drained.
Pests and diseases: Jerusalem artichokes get aphids but are not bothered much by them. If drainage

Jerusalem artichoke

113

flowers are cheerful and you may decide to forfeit a few tubers to enjoy the flowers.

This is a good crop to start on a vacant lot, along a rail right-of-way, or as a screen or windbreak in a garden. The plants take lots of room but grow well without too much attention.

HARVESTING, EATING, STORING

When the leaves die back, dig up the tubers with a fork. Leave a few in the soil for next year. Tubers can be eaten raw, boiled, steamed, or creamed. Wash and store the extras in plastic bags in the refrigerator.

BY THE WAY...

Pigs love the tubers. The classic manner for getting rid of an infestation of Jerusalem artichokes is to let the pigs root for them.

Asparagus

Common name: asparagus
Botanical name: *Asparagus officinalis*
Origin: Mediterranean

DESCRIPTION

A long-lived hardy perennial with fleshy roots, the asparagus plant has fernlike foliage and grows about 4 feet tall.
Varieties: Paradise and Mary Washington are both rust-resistant varieties.
Grown from: Seeds (700 per ounce) or 1-year-old roots called crowns.
Time from planting to harvest: 3 years from seeds, 2 years from crowns.

Parts eaten: The immature stalks.
Yield from a 10-foot row: 3 to 5 pounds.

GROWING ASPARAGUS

Space between plants: Plan 12 to 18 inches between plants and 18 inches between rows. Rows make harvesting and weeding easier.
Light: Asparagus prefers full sun but will tolerate a slight amount of shade.
Temperature: This is a hardy vegetable that thrives especially well in areas with 2 or 3 months of winter.
Water: It is very important that asparagus gets enough water when the spears are forming. The plant will survive without extra watering, but the stalks may be stringy and woody.
Soil: Prefers good drainage which is also important in preventing crown rot.
Pests and diseases: Asparagus beetles and rust are the asparagus' main enemies. The best prevention

Asparagus seedling

for rust is to buy one of the rust-resistant varieties.

Cultural hints: Since an asparagus bed is virtually impossible to move, select the spot for it carefully. Spade down 8 to 10 inches and mix in lime and fertilizer while digging. Vintage manure is great if you can get it. It provides organic matter for the hungry asparagus.

Pampered plants grown from seeds often do better than plants grown from abused crowns. If you buy crowns, be sure they do not dry out. Buy twice as many as you need, select and plant the plumpest, then throw away the rest.

To plant asparagus crowns dig out a trench or furrow 10 inches wide and 8 to 10 inches deep. Put in 2 to 4 inches of loose soil mixed with manure or peat moss and a complete fertilizer. Plan to use ¾-pound of 5-10-10 fertilizer for each 10-foot row. Place the roots, well spread out, on the enriched soil and cover with 2 more inches of soil. As the spears grow, gradually fill in the trench to the top.

It takes heavy fertilizing and a soil pH over 6.0 to grow asparagus. Apply high-nitrogen fertilizer after harvesting the spears.

HARVESTING, EATING, STORING

Do not harvest the first 2 seasons so the crowns can fully develop. During the third season, snap off the spears or cut them off with an asparagus knife, at ground level when the stalks are somewhere between 2 inches and 2 feet. If the stalk starts to feather out, it is too late to eat it.

Stop harvesting when the stalks start coming up pencil thin. If you persist and eat them all, you will kill the plants.

Asparagus spears will wilt if you do not refrigerate them immediately. In the event that you cannot eat

Asparagus

them right away, asparagus spears can be frozen.

BY THE WAY...

Asparagus, contrary to legend, does not prefer to be sprinkled with salt and grown in old tin cans.

Basil

Common name: basil
Botanical names: *Ocimum basilicum, Ocimum crispum, Ocimum minimum*
Origin: India, Central America

DESCRIPTION

These tender annuals grow 1 to 2½ feet tall with square stems and opposite leaves. Basil may have either green or purple-red leaves and spikes of small whitish or lavender flowers.
Varieties: The most common kinds of basil are two varieties of *Ocimum basilicum:* the green sweet, or broad-leaved, basil and the purple dark opal. Lettuce-leaved basil *(Ocimum crispum)* with curly leaves and bush basil *(Ocimum minimum)* with small leaves are less common but equally fragrant.
Grown from: Seeds.
Time from planting to harvest: About 60 days.
Parts eaten: The tender tips and leaves.
Yield from a 10-foot row: Enough for the whole neighborhood.

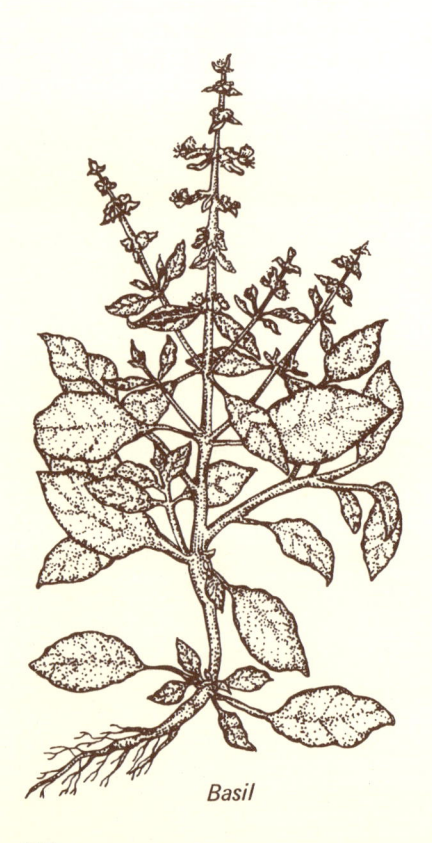

GROWING BASIL

Space between plants: 6 to 12 inches.
Light: Tolerates light shade and will grow on sunny windows or under lights.
Temperature: Basil can stand heat better than cold but it does not like it too hot either.
Water: Like a coleus, basil needs enough water not to wilt. Its leaves wilt when it needs water.
Soil: Light soil with good drainage.
Pests and diseases: Not bothered much by major pests or diseases.
Cultural hints: Basil plants can be started inside for use in a bright window or for planting outside after the danger of frost is over. Seeds can be planted any time after your last spring frost. Seeds often last through the winter and will produce good plants if the soil is not stirred up by overly ambitious gardeners in early spring.

See the step-by-step discussion of herbs for more information about growing basil.

HARVESTING, EATING, STORING

Pick the basil as needed by cutting 5 or 6 inches out of the tops. This encourages branching and slows down flower production as well.

Basil

Basil seedling

Four-angled bean seedling

Fresh basil is delicious in salads. When dried it makes a flavorful contribution to meat, fish, poultry, eggs or vegetables. Cut the stems, tie them in loose bunches and hang them in a protected place. When the leaves become brittle, rub them off the stems, crumble, and store in a jar with a tight-fitting lid. Basil can also be frozen for later use.

BY THE WAY...

In India basil is considered a holy herb. In Italy it is a love gift. In Romania it is an engagement token. And in Greece, basil is a symbol of death and hatred.

nual vine that grows like a ground cover. It has red-brown flowers and produces 1- to 3-inch pods that look like green hot dogs with fins. *Psophocarpus tetragonolobus* is a twinning perennial that prefers to grow to the top of an 8-foot stake. It has bluish-white flowers and long, thin, green pods that also look like hot dogs with fins. The pods are 6 to 9 inches long. The perennial four-angled bean also produces an eatable tuber if the growing season is 8 or more months long.

Varieties: Plant whatever variety is available in your area.

Grown from: Seeds or tubers.

Bean, Four-Angled

Common names: bean, four-angled bean, winged bean, asparagus bean, asparagus pea

Botanical names: Two separate plants are called by the above common names: *Lotus tetragonolobus* and *Psophocarpus tetragonolobus*

Origin: India

DESCRIPTION

Lotus tetragonolobus is a hairy an-

Four-angled bean

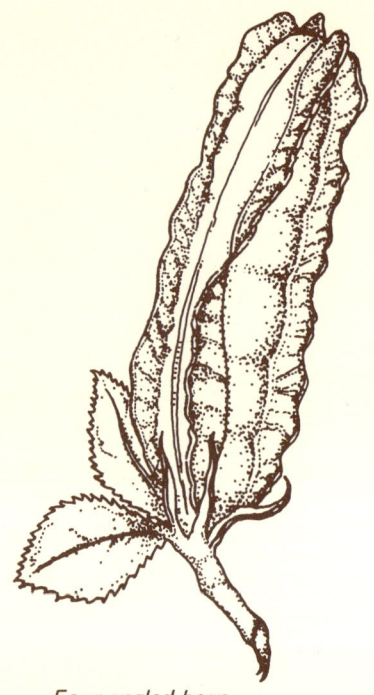

Four-angled bean

Soil: Well-worked soil that drains well.
Pests and diseases: No serious problem.
Cultural hints: The perennial four-angled bean can be trained on wire or a trellis instead of a pole. Plant the seed ½ to 1 inch deep.

HARVESTING, EATING, STORING

Pick the annual's pods when they are 2 inches long; pick the perennial's pods when they are 4 or 5 inches long though they will grow longer. They are good steamed and buttered. To eat them you suck the pulp off the stringy core. It is messy, but tasty. You can cook the dried seeds like dried beans, and the tuber can be cooked like a sweet potato. The pods do not store well, so give the extras to your friends — they probably have never seen a flying green hot dog before.

BY THE WAY...

Because of the high protein content of the beans, and because the tubers of the perennial variety are also eatable, the four-angled bean is an important crop in the battle against hunger.

Time from planting to harvest: Pods 70 days after planting the seeds. For tubers, you have to wait at least 8 months.
Parts eaten: Immature pod of both varieties. Dried seeds and tubers of the perennial variety.
Yield from a 10-foot row: 4 to 5 pounds of pods.

GROWING FOUR-ANGLED BEANS

Space between plants: 15 inches.
Light: Both kinds of four-angled bean need full sun.
Temperature: Four-angled beans are sensitive to cold and prefer moderate temperatures.
Water: Water before the soil dries out.

Bean, Lima

Common names: bean, lima bean, butter bean, civit bean
Botanical name: *Phaseolus lunatus*
Origin: South Mexico, Central America

DESCRIPTION

This tender, very large-seeded an-

nual bean grows as either a bush or a vine that needs support. Its flat seeds are often eaten when they are green, before they are mature.
Varieties: King of the Garden (88 days) is a large-seeded pole lima. Fordhook 242 (75 days) is a large-seeded bush lima. Henderson Bush (65 days) is a small-seeded bush lima.
Grown from: Seeds (25 to 70 per ounce), planted 1 to 1½ inches deep.
Time from planting to harvest: 60 to 75 days for bush limas and 85 to 110 days for pole limas.
Parts eaten: The seeds.
Yield from a 10-foot row: If the summer is wet and cloudy and the soil is rich, poor bean crops will result. Under the same weather conditions, poor soil will, surprisingly, produce a good crop. If you are blessed with a sunny dry summer, good soil will yield a good crop and, more predictably, poor soil will produce a poor crop.

GROWING LIMA BEANS

Space between plants: Plant bush beans 8 to 10 inches apart in rows 2 to 4 feet apart. Plant pole beans 15 to 18 inches apart in hills spaced every 3 or 4 feet.
Light: Limas love full sun.
Temperature: They need a minimum 65°F soil temperature for 5 days in order to germinate. Cold, wet weather causes the flowers to drop; temperatures above 80°F mean the pods will not set.
Water: Keep water off the leaves if possible. Stay away from the plants when they are wet with dew or rain. Working the plot when the plants are wet spreads disease.
Soil: Limas will grow in any well-drained soil. High soil moisture and high nitrogen levels slow maturity.

Pests and diseases: Aphids, whiteflies, spotted cucumber beetle and, if you are east of the Rockies, the Mexican bean beetle will compete for your limas.
Cultural hints: Lima beans need a long stretch of pleasant weather, not too cold and not too hot, which means the slower growing pole beans are hard to fit into short growing seasons.

The large seed sometimes has trouble pushing through the soil. If your soil tends to cake, cover the seed with sand, vermiculite, or peat moss and vermiculite. Before planting, treat bean seeds with nitrogen-fixing bacteria inoculant to help these bacteria convert inorganic nitrogen compounds into usable organic compounds.

Pole limas need support to keep the pods from touching the ground. The support system should be installed before you sow the seeds.

Since the roots are very close to the surface, weeding and cultivating should be done with a light touch.

See the step-by-step discussion of beans for more information about growing lima beans.

HARVESTING, EATING, STORING

The pods should be picked while beans are still tender. Freeze the extra limas.

Lima bean seedling

Lima bean   *Mung bean*

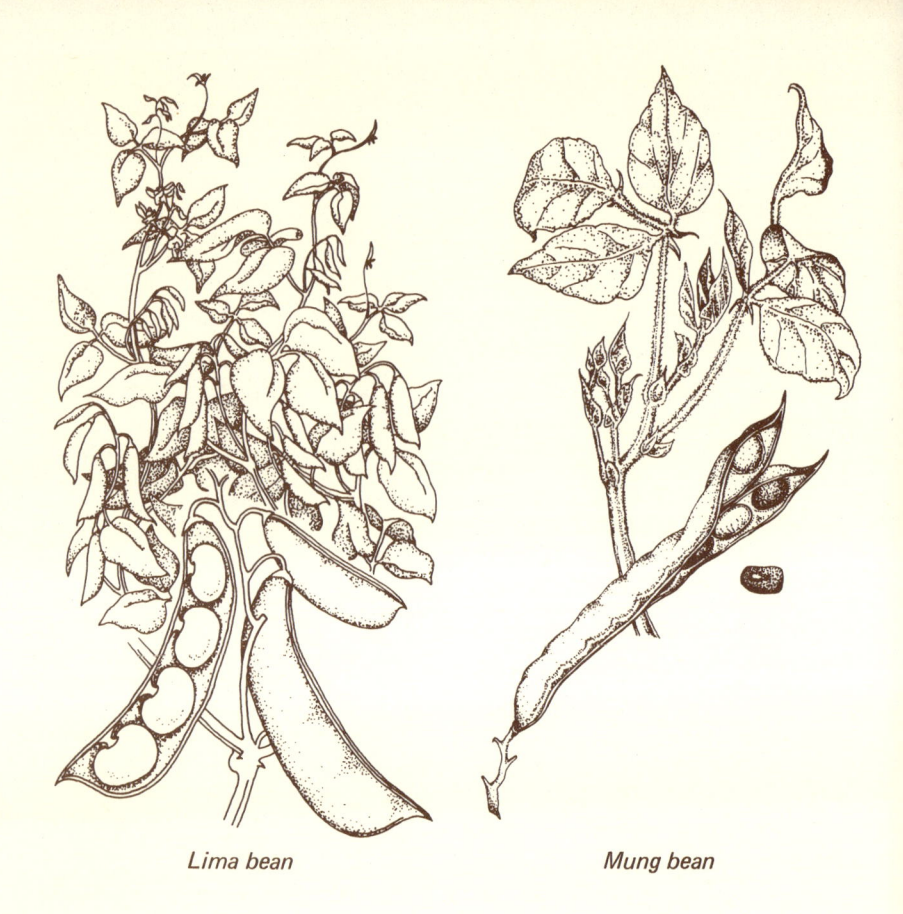

BY THE WAY...

Lima beans, like snap beans, corn, tomatoes and peppers originated in the Americas.

Bean, Mung

Common names: bean, mung bean, golden gram, green gram
Botanical name: *Phaseolus aureus*
Origin: India, Central Asia

DESCRIPTION

The mung bean is a bushy or floppy annual that grows about 2½ to 3 feet tall. It has many branches with large hairy beanlike leaves. The flowers are yellowish-green with purple streaks and produce long, thin, hairy pods containing 9 to 15 small greenish-yellow seeds. The seeds are used to produce bean sprouts.
Varieties: You can usually buy mung beans at health food stores or Oriental specialty shops. Try growing any mung beans you can buy.
Grown from: Seeds.
Time from planting to harvest: 4 to 5 days for sprouts, 60 to 90 days for pods.
Parts eaten: Seeds.

Yield from a 10-foot row: 1 to 2 pounds.

GROWING MUNG BEANS

Space between plants: 18 to 20 inches between plants and 20 to 24 inches between rows.
Light: Full sun.
Temperature: The mung bean can take high temperatures but not cold weather.
Water: Too much water decreases the yield. The mung bean does better under dry conditions. Water sparingly.
Soil: Mung beans prefer a well-worked, well-drained, fertile soil.
Pests and diseases: The mung bean has no serious enemies.
Cultural hints: Keep weeds pulled out. Hill up the earth around the plants as they start to grow.

See the step-by-step discussion of beans for more information about growing mung beans.

HARVESTING, EATING, STORING

Remove the pods before they split. Remove the seeds from the pod by hand or by placing pods on a mat and pounding them with a stick. Store the seeds in a jar.

BY THE WAY...

These are the beans that produce the sprouts for Chinese dishes and salads. They are a good source of vitamin C.

Bean, Snap

Common names: bean, green bean, snap bean, string bean, French bean, wax bean, pole bean, bush bean, kidney bean, navy bean, green shell bean, stringless bean
Botanical name: *Phaseolus vulgaris*
Origin: South Mexico, Central America

DESCRIPTION

Beans are tender annuals that grow either as bushes or vines. Their leaves are usually composed of 3 leaflets; their flowers are pale yellow, lavender or white. The size and color of the pods and seeds are quite variable. Beans are able to take nitrogen from the air and, with the help of nitrogen-fixing bacteria, increase the amount of nitrogen available in the soil.
Varieties: Some reliable bush-type snap beans include Provider (50 days), Spartan Arrow (51 days), Contender (53 days), Tendercrop (53 days). Green pole-growing varieties of snap beans include Blue Lake (60 days), Kentucky Wonder (65 days). Yellow (wax) bush-type snap beans try Cherokee Way (52 days), Pencil Pod Black Wax (56 days).
Grown from: Seeds (100 per ounce).
Time from planting to harvest: 50 to 60 days for bush beans, 60 to 90 days for pole beans. Allow 60 to 100 days for dry shell beans.
Parts eaten: Tender pods, semi-

Mung bean seedling

Green bean

Water: Water the beans when the soil starts to dry out. Too much rain can cause the flowers and small pods to drop off.
Soil: Beans will grow in almost any soil as long as it is well drained. Too-fertile a soil may produce lots of leaves and few beans.
Pests and diseases: Mexican bean beetle, bean leaf beetle, anthracnose, blights, rusts and mildews all attack beans. Working with beans while their leaves are wet can spread disease.
Cultural hints: Plant bush beans every 2 weeks to extend the harvest. Or start with bush beans and follow up with pole beans. Bush beans mature more quickly than pole beans and do not need support; pole beans produce more and can be harvested over a longer period of time. Beans will produce at least 2 crops, sometimes more, if they are kept harvested.

See the step-by-step discussion of beans for more information about growing snap beans.

HARVESTING, EATING, STORING

Keep removing the pods before they become mature or the plant will stop producing. Once the seeds mature the plant dies. For a change, try green beans raw in salads. Freeze, can or dry your excess crops.

mature pods and dry beans.
Yield from a 10-foot row: 5 to 6 pounds.

GROWING SNAP BEANS

Space between plants: Bush beans should be planted 4 to 6 inches apart, pole beans 9 to 12 inches apart. Beans can be planted quite close together and the yield will not be too badly affected.
Light: Beans will tolerate partial shade.
Temperature: Since beans are sensitive to cold, they should be planted only after the soil has warmed up. Excessively hot weather causes them to drop their flowers.

Green bean seedling

BY THE WAY...

The American Indians mixed dried beans and corn, a combination called succotash, to make a high protein food that could be easily transported. Since 1894, when Burpee introduced the Stringless Green Pod, most string beans have been stringless.

and do best in the cooler parts of the country but will go to seed without making roots if they get too cold when young. Beets are planted as a winter crop in the South. At high temperatures they turn woody.
Water: Provide plenty of water for tender roots.
Soil: Beets thrive in well-worked, loose soil that is high in organic mat-

Beet

Common name: beet
Botanical name: *Beta vulgaris*
Origin: South Europe

DESCRIPTION

This hardy biennial is grown as an annual. It has a round or tapered swollen root from which a rosette of large leaves sprouts. The root can be red, yellow, or white, which makes it possible to have Harvard, Princeton and Yale beets!
Varieties: Early Wonder (53 days), Burpee's Golden (55 days), Ruby Green (56 days), Cylindra, also called Formanova or Tendersweet (60 days), Long Season, also called Winter Keeper (80 days).
Grown from: Seeds (clusters or clumps contain several seeds). There are 1,600 seeds in an ounce.
Time from planting to harvest: 40 to 80 days.
Parts eaten: The leaves and roots.
Yield from a 10-foot row: 6 to 10 pounds of roots and leaves.

GROWING BEETS

Space between plants: Thin the beets 4 to 6 inches apart in rows spaced 12 inches apart.
Light: Tolerate partial shade.
Temperature: Beets can stand frost

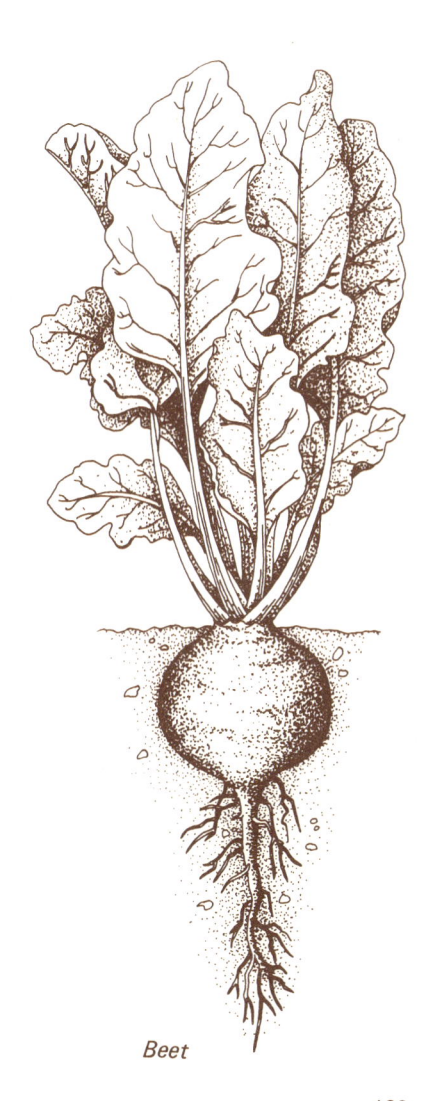

Beet

Beet seedling

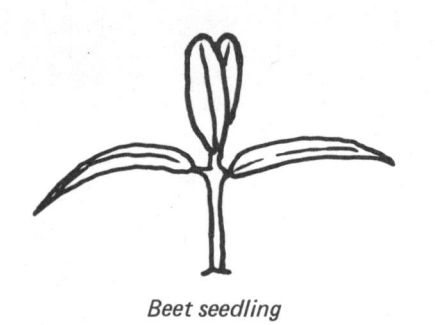

ter and has no rocks or brickbats. Beets sulk in acid soil. Do not use new manure. It causes more problems than it solves.
Pests and diseases: Not many pests bother beets. Of course, there are usually some illiterate insects that you have to shoo away.
Cultural hints: To speed up a crop, start the beets inside. If you can crush the seed clusters without crushing the seed you will avoid the work of thinning the beets. Otherwise there will be several seedings in each spot. They can be separated and transplanted if you are careful. This is a good plant to grow in a band rather than a row.

See the step-by-step discussion of root crops for more information about growing beets.

HARVESTING, EATING, STORING

Eat the beets as they grow. Start with the greens that are thinned to provide growing space, continue with small tender beets and greens served separately, then end up with a big harvest of both. Freeze or pickle your excess crops.

BY THE WAY...

Twist off the leaves, rather than cutting them off, to prevent "bleeding." Bleeding causes less intense color and some claim a less delicious beet. For a beet without a bottom, see chard.

Broad Bean

Common names: bean, broad bean, horsebean, fava bean, Scotch bean, Windsor bean
Botanical name: *Vicia faba*
Origin: Central Asia

DESCRIPTION

A bushy, hardy annual, the broad bean grows 3 to 4 feet high and has square stems with leaves divided into leaflets. The white flowers are splotched with brown. The pods are 6 to 8 inches long and contain 4 to 6 or more light brown seeds when mature.
Varieties: Try your luck with whatever broad bean seed is available.
Grown from: Seeds (20 to 50 per ounce).
Time from planting to harvest: 85 days.
Parts eaten: Eat the young, immature pods or wait and harvest the mature seeds.
Yield from a 10-foot row: Some people are unlucky. Their broad bean crop is attacked by all of its enemies, and they get a zero crop.

Broad bean seedling

Other gardeners average around 3 pounds per 10-foot row.

GROWING BROAD BEANS

Space between plants: 8 to 10 inches, in rows 4 feet apart.
Light: Full sun is required for broad beans.
Temperature: Broad beans need cool weather to set their pods. They prefer weather below 70°F and should be planted very early in your growing season. They will not produce in the summer's heat.
Water: Water before the soil dries out. Try to avoid wet soil conditions which, combined with high temperatures, are an invitation to root rots.
Soil: Fertile soil, high in organic matter with excellent drainage, is best for broad beans. They prefer an alkaline soil.
Pests and diseases: Slugs, aphids, root rots and rusts. Black aphids adore broad beans, so be prepared with spray, or pray a lot and pinch out the aphid-infested tender tips.
Cultural hints: Planted 1 to 2 inches deep, broad beans are grown more like peas than snap beans. If you have a collection of old Christmas trees, cut off the branches and stick them between plants to give them some protection and support.

In cold areas broad beans can be grown as a substitute for lima beans.

HARVESTING, EATING, STORING

Pick the young, tender pods and cook them like string beans; or pick the pods when the seeds have become dry and light brown. You can also soak the dried beans overnight, drain and deep fry them for a snack.

BY THE WAY...

Upper class Greeks and Romans

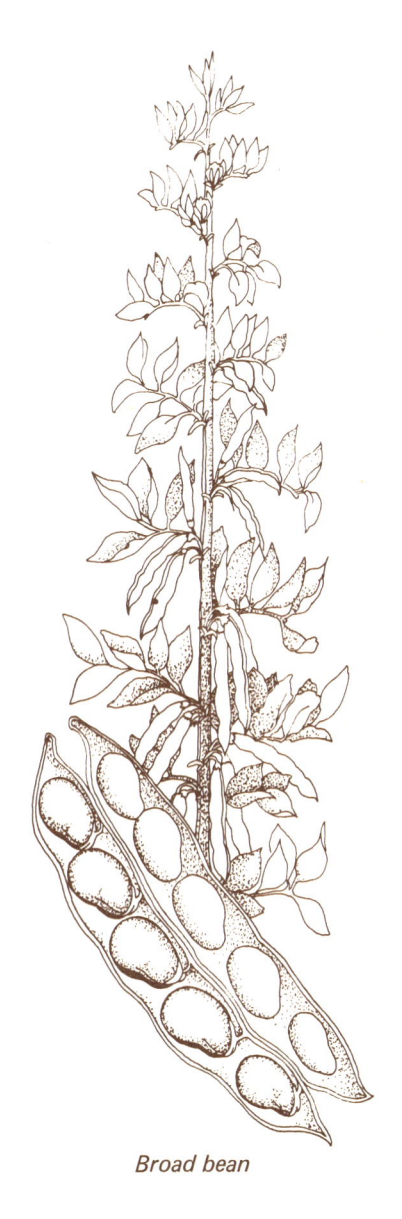

Broad bean

thought that eating "horse beans" would cloud their vision. But fava beans were a filling staple for Roman legionnaires, and later fed the English poor.

125

Broccoli

Common names: broccoli, Italian broccoli, Calabrese, brocks
Botanical name: *Brassica oleracea italica*
Origin: Mediterranean. Today's broccoli is a horticultural hybrid.

DESCRIPTION

This hardy biennial grown as an annual grows 1½ to 2½ feet high. It looks a bit like a cauliflower that has not quite got itself together. The flower stalks are green, purple or white. When it comes to the white-budded ones, the U.S. government has trouble deciding where a broccoli stops and where a cauliflower starts. The flowers of all of them are yellow, but they are usually eaten while they are still in bud before they bloom.
Varieties: Green Comet (40 days), De Cicco (48 days), Cleopatra (55 days), Spartan Early (55 days) and Waltham 29 (75 days).
Grown from: Most people prefer to start with transplants but broccoli can also be grown from seed (9,000 per ounce).
Time from planting to harvest: If you sow seeds, your broccoli will take from 100 to 150 days to mature, depending on the variety. Some broccoli transplants will produce in 40 to 80 days.
Parts eaten: The flower buds, stems and leaves.
Yield from a 10-foot row: 4 to 6 pounds — more if you eat the leaves and all.

GROWING BROCCOLI

Space between plants: 18 to 24 inches between plants, 24 inches between rows.
Light: Tolerates partial shade.
Temperature: Broccoli is a cool weather crop and does poorly at day temperatures above 80°F.
Water: Though broccoli tolerates a wide range of water availability, it tastes better if it has been watered regularly.
Soil: Rich, well-worked soil, high in organic matter with good drainage.
Pests and diseases: Broccoli inherits the cabbage family's traditional enemies — pigeons, cutworms, rabbits, and caterpillars.
Cultural hints: Plant your broccoli late in the spring and frustrate the cutworms. Remember when cultivating and weeding that broccoli is shallow-rooted. Cut out and eat the central flower head when it is still in tight bud to encourage side shoots.

See the step-by-step discussion of cabbage for more information about growing broccoli.

HARVESTING, EATING, STORING

Harvesting can continue over a relatively long period. Start with the center top and then pick the side shoots in order of maturity. Cut off the buds with a portion of the stalk before the flowers open. You can eat broccoli in full bloom but the brocks stop coming after the bloom.

Enjoy broccoli raw or cooked until it is just tender. Freezing is a

Broccoli seedling

Broccoli

good way to preserve your excess harvest.

BY THE WAY...

Americans did not discover broccoli until the 1920s even though this vegetable had been an Old World favorite.

Brussels Sprout

Common names: Brussels sprouts, sprouts
Botanical name: *Brassica oleracea gemmifera*
Origin: Europe, Mediterranean

DESCRIPTION

Brussels sprouts are tall, erect hardy biennials that are grown as annuals. They are another variation on the cabbage. The leaves that grow from the stalk are large, like collards, and miniature 1- to 2-inch "cabbages" grow between them on a stout main stem.
Varieties: Jade Cross (85 days).
Grown from: Seeds (9,000 per ounce) or transplants.
Time from planting to harvest: 85 to 95 days to mature from seeds, 75 to 90 days from transplants.
Parts eaten: The sprouts and leaves.
Yield from a 10-foot row: 5 to 8 pounds of sprouts.

GROWING BRUSSELS SPROUTS

Space between plants: 15 to 24 inches.
Light: Partial shade.
Temperature: Brussels sprouts dislike hot weather and do not care for night temperatures above 65°F.
Water: They need a regular water supply to keep them growing. Make sure the soil does not completely dry out.
Soil: Well-worked soil with high organic content and good moisture retention will yield the best sprouts.
Pests and diseases: Cutworms, cabbage worms, pigeons and rabbits nibble on this vegetable.
Cultural hints: If you live in an area with cold winters, you can pluck off the tip of the plant early in the autumn. This forces the plant to mature all of its sprouts at once. The general growing and harvesting plan

Brussels sprout seedling

Cabbage

Common name: cabbage
Botanical name: *Brassica oleracea capitata*
Origin: South Europe

DESCRIPTION

Grown as an annual, the hardy biennial cabbage has an enlarged terminal bud made of crowded and expanded overlapping leaves shaped into a head. The leaves are smooth or crinkled in shades of green or purple. Like human heads, cabbage heads can be pointed, round or flat. A cabbage stem can run from virtually nothing to 20 inches.
Varieties: Stonehead (60 days), Jersey Wakefield (62 days), Golden Acre (65 days), Red Acre (76 days), Market Prize (78 days), Savoy King (90 days), Badger Ball Head (98 days), Flat Dutch (105 days).
Grown from: Seeds (8,500 per

Brussels sprout

for sprouts is much like that for broccoli.

See the step-by-step discussion of cabbage for more information about growing Brussels sprouts.

HARVESTING, EATING, STORING

Start from the bottom, and remove the leaves and sprouts as the season progresses. Harvesting can continue after frost, until all the sprouts are gone. The leaves can be cooked like collards or cabbage. Freeze your excess harvest.

BY THE WAY...

Some people claim that adding a walnut to a pot of sprouts will cut down the cabbagey cooking odor.

Cabbage seedling

Cabbage

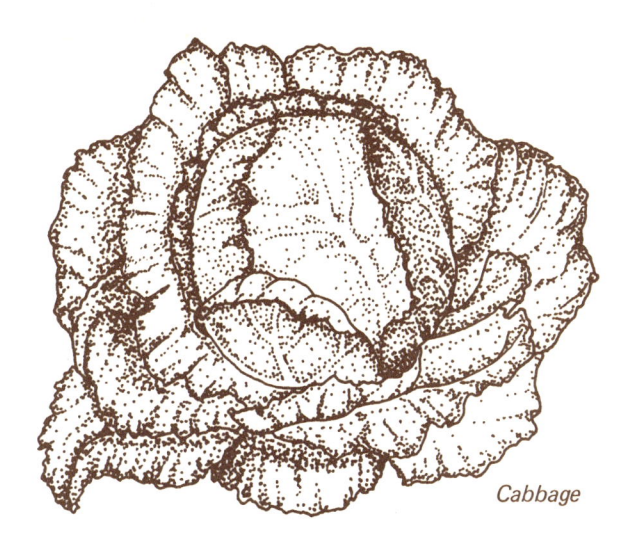

ounce) or transplants.
Time from planting to harvest: Cabbages mature in 80 to 180 days from seed, depending on their variety. If you use transplants the cabbages will be ready to pick in 60 to 105 days.
Parts eaten: The head.
Yield from a 10-foot row: 5 to 8 heads.

GROWING CABBAGE

Space between plants: 18 to 24 inches.
Light: Full sun is required.
Temperature: Cabbages do best in a cool growing season with day temperatures under 80°F and night temperatures 20°F lower. If the plants are cold for too long a period, or if the weather is too warm, they will bolt (go to seed) without forming a head. If the head is already formed, it will split in hot weather.
Water: Abundant soil moisture and cool moist air are needed for the best growth. Cut down the watering as they approach maturity to prevent splitting.

Soil: Plant cabbage in rich, well-drained soil that is high in organic matter and holds moisture without getting soggy.
Pests and diseases: Caterpillars, cutworms, aphids, flea beetles. Yellows and a number of other diseases are best controlled by using resistant varieties. If possible, rotate crops to frustrate the insects and diseases.
Cultural hints: Keep plants growing quickly. They love rich soil and plenty of water. Avoid over-crowding the seedlings; take care when transplanting that the roots have plenty of room. Keep the surface of the soil from caking. Eliminate the weed competition.

See the step-by-step discussion of cabbage for more growing information.

HARVESTING, EATING, STORING

Cut off the head, leaving the stem with a couple of leaves. Often a few small heads will grow on the stalk — super Brussels sprouts. Savoy cabbage is especially good stuffed.

Store the heads in a cool moist place — or make sauerkraut.

BY THE WAY...

Cabbages are decorative in the flower garden. The purple cabbages and the savoys look good in a mixed border. The flowering cabbages look like enormous variegated blossoms. Decorative cabbages can be grown in containers on the patio or even indoors.

Cabbage, Chinese

Common names: Chinese cabbage, white cabbage, flowering cabbage, celery cabbage, pak-choy, Michihli, Napa cabbage
Botanical name: *Brassica chinensis*
Origin: China

DESCRIPTION

A hardy biennial grown as an annual, Chinese cabbage has broad, thick, tender leaves and heavy midribs. Plants can be either loosely or tightly headed and grow 15 to 18 inches tall. The variety with a large compact heart is called celery cabbage, pak-choy or Michihli.
Variety: Chihli, also called Michihli, is a variety of Chinese cabbage that matures in 75 days.
Grown from: Seed (9,500 per ounce).
Time from planting to harvest: 50 to 80 days.
Parts eaten: Leaves and leaf stalks.
Yield from a 10-foot row: 10 or more heads.

GROWING CHINESE CABBAGE

Space between plants: 9 to 12 inches between plants in rows spaced 15 to 18 inches apart.
Light: Chinese cabbage will tolerate partial shade.
Temperature: Chinese cabbage can be grown only in cool weather since it goes to seed quickly in hot weather and long days.
Water: Water frequently to help them grow fast and tender. Do not let the soil dry out. If growing slows down, it will sometimes go to seed.
Soil: They need well-worked, well-fertilized soil, high in organic matter. The soil should be able to hold moisture.
Pests and diseases: Occasionally a caterpillar or some aphids will stop by. Just compost the outside leaves.
Cultural hints: Because of its tendency to go to seed, Chinese cabbage is usually grown as a fall crop in the North and a winter crop in the South. It can be started inside and transplanted out in the spring, but transplanting sometimes shocks it into going to seed.

See the step-by-step discussion of cabbage for more information about Chinese cabbage.

HARVESTING, EATING, STORING

Cut off the whole plant at the soil line. The Chinese cabbage does not

Chinese cabbage seedling

Chinese cabbage

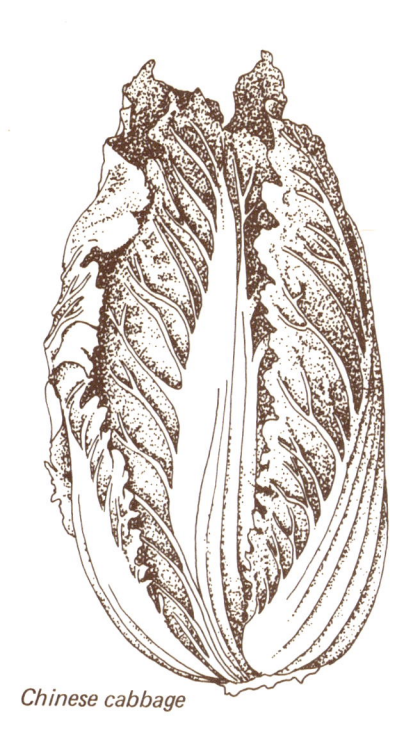

have a strong flavor. It is delicious eaten raw or in Oriental stir-fry dishes. Store in the refrigerator.

BY THE WAY...

In Chinese, call this cabbage cousin *pe-tsai*. In Japanese, say *hakusai*.

Carrot

Common name: carrot
Botanical name: *Daucus carota*
Origin: Europe, Asia

DESCRIPTION

Carrots are hardy biennials grown as annuals. They have a rosette of finely-divided fernlike leaves growing from a swollen, fleshy taproot. The root, which varies in size and shape, is generally a tapered cylinder that grows up to 10 inches long in different shades of orange.

Varieties: Pioneer Hybrid (67 days), Nantes or Coreless (68 days), Red Cored Chantenay (70 days), Danvers 126 (75 days), Spartan Bonus (77 days). If your soil is heavy clay, plant the short varieties.
Grown from: Seeds (23,000 per ounce).
Time from planting to harvest: 55 to 80 days.
Parts eaten: The roots are excellent people food. The tops can be used to flavor soup stocks or as duck food, if you happen to have a pet duck.
Yield from a 10-foot row: 7 to 10 pounds.

GROWING CARROTS

Space between plants: 3 inches.
Light: Partial shade is tolerated.
Temperature: In areas with high soil temperatures the roots will grow short and pale unless you mulch.
Water: To keep them growing quickly, give carrots plenty of water. As they approach maturity, hold off on water to prevent cracks.
Soil: Carrots need rich soil, well worked and well drained.
Pests and diseases: Cutworms and rabbits damage carrots.

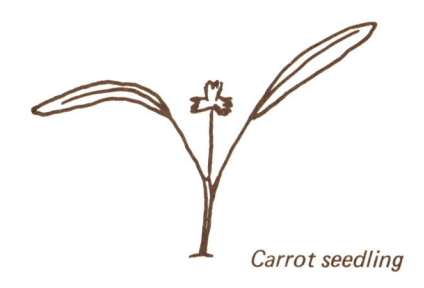

Carrot seedling

Cultural hints: Seeds take a long time to germinate, and when they are planted in the cold, raw spring they may give up before they come up. Wait to plant them and you will be the first on your block to harvest carrots. Plant successive crops every 2 to 3 weeks until 3 months before frost.

See the step-by-step discussion of root crops for more information about growing carrots.

HARVESTING, EATING, STORING

Harvest carrots when they are small. Pull them up by hand or use a spading fork to gently pry them out of the earth. Because they are very special, share carrots with friends when they are fresh. After several weeks in the refrigerator you won't be able to tell them from store-bought carrots.

BY THE WAY...

Grandma said, "Eat carrots, they are good for your eyes!" She was right. Night blindness is sometimes caused by a vitamin A deficiency.

Cauliflower

Common name: cauliflower
Botanical name: *Brassica oleracea botrytis*
Origin: Europe, Mediterranean. Today's cauliflower is a horticultural hybrid.

DESCRIPTION

Cauliflower is a single-stalked, half-hardy biennial member of the cabbage family grown as an annual. The edible flower buds form a solid head called a curd which may be white, purple or green. Sometimes only its mother can tell which is cauliflower and which is broccoli. Broccoli is generally the better behaved.

Carrots

Blanching cauliflower   *Cauliflower*

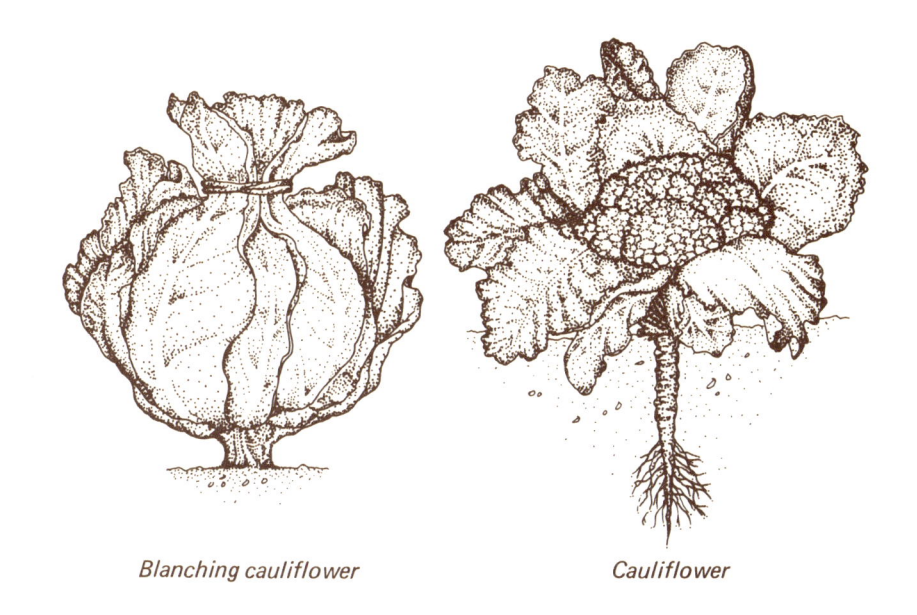

Varities: Super Snowball (55 days), Snowball Imperial (58 days), Snowball M (59 days), Self-Blanche (70 days), Greenball (95 days), Royal Purple (95 days).
Grown from: Seeds (10,000 per ounce) or, more commonly, transplants.
Time from planting to harvest: 85 to 130 days from seed, 55 to 100 days from transplants.
Parts eaten: Flower buds and stalks.
Yield from a 10-foot row: 6 or 7 heads, if you are lucky.

GROWING CAULIFLOWER

Space between plants: 18 to 24 inches.
Light: Tolerates partial shade.
Temperature: Thrives only in moderate temperatures; they will not grow in hot or cold weather.
Water: It needs evenly moist soil. Do not let the ground completely dry out.

Soil: Rich, moisture-holding soil, high in organic matter, with good drainage.
Pests and diseases: Cutworms, aphids, mildew, clubroot, caterpillars and the rest of the cabbage family's traditional enemies attack the cauliflower even more vigorously than cabbages or broccoli.
Cultural hints: Cultivate regularly to keep down the weed competition and to prevent a crust from forming on the soil's surface. Take care not to damage the roots.

The object with cauliflower is to achieve a perfect curd, or head, with all the flowerets pressed tightly together. Unless it's supposed to be green or purple, the color should be untinged creamy-white. Since too much sun or rain can damage the curds, you have to tie the leaves over the top of the curd when it gets to be about the size of an egg a week or two before harvesting. To blanch (whiten) cauliflower, take 3 or 4 leaves and gather them to-

Cauliflower seedling

on top of a large brown turniplike root.
Grown from: Seeds (70,000 per ounce) or transplants.
Time from planting to harvest: 110 to 120 days from seed.

gether over the curd. If you secure them with colored rubber hands you can keep track of cauliflowers tied at different times. Self-blanching cauliflower does not need to be tied, but it will not blanch in hot weather.

See the step-by-step discussion of cabbage for more information about growing cauliflower.

HARVESTING, EATING, STORING

Leave a ruff of surrounding leaves on the head when you cut it off. The leaves are also edible. Cauliflower freezes well.

BY THE WAY...

Mark Twain called the cauliflower a cabbage with a college education.

Celeriac

Common names: celeriac, turnip-rooted celery, celery root, knob celery
Botanical name: *Apium graveolens rapaceum*
Origin: Europe and Africa

DESCRIPTION

This hardy biennial grown as an annual has a rosette of leaves growing

Celeriac

Parts eaten: Leaves and roots.
Yield from a 10-foot row: 16 to 20 roots.

GROWING CELERIAC

Space between plants: 6 to 8 inches.
Light: Celeriac tolerates light shade.
Temperature: Likes cool temperatures, but not cold or hot. It prefers a variation between day and night temperatures.
Water: Frequent watering is very important. Celeriac, like celery, is shallow-rooted and a lack of soil moisture can stop its growth.
Soil: Rich, well-drained soil that holds moisture.
Pests and diseases: Once through its awkward youth, celeriac grows quite well. There is not much you can do about the few pests and diseases that afflict it.
Cultural hints: Celeriac is easier to grow than celery but it is still a good idea to start with healthy transplants that are a couple of months old. They must be kept moist, especially when young. Young plants are not much competition for weeds and are often petulant. In order to produce a symmetrical, unbranched root, rub off the side roots — but do not go too far or you will rub out the celeriac.

HARVESTING, EATING, STORING

The leaves can be taken off any time after the plant looks as if it is going to survive. Pull up the roots when they are about the size of a baseball. Peel, dice and cook them. Then marinate them in vinegar and oil seasoned to your taste. They make an interesting addition to any luncheon.

You can dry the leaves to use as an herb in soups and stews. Keep the roots in the refrigerator, or store them in moist sand in a cool place away from cats. They will also keep in the ground.

See the step-by-step discussion of root crops for more information about growing celeriac.

Celeriac seedling

BY THE WAY...

Celeriac is not widely known in the United States, but it is popular in Europe. It is relatively easy to grow but a pain to prepare for eating.

Celery

Common name: celery
Botanical name: *Apium graveolens dulce*
Origin: Europe

DESCRIPTION

A hardy biennial grown as an annual, celery has a tight rosette of stalks, 8 to 18 inches tall, which are topped with many divided leaves. It belongs to the same family as dill, parsley and fennel. The flowers look like coarse Queen Anne's Lace and are carried on tall stalks.
Varieties: Summer Pascal (115

Celery

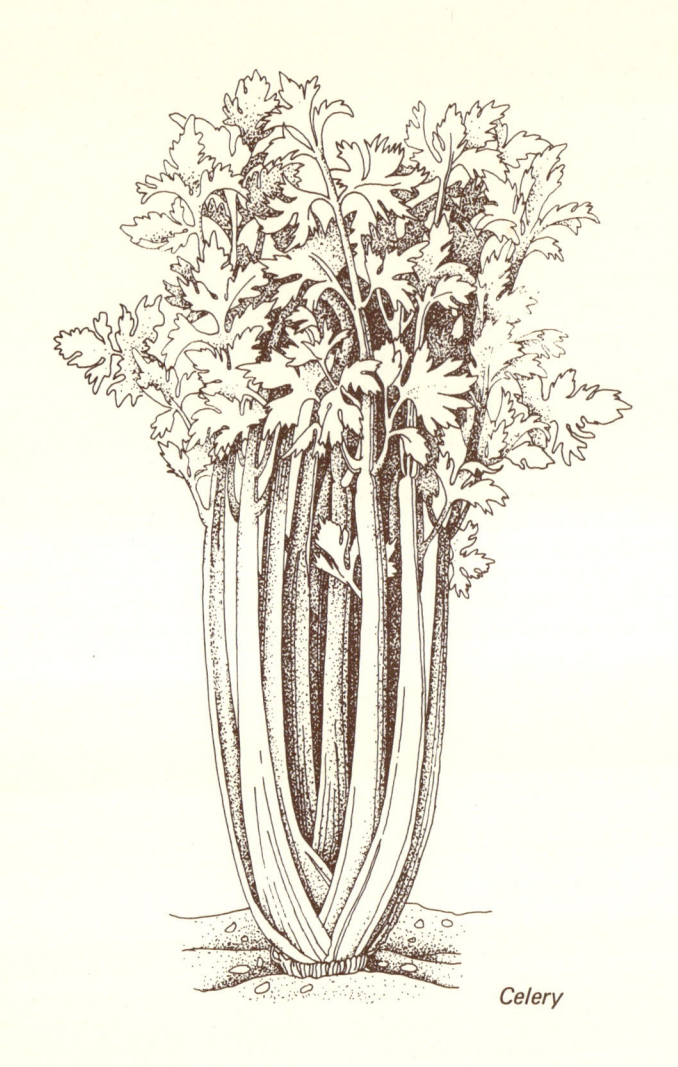

days), Golden Plume (118 days), Utah 52-70 (125 days).
Grown from: Seeds (70,000 per ounce) are very slow to germinate. Try to find transplants.
Time from planting to harvest: From transplants, celery is ready in 100 to 130 days. Seeds take 10 to 20 days longer.
Parts eaten: Leaves, stalks and seeds.
Yield from a 10-foot row: 20 stalks.

GROWING CELERY

Space between plants: 6 to 10 inches in rows 2 feet apart. For a bleached look, keep the celery crowded.
Light: Tolerates light shade.
Temperature: Does best in cool weather and especially enjoys cool nights. Cold weather will slow down growth and 2 weeks at 40°F to 50°F, or a month of 50°F to 60°F, while the

plants are small, will start the formation of a seed stalk.

Water: It is very important to water celery, a moisture loving plant. Lack of water may slow growth and trigger the plant into sending up flower stalks.

Soil: Celery prefers rich soil, high in organic matter and moisture-holding capacity, but with good drainage. Celery needs a lot of fertilizer to keep it growing quickly.

Pests and diseases: Pests are not much trouble. Pink rot, black heart, and blights, however, can be real bothers when they show up. They can be prevented to some extent by making sure that magnesium and calcium are available in the soil.

Cultural hints: Celery plants grow slowly at first and are bothered by weeds. Since their roots are very near the surface, take care when getting rid of weeds.

Celery has to be kept growing quickly or it gets very stringy. Good supplies of moisture and fertilizer are important. Grow celery in the spring in the North, and in the late summer in the South.

Growing blanched celery suitable for a Gay 90s luxury hotel is a lot of work. Proper blanching (whitening) should start 10 days to 2 weeks ahead of the harvest date. To blanch, cover the plants to protect them from the sun. The more sun they get, the more chlorophyl they produce and the greener they turn.

There are a number of blanching materials to choose from, but none of them should be left on too long or the celery stalks will become pithy and rot. Soil can be mounded around each side of the celery row. Build up the soil to the tops of the stalks. Some people use plastic next to the plants on both sides of the row for less mess. If the weather is warm, however, this is not a good method. The hearts tend to decay.

Celery seedlings

Boards tilted to shade the celery up to their tops can be kept in place with stakes at the bottom and hooks and eyes at the top. Heavy paper, such as freezer paper or layers of newspaper, can also be used. Wrap it around each plant and fasten with a rubber band. Or try cylinder-shaped tiles. They will fit over the tops of the celery when you gather the stalks together.

HARVESTING, EATING, STORING

Cut off the stalks at or slightly below the soil level. Try braised celery for a change. The leaves can be dried to be used in soups and stews. The seeds can be kept in screw-top jars.

BY THE WAY...

Though celery originated around the Mediterranean, it was brought to Michigan from Scotland where it was grown by Dutch farmers during the last half of the 19th century.

Chard

Common names: chard, Swiss chard, sea kale, Swiss beet, sea-kale beet
Botanical name: *Beta vulgaris cicla*

Chard seedling

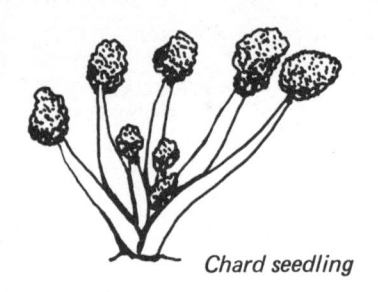

Origin: Europe, Mediterranean

DESCRIPTION

Chard is basically a beet without a bottom. It is another biennial that is grown as an annual. Chard is a very decorative plant with a rosette of large, dark green leaves and juicy red or white leaf stems.

Chard

Varieties: Lucullus (50 days), Fordhook Giant (60 days), Rhubarb (60 days).
Grown from: Seeds (1,600 per ounce) or seed clusters containing several seeds.
Time from planting to harvest: 55 to 60 days.
Parts eaten: Leaves and leaf stalks.
Yield from a 10-foot row: 9 pounds or more.

GROWING CHARD

Space between plants: Thin the seedlings to 9 to 12 inches apart.
Light: Tolerates light shade.
Temperature: Chard prefers cool temperatures. High temperatures slow down the leaf production.
Water: Chard needs enough soil moisture to keep the leaves growing quickly.
Soil: Chard needs fertile, well worked soil with good drainage and high organic content. Like beets, it is not fond of acid soil.
Pests and diseases: Aphids are sometimes a problem.
Cultural hints: Chard will grow and produce steadily all summer. If the soil is fertile and the weather does not get too cold, harvesting can continue on into the second year.

HARVESTING, EATING, STORING

You can start harvesting chard when the outside leaves are 3 inches long. Don't let them get much over 10 inches long or they will taste earthy. Some people like to take off the outside leaves a few at a time while others prefer to cut off the entire plant at 3 inches and let it grow back.

Chard is delicious steamed or cooked like spinach. The extras can be frozen, but will lose much in translation.

BY THE WAY...

Chard is one of the easiest, most productive crops. More tolerant to heat than spinach, chard is one crop that can be harvested all summer. It can also hold its own in a flower bed.

Chayote

Common names: chayote, chocho, chuchu, sou-sou, vegetable pear, one-seeded cucumber, Merliton
Botanical name: *Sechium edule*
Origin: Central America

DESCRIPTION

The chayote is a tender perennial vine that can climb to 30 feet by means of tendrils. It has hairy leaves the size and shape of maple leaves. The fruit looks like a greenish or whitish flattened pear. Male and female flowers are born on the same vine.
Varieties: Plant whatever variety is available.
Grown from: The whole fruit.
Time from planting to harvest: 120 to 150 days.
Parts eaten: The young shoots, the fruit, and if the plant lives long enough, the tubers.
Yield from a 10-foot row: If a chayote really gets started before a frost, you will have enough to give away. The shorter your growing season, the less there will be to eat.

GROWING CHAYOTE

Space between plants: 24 to 30 inches between plants and 4 to 5 feet between rows.
Light: Chayote tolerates partial shade.
Temperature: It prefers warm to hot temperatures and cannot survive temperatures below freezing.
Water: Keep watering to keep the plant growing.
Soil: Well-fertilized, well-drained soil, high in organic matter.
Pests and diseases: Aphids and other common pests.
Cultural hints: The whole fruit is planted with the fat side stuck halfway down in the soil at an angle. In areas where the season is short, chayote can be grown in a pot and then set out in the soil, or kept in a pot and brought back inside when the weather turns cold. In addition to being tender, it is also affectionate — the tendrils reach out for everything. Since it can get quite heavy, grow it over an arbor or a trellis.

HARVESTING, EATING, STORING

Cut the chayote off the vine while it is young and tender, before the flesh becomes really hard. They can be prepared any way you prepare squash. If you let the chayotes ripen too long they will taste like vintage wash cloths instead of like mild-flavored squash. If a chayote over-ripens, take out the insides, remove the seed (a large seed, in what looks

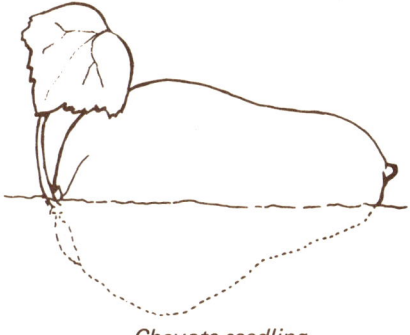

Chayote seedling

Chayote

like a terry cloth bag), mash the insides with cheese or meat, restuff and bake. The tubers of really mature plants are edible and filling, but not very flavorful. Freeze extra chayotes either diced or stuffed.

BY THE WAY...

Chayotes are very popular in Mexico and Central America. They also have a place in American Creole cooking.

Chicory

Common names: chicory, witloof, French endive, Belgian endive, succory
Botanical name: *Cichorium intybus*

Origin: Asia, Europe

DESCRIPTION

A hardy perennial with a long, fleshy taproot and a flower stalk that rises from a rosette of leaves. The chicory looks similar to a dandelion except the flowers grow on a branched stalk and are pale blue. This kind of chicory can be used to produce blanched Belgian endive. If you want the chicory that has lacy leaves and is sometimes called escarole, plant *Chicorium endivia*. The growing process for blanched endive requires 2 stages. The first stage produces a root. The second stage produces the tender top.
Varieties: Any variety — even wild, roadside chicory.
Grown from: Seeds.
Time from planting to harvest: It takes over 100 days to produce a mature chicory root. The leaves can be eaten at any point, but if you want the traditional blanched endive, you will have to wait another 3 or 4 weeks after the root matures.
Parts eaten: The leaves are eaten and the roots are sometimes

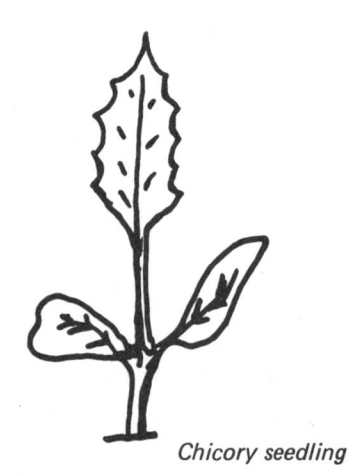

Chicory seedling

roasted and ground to add to coffee.
Yield from a 10-foot row: 30 to 50 shoots.

GROWING CHICORY

Space between plants: For the root development stage, thin the plants to 3 or 4 inches apart. During the second stage, the roots are planted almost touching each other.
Light: Chicory tolerates partial shade in stage 1 and in stage 2 is often forced with no light.
Temperature: Chicory is very hardy and tolerates cold. If the temperature alternates a lot between hot and cold, the roots tend to produce a number of buds rather than 1 bud. Thorough chilling or freezing is necessary to produce good results in the second stage.
Water: The more even the water availability, the more even the growth of the central bud and the less development of secondary shoots. Try not to let the soil dry out.
Soil: Well-worked soil with good drainage and high organic content. The fewer the lumps, the less forking or splitting of the roots.
Pests and diseases: Anything that will bother a dandelion.
Cultural hints: Do not start the seed too early in the growing season or the plant will go to seed.

Chicory

HARVESTING, EATING, STORING

During the first stage of growth in well-cultivated soil, rich in organic matter, endives should develop large roots. Before freezing weather, take up the roots and cut off the tops leaving about 1 inch of stalk. Trim the bottoms evenly and pack the roots in large 12-inch pots using a mixture of equal parts damp sand and damp peat moss. Cover the pots with plastic and then mulch. Keep them below 40°F.

About 3 to 4 weeks before serving, put a pot under the sink or in some other warm, dark spot. Water and let the leaves grow 6 or more inches long. Cut off the *chicons* (sprouts) 1/2 inch above the root. Then let the roots resprout. Enjoy the sprouts braised or in salads. Refrigerate cut sprouts until ready to serve.

BY THE WAY...

Chicory root can be used as a flavoring in coffee or as a coffee substitute. Wash and dice the root, then dry it and roast it before grinding.

Chive

Common name: chives
Botanical name: *Allium schoenoprasum*
Origin: Europe

DESCRIPTION

This hardy perennial relative of the onion has tufts of thin hollow leaves 6 to 10 inches long. In the late spring, the lavender balllike blossoms are very attractive.
Grown from: Seeds or separated clumps.
Time from planting to harvest: You can start snipping chives after 90 days, but the plant will produce much better the second year. Starting with clumps, you can have chives in 60 days.
Parts eaten: The leaves and sometimes the flowers.
Yield from a 10-foot row: Enough for the whole neighborhood.

GROWING CHIVES

Space between plants: Each individual bulb can be grown almost touching the next. Small clumps (25 plants) can be set out 6 to 8 inches apart in rows. They fill in and make a nice border.
Light: Chives can grow in partial shade outdoors or in a window inside.
Temperature: They do well in cool weather and are very hardy, surviving cold and hot weather.
Water: Watering is important for good growth, but chives will survive neglect. Try not to let the soil dry out or the leaves will become brown.
Soil: Chives will grow almost anywhere, but sandy soil with high organic matter and good drainage is preferred.
Pests and diseases: Thrips sometimes attack plants that lack water.
Cultural hints: Chives need little encouragement. Separate the clumps from time to time. If you grow chives indoors have several pots that can take turns being clipped.

See the step-by-step discussion of herbs for more information about growing chives.

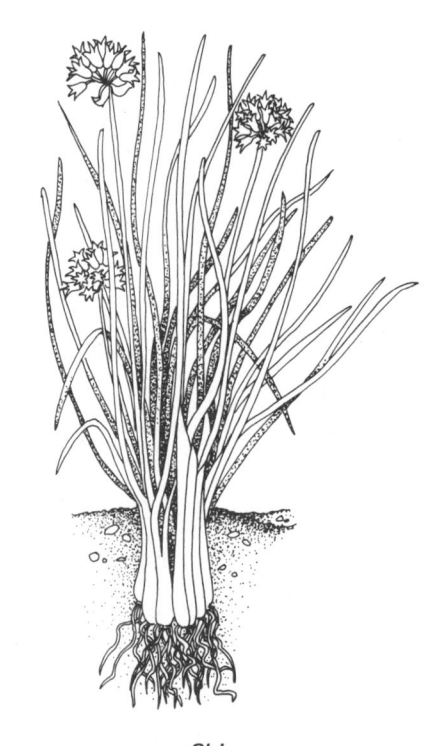

Chive

Chive seedling

Collard seedling

HARVESTING, EATING, STORING

Snip off the ends with scissors, leaving about 5 inches of leaf. Used raw, they add a mild onion flavor to any dish. They are often mixed with cottage cheese, sour cream or cream cheese. The blossoms can be eaten too and are best when just coming into bloom. Chives can be frozen but for a fresh supply, grow them indoors in pots.

BY THE WAY...

The chive blossom appears, dried or fresh, in many Japanese dishes.

Collard

Common name: collards
Botanical name: *Brassica oleracea acephala*
Origin: Europe

DESCRIPTION

A hardy biennial grown as an annual, the collard grows 2 to 4 feet high and has tufts or rosettes of leaves growing on sturdy stems. Collard is a kind of kale, or non-heading cabbage. The name collard is also given to young cabbage plants that are harvested before they have headed.
Varieties: Georgia (75 days), Vates (75 days) from transplants.
Grown from: Seeds (8,000 to 9,000 per ounce) or transplants.
Time from planting to harvest: 75 to 85 days from transplants, 85 to 95 days from seeds.
Parts eaten: Leaves.
Yield from a 10-foot row: 8 pounds or more.

GROWING COLLARDS

Space between plants: Collards should be grown 2 feet apart in rows 3 to 4 feet apart.
Light: Tolerate partial shade but prefer full sun.
Temperature: Collards are quite tolerant of both heat and cold. They will take more heat than cabbage and more cold than cauliflower.
Water: Regular watering keeps the leaves from getting tough.
Soil: Collards need well-drained, fertile soil high in organic matter.
Pests and diseases: Cabbage worms are the collards' chief enemy. Collards have fewer pests than the other cabbages.
Cultural hints: In the South get ahead of the warm weather by planting collards in February or March. In

Collards

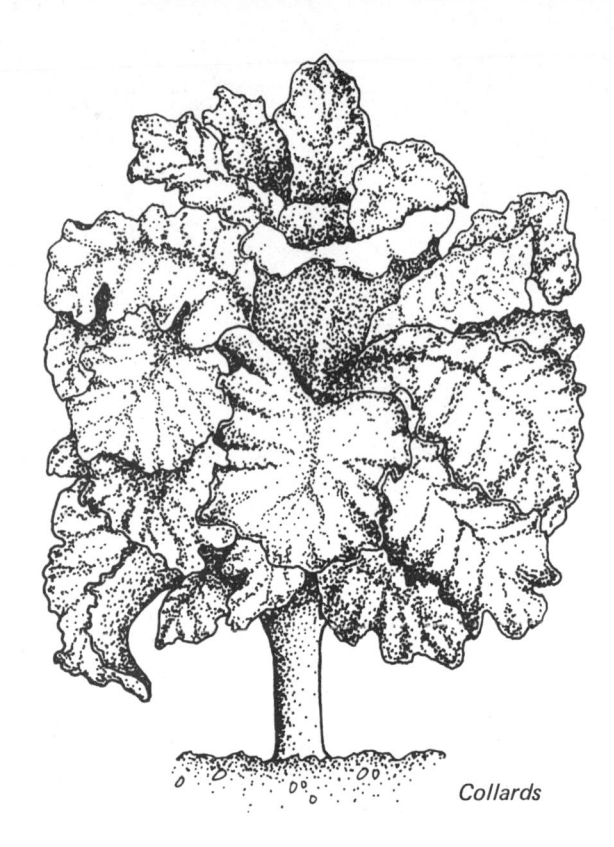

the North, plant in early spring and again in July or August. Stake the plants if they get too heavy. Since the leaves are cut up before cooking, do not worry about any lacework made by pests.

See the step-by-step discussion of cabbage for more information about growing collards.

HARVESTING, EATING, STORING

Harvest the leaves from the bottom up before they get old and tough. They can be steamed or boiled. Serve them alone or combine them with ham or salt pork and serve with corn bread. Collards can be frozen or canned.

BY THE WAY...

A primitive, uneducated member of the cabbage family, collards do not form heads. They were England's main winter vegetable for centuries.

Corn

Common names: corn, sweet corn
Botanical name: *Zea mays*
Origin: Central America

DESCRIPTION

Corn, a tender annual that can grow

4 to 12 feet high, depending on the variety, is a member of the grass family. It produces 1 to 2 ears on a stalk. The pollen from the tassels must fall in the silks to produce kernels. If pollination does not occur, all that will grow is the cob. The kernels of sweet corn can be yellow, white, black, red or a combination of colors.

Varieties: Your local extension service can give you suggestions for the best corn to grow in your area. Polar Vee (55 days), Sugar and Gold (white and yellow kernels, 60 days), Earliking (66 days), Butter and Sugar (white and yellow kernels, 78 days), Golden Cross Bantam (84 days). For late crops, try Aristogold Bantam Evergreen (90 days) or Silver Queen (92 days).
Grown from: Seeds (100 or less per ounce).
Time from planting to harvest: 55 to 95 days, depending on the variety.
Parts eaten: The ears.
Yield from a 10-foot row: Only 5 to 8 ears.

GROWING CORN

Space between plants: When planting early in cold soil, plant the seeds thickly. Thin the short varieties 2 feet apart, the tall varieties 3 feet apart.
Light: Full sun.
Temperature: The optimum growing temperature is 85°F.
Water: Corn requires water but rain or water on the tassels at the time of pollination can reduce the number of kernels on a cob — and sometimes can destroy the whole crop.
Soil: Well-worked, fertile soil with good drainage.
Pests and diseases: Corn attracts the corn earworm, the European corn borer and about 348 other insects — but usually not at the same time. Raccoons are very fond of sweet corn and can find the right ear at the right time, even in the center of a city. Smut, wilt and blight are the more frequent diseases.

See the step-by-step discussion of corn for more information about growing this popular eatable.

HARVESTING, EATING, STORING

Harvest when the kernels are soft and plump and the juice is milky. Have the water boiling when you go out to harvest and rush the corn from the stalk to the pot, then to the table. The goal is to cook the corn before the sugar in the kernels changes to starch.

Storage is rarely a problem with sweet corn — there is never any left.

BY THE WAY...

Corn is the number 1 crop in the United States and, along with rice,

Corn seedling

Corn

wheat, and potatoes, is one of the top 4 crops in the world. Although people eat sweet corn, popcorn, corn bread, and corn flakes, they eat most corn second-hand — 80 percent of the U.S. corn crop goes into the production of meat.

Cress

Common names: cress, garden cress, peppergrass
Botanical name: *Lepidium sativum*
Origin: Asia

DESCRIPTION

Cress is a hardy annual with finely divided green leaves that have a biting flavor. Garden cress is different from water cress, though they both taste peppery.
Varieties: Sometimes cress is hard to find so plant whatever variety is available.
Grown from: Seeds, indoors or out.
Time from planting to harvest: A mere 15 days in the ground for sprouts.
Parts eaten: Stems and leaves.
Yield from a 10-foot row: Enough for the whole neighborhood.

GROWING CRESS

Space between plants: Sow cress thickly in rows or broadcast the seeds.
Light: Shade or semi-shade.
Temperature: Cress can tolerate a wide range of temperatures.
Water: Cress needs even moisture. Try not to wet the leaves since the soil that lodges there when water splashes on them is impossible to wash out without damaging the leaf.
Soil: Well worked soil with good drainage is best for cress.
Pests and diseases: Nothing of importance bothers cress.
Cultural hints: When grown indoors, cress must have good circulation or it tends to rot. Sow seeds every 10 to 14 days for a continuous supply of cress for salads and sandwiches. Cress can be sprouted on water-soaked cotton.

Cress

HARVESTING, EATING, STORING

Often the plants are eaten at their seed leaf stage. Cut off the cress with scissors and enjoy in salads or sandwiches. Cress does not store well so just keep on sprouting it.

BY THE WAY...

The English nibble "small salads" of cress and mix the young sprouts with white mustard for dainty cress sandwiches.

Cucumber

Common name: cucumber
Botanical name: *Cucumis sativus*
Origin: Asia

DESCRIPTION

Cucumbers are weak-stemmed, tender annuals that can sprawl on the ground or be trained to climb. Both the large leaves and the stems are covered with short hairs. The flowers are yellow and the sexes are separate. Only the female flowers can produce cucumbers. Some plants have both sexes on the same vine; there may be 10 males to every female flower. The English forcing cucumber does not require pollination.

Varieties: In the United States, cucumbers are divided into slicing (large-sized that stay green for a long time), pickling (small, stubby), and forcing (which must be grown in a greenhouse). There are dozens of varieties, including "burpless" and round, yellow Lemon Cucumbers. Contact your local extension service to find out which variety is best for your area.

Grown from: Seeds (1,000 per ounce).

Time from planting to harvest: Depending on the variety, cucumbers are ready to pick from 50 to 75 days.

Parts eaten: The fruit and sometimes the male flowers.

Yield from a 10-foot row: 6 to 10 pounds.

Cucumber seedling

Cucumber

keep the roots cool and the soil moist.

Water: Cucumbers are 95 percent water and need plenty of water to keep growing fast. Do not let the soil dry out. In hot weather the leaves may wilt during the day, even when the soil moisture is high, because the plant is using water faster than its roots can supply it.

Soil: Well-drained soil that is high in organic matter. Mulch to avoid soil compaction caused by heavy watering. Cucumbers love well-rotted manure.

Pests and diseases: Aphids, cucumber beetles, scab, mosaic, and mildew.

Cultural hints: Cucumbers can be trained on a trellis or fence. Some varieties can be grown in containers such as tubs and hanging baskets. If the area is insect-free, use a watercolor brush to transfer pollen from male to female blossoms. To keep production going, keep the cucumbers cut off. Mature cukes left on the vine suppress the production of more flowers.

See the step-by-step discussion of cucumbers for more growing information.

GROWING CUCUMBERS

Space between plants: Single plants should be 6 to 12 inches apart. Plant many seeds to take care of all the early hazards. If more survive than you need, thin them out.
Light: Tolerate partial shade.
Temperature: They prefer warm weather with night temperatures of 60°F to 65°F and day temperatures up to 90°F. High temperatures are no problem if the soil is mulched to

HARVESTING, EATING, STORING

Pick the fruits while they are immature. When the seeds start to mature, the plant will stop producing. Enjoy cukes raw or braised. Male flowers can be dipped in egg batter and fried. Share the excess harvest or pickle because cucumbers will not keep in the refrigerator for long periods without being dipped in wax.

BY THE WAY...

In the Gay 90s the hallmark of an elegant tea party was to serve cucumber sandwiches, made open-faced on thin-sliced bread.

Dill

Common name: dill
Botanical name: *Anethum graveolens*
Origin: Southeast Europe

DESCRIPTION

Dill is a biennial grown as an annual that grows 2 to 4 feet tall. A plant with finely cut leaves and small yellow flowers growing in a flat-topped cluster, it has a delicate feathery look and makes a good background for flowers or vegetables.
Grown from: Seeds (12,000 per ounce).
Time from planting to harvest: 70 days for foliage, 90 days or more for seeds.
Parts eaten: Leaves and seeds.
Yield from a 10-foot row: Enough for the neighborhood.

GROWING DILL

Space between plants: 8 to 12 inches between plants and 30 inches between rows. This is a good plant to grow in a clump or mass rather than in a row.
Light: Dill will tolerate partial shade. In light shade they can be planted closer together than in full sun since they will not get as bushy.
Temperature: Dill can take a wide range of temperatures.
Water: Dill does better when kept on the dry side.
Soil: Poor, sandy soil with excellent drainage produces stronger-flavored plants.
Pests and diseases: Dill is usually quite trouble-free.
Cultural hints: If it has enough light, dill is very easy to grow. Seeds can be planted in the spring or late fall. Once established, dill will often seed itself and come up year after year. When young, dill can easily be pulled out of spots where it is not wanted and tossed into a salad or sandwich.

See the step-by-step discussion of herbs for more information about growing dill.

HARVESTING, EATING, STORING

Snip off the leaves or young flower heads for soup or salad. For pickling, cut whole stalks when the plant is more mature. Gather mature seed for planting or drying. Dill makes a flavorful contribution to fish, potatoes, or rye bread.

Dill dries very easily. Cut off the feathery stalk, hang it upside down in a dry place. When it is brittle, crumble and store in a tightly sealed jar.

Dill

Dill seedling

BY THE WAY...

Carrying a bag of dry dill over the heart is supposed to ward off the evil eye. Dill water was once used to quiet babies and get rid of gas.

Eggplant

Common names: eggplant, aubergine, guinea squash
Botanical name: *Solanum melongena*
Origin: East Indies, India

DESCRIPTION

Eggplant is a very tender, perennial plant with large greyish-green hairy leaves. It is related to the tomato, the potato and the pepper. Its star-shaped flowers are lavender with yellow centers. The round or egg-shaped fruit is creamy-white, yellow, brown, purple and sometimes almost black. Eggplants will grow 2 to 6 feet tall, depending on the variety.
Varieties: Black Magic Hybrid (73 days), Jersey King Hybrid (75 days), Black Beauty (80 days).
Grown from: Seeds (6,500 per ounce) or transplants.

Time from planting to harvest: 100 to 150 days from seeds; 70 to 85 days from transplants.
Parts eaten: The fruit.
Yield from a 10-foot row: In a peak, pest-free year you may have 20 eggplants.

GROWING EGGPLANTS

Space between plants: 2 to 3 feet between plants and about 3 feet between the rows.
Light: Full sunlight is essential.
Temperature: Eggplants are very sensitive to cold. They need a growing season with day temperatures between 80°F and 90°F and night temperatures between 70°F and 80°F. Sometimes the soil temperature can get too warm for the roots.
Water: Try to maintain even soil moisture so they can grow steadily. The roots will rot if there is too much water.
Soil: Eggplants will grow in almost any soil but they do better in rich soil, high in organic matter, that is free of rocks and has excellent drainage.
Pests and diseases: Watch out for cutworms, aphids, flea beetles, Colorado potato bugs, spider mites, tomato hornworms, and fungous and bacterial diseases.
Cultural hints: Eggplants must be treated with great solicitude. They are very picky about temperature and moisture requirements until

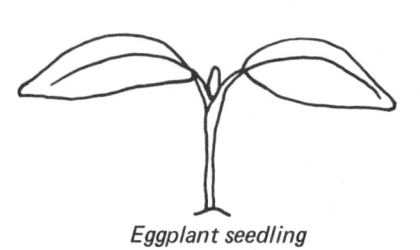

Eggplant seedling

they are well-established in the garden. If plants are large or growing in a windy spot it is a good idea to stake them. If unpollinated, the flowers produce only tiny fruits.

See the step-by-step discussion of tomatoes for more information about growing eggplant.

HARVESTING, EATING, STORING

Cut the fruit from the plant with a sharp knife. The fruit does not break off very easily. Pick it young, before the flesh become pithy. The purple fruit should be picked when they are still shiny purple, rather than streaked with brown. Freeze the excess harvest.

BY THE WAY...

This is a handsome plant and can be grown at the back of a flower bed.

Endive

Common names: endive, escarole
Botanical name: *Cichorium endivia*
Origin: South Asia

DESCRIPTION

Endive or escarole is a half-hardy biennial grown as an annual. It has a large rosette of toothed and curled or wavy leaves that are used in salads as a substitute for lettuce.
Varieties: Full Heart Batavian (90 days) has smooth leaves. Salad King (98 days) has curled leaves.
Grown from: Seeds (26,000 per ounce).
Time from planting to harvest: 90 to 100 days.
Parts eaten: The leaves.
Yield from a 10-foot row: 10 heads.

GROWING ENDIVE

Space between plants: Thin the seedlings to 12 inches apart in rows 18 inches apart.

Eggplant

Endive seedling

151

Endive

Light: Endive tolerates partial shade.
Temperature: Endive prefers a mild climate but is more tolerant of heat than lettuce.
Water: Keep it growing quickly. Lack of water and slow growth make for bitter leaves.
Soil: Well-drained, well-fertilized soil, high in organic matter.
Pests and diseases: No serious pests or diseases. If the plant is tied up while the inside is wet, some of the leaves may rot.
Cultural hints: Grow endive like lettuce. If you prefer pale yellow rather than green endive in your salad or soup (it is good in soup) you can tie up the plants with a bit of raffia, lay a board over the whole row, or put a flowerpot over each plant.

See the step-by-step discussion of lettuce for more information about growing endive.

HARVESTING, EATING, STORING

Cut off the endive at the soil line and wash it well before serving it in a salad, soup, or sandwich. Store it in the refrigerator crisper.

BY THE WAY...

Endive or escarole is different from Belgian endive, though they both belong to the genus *Chicorium*.

Fennel

Common names: fennel, Florence fennel, finnochio
Botanical name: *Foeniculum vulgare dulce*
Origin: Mediterranean

DESCRIPTION

A stocky perennial grown as an annual, fennel looks a bit like celery with very feathery leaves. Ordinary fennel *(Foeniculum vulgare)* is also a perennial. Its leaves are picked for soups, sauces, and salads.
Grown from: Seeds (4,500 per ounce).
Time from planting to harvest: 70 to 90 days.
Parts eaten: Leaves, swollen stems, seeds.
Yield from a 10-foot row: 20 stalks.

GROWING FENNEL

Space between plants: Thin fennel 4 to 6 inches apart.
Light: Full sun.
Temperature: Fennel tolerates both warm and cool temperatures.
Water: Keep fennel on the dry side but give it enough moisture to sustain growth.
Soil: Fennel wants its soil well-drained and high in organic matter.
Pests and diseases: If you see a worm on the leaves, tell it it is on the wrong plant and escort it away. Not much is supposed to bother fennel.
Cultural hints: When the seedlings are about 4 inches tall you might give them a side dressing of liquid fertilizer. Pour with a light hand about 4 inches on either side of the plant.

See the step-by-step discussion of herbs for more information about growing fennel.

Fennel

Fennel seedling

HARVESTING, EATING, STORING

Fennel is featured in many Italian dishes. You can pinch the leaves for flavoring as soon as you get up the courage. They look like dill leaves and taste like anise. Harvest the bulbous stalk when it is 3 inches or more in diameter. You can freeze or dry the leaves. You will probably want to eat the stalks fresh but they can also be frozen.

BY THE WAY...

In the good old days, fennel sharpened eyesight, stopped hiccups, freed one from loathings, acted as an aphrodisiac, and promoted weight loss.

Garlic

Common name: garlic
Botanical name: *Allium sativum*
Origin: South Europe

Garlic

DESCRIPTION

Garlic is a hardy perennial plant that looks a lot like an onion, except that the bulb is segmented into cloves. The flower head looks like a tissue paper dunce cap and is filled with small flowers and bulblets.
Varieties: Seller's choice — you plant the variety you can find.
Grown from: Cloves or bulblets are planted with the fat end down. Use the plumpest ones for cooking and plant the others.
Time from planting to harvest: 70 to 100 days.
Parts eaten: Leaves and cloves.
Yield from a 10-foot row: Enough for the neighborhood.

GROWING GARLIC

Space between plants: 4 to 6 inches apart, 1 to 2 inches deep. Space the rows about 1 foot apart.
Light: Full sun.
Temperature: Cool temperatures in the garlic's early growth period are necessary. Plant garlic in the spring in the North and in the fall in the South. Garlic is not affected by heat in the later stages of its growth.
Water: Keep the soil on the dry side.
Soil: Garlic grows best in well-worked soil with good drainage and high organic content.
Pests and diseases: If it gets too warm and moist, onion thrips and mildew will bother garlic.
Cultural hints: For strong flavor, keep them slightly dry and hold off fertilizing. The bulbs should be kept weeded. Cut down on the watering when the bulbs are near maturity.

See the step-by-step discussion of onions for more information about growing garlic.

HARVESTING, EATING, STORING

Dig up the bulbs when the leaves

Garlic seedling

dry, or before the first frost in the North. The leaves can be cut and used like chives. The cloves are used whole, minced or mashed for flavoring. (Some recipes for garlic soup call for as many as 15 cloves.)

Dry the cloves with good air circulation. If you like, you can twist their leaves into a long braid and hang it near the stove.

BY THE WAY...

There is an old story that when the Devil walked out of the Garden of Eden after the fall of Adam and Eve, onions sprang up from his right hoof-print and garlic from his left.

Grape

Common name: grape
Botanical name: various varieties and hybrids of the genus *Vitis*
Origin: Asia, America

DESCRIPTION

Woody perennial vines of various degrees of hardiness, grapes bear round, smooth-skinned fruit that are bluish, reddish-purple or greenish-white. The European wine grape *(Vitis vinifera)* also produces important eating grapes: Thompson seedless, the green grape in grocery stores, and Tokay, the red grape in stores. The most commonly grown American grapes are garden grapes descended mostly from *Vitis labrusca*. They are grown primarily for juice and jelly making.
Varieties: Concord, Delaware, Fredonia, Niagara.
Grown from: Cuttings or plants.
Time from planting to harvest: Cuttings take about 2 years to bear fruit. Concord grapes need a growing season of about 160 days.
Parts eaten: Fruit and leaves.
Yield from a 10-foot row: 20 to 25 pounds.

GROWING GRAPES

Space between plants: 5 to 10 feet.
Light: Full sun.
Temperature: Grapes do best when the temperature is cool in the first half of the growing season and hot in the second half.
Water: Lack of water when fruit is growing prevents grapes from growing full size and can delay maturity.
Soil: Grapes tolerate a wide range of soils, but the drainage should be excellent.
Pests and diseases: Rabbits, deer, people and phylloxera, a gall-forming aphid that nearly eliminated the wine industry when it was introduced into Europe.
Cultural hints: Grape vines need to be trained on a trellis, fence or arbor to keep them up from underfoot, to provide good air circulation and to expose as much of the plant to the sun as possible. The current year's grapes grow from the preceding year's growth. Almost all the earlier woody growth can be eliminated. Do not be afraid to prune off a lot since

Grape

the vines can grow 30 feet or more each year.

See the step-by-step discussion of grapes for more growing information.

HARVESTING, EATING, STORING

Grapes do not become sweeter after being picked. Their color comes before they are completely sweet, so test before picking off a bunch. The leaves can be used to make Greek dolmades (stuffed grape leaves) or other Mediterranean dishes. Make jelly or jam with the excess crop.

BY THE WAY...

Right after the flood, Noah went into the farming business and the first thing he did was plant grapes.

Horseradish

Common name: horseradish
Botanical name: *Armoracia rusticana*
Origin: Eastern Europe

DESCRIPTION

Horseradish is a hardy perennial member of the cabbage family though it looks like a giant, 2-foot radish.
Variety: New Bohemian.
Grown from: Crowns or roots.
Time from planting to harvest: Plants grown from crowns can be

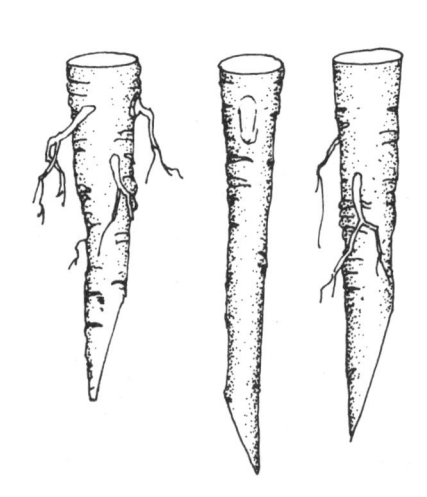

Horseradish root

harvested in 150 days. Plants grown from roots cannot be harvested until the second year.
Parts eaten: Roots.
Yield from a 10-foot row: 6 to 8 roots.

GROWING HORSERADISH

Space between plants: 12 to 24 inches.
Light: Tolerates partial shade.
Temperature: Horseradish is a very cold-hardy plant which does well in the North and in cool high-altitude areas in the South.
Water: Grown in evenly moist soils, the roots will be tender and flavorful. They get woody in dry soils.
Soil: Horseradish needs deep, well cultivated soil that is rich and drains well or the roots will split.
Pests and diseases: None.
Cultural hints: There is a handy convention to remember when taking horseradish cuttings for planting. Cut the end closest to the mother root square, and then trim the other end with a slant so that you'll know which end is up at planting time. Plant the cutting on a slight slope in a trench with the slanted end down. Fill in with soil until the square-cut end is just barely covered.

If unrestrained, horseradish can take over. To keep it in check and to encourage a single root, cut off the side roots about 4 inches down at mid-summer.

HARVESTING, EATING, STORING

Horseradish can be dug as needed. In areas where the ground freezes hard, dig and wash the roots in the fall. Store them in plastic bags at 32° to 38°F. Both roots and grated horseradish can be frozen or refrigerated in jars with tight, screw-on lids.

Since the fumes are very

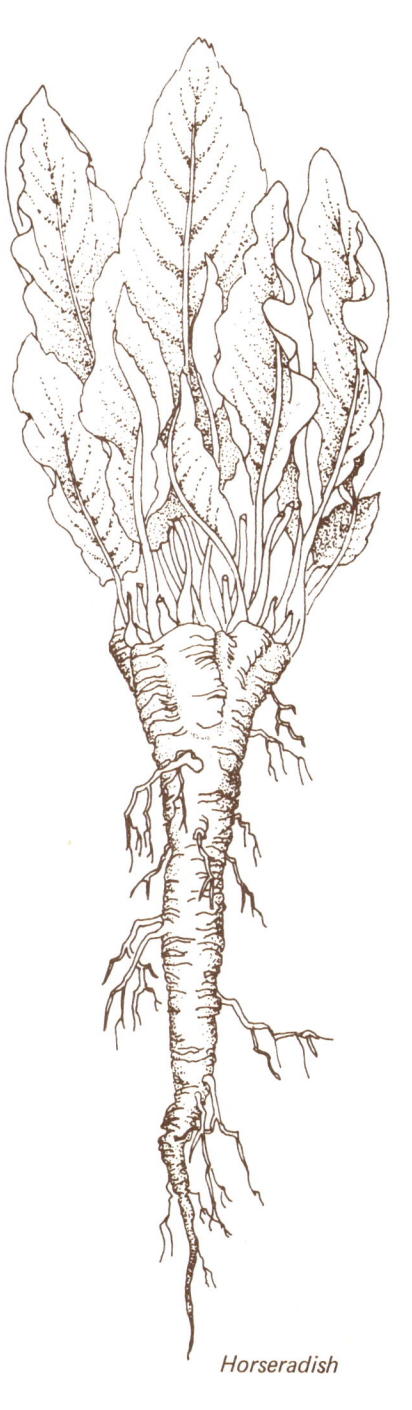

Horseradish

strong, grating is best done outdoors. If you must do it indoors, use a blender. Peel and cube the roots and place them in the blender, with enough water to cover the blades and a few crushed ice cubes. Run the blender on grating speed, adding more water or ice cubes until the desired consistency is reached. Add 2 to 3 tablespoons of white vinegar and 1/2 teaspoon salt to each cup of grated horseradish. The vinegar stops the enzymatic action. If you want mild horseradish, add vinegar right away. Wait 3 minutes before adding vinegar if you like your horseradish hot-hot.

BY THE WAY...

Ninety-eight percent of all commercial horseradish is grown in 3 Illinois counties near St. Louis.

Kale

Common names: kale, borecole, collard, green cabbage, German greens
Botanical name: *Brassica oleracea acephala*
Origin: horticultural hybrid

Kale seedling

DESCRIPTION

Kale is a hardy biennial plant grown as an annual. It looks like cabbage with a permanent wave. Scotch kale has grey-green leaves that are extremely crumpled and curly. Siberian or blue kale usually is less curly and is a bluer shade of green. There are also decorative forms with lavender and silver variegated leaves.
Varieties: Dwarf Blue Curled (55 days), Dwarf Blue Scotch (55 days), Vates (55 days), Dwarf Green Curled (60 days).
Grown from: Seeds (9,000 to 10,000 per ounce) or transplants.
Time from planting to harvest: 55 days from transplants, 70 to 80 days from seeds.
Parts eaten: The leaves.
Yield from a 10-foot row: 10 heads.

GROWING KALE

Space between plants: Thin to 12 to 15 inches apart.
Light: Tolerates partial shade.
Temperature: A cool weather crop, kale will last through the winter as far north as Maryland and central Indiana. Hot dry weather produces poor plants.
Water: Regular watering keeps it growing fast and prevents toughness.
Soil: Good drainage is important. The soil should be high in organic matter. Fertilize to produce the best plants.
Pests and diseases: Kale has no serious enemies.
Cultural hints: Plant kale early in the spring and again at midsummer.
    See the step-by-step discussion of cabbage for more information about growing kale.

Kale

HARVESTING, EATING, STORING

Leave kale in the garden until needed. Thinned plants can be used as greens. As the remaining plants mature, you can take outside leaves as long as the plant lives or you can cut off the entire plant at once. But harvest kale before it gets old. Old kale is tough, as is kale that had a hard childhood and adolescence.

Kale tastes good slightly steamed and, like collards and mustard greens, it combines well with ham or salt pork.

BY THE WAY...

Kale is very ornamental whether it's grown in the garden or in a flowerpot. When you tire of it as a decoration, throw it in the soup and enjoy its vitamin A.

Kohlrabi

Common names: kohlrabi, turnip-rooted cabbage, stem turnip, turnip cabbage
Botanical name: *Brassica caulorapa*
Origin: horticultural hybrid

Kohlrabi seedling

Kohlrabi

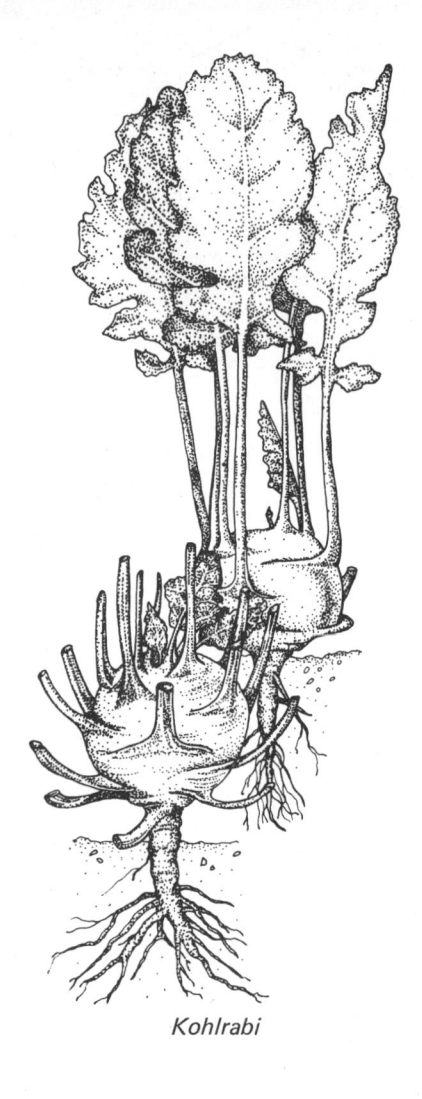

DESCRIPTION

Kohlrabi is a hardy biennial grown as an annual. It has a swollen stem that makes it look like a turnip on tiptoes. The swollen stem can be white, purple or green and is topped with a rosette of blue-green leaves. It is a member of the cabbage clan.
Varieties: Early White Vienna (55 days), Early Purple Vienna (60 days).
Grown from: Seeds (8,000 to 9,000 per ounce).
Time from planting to harvest: 55 to 75 days.
Parts eaten: The swollen stem and leaves.
Yield from a 10-foot row: 20 "turnips."

GROWING KOHLRABI

Space between plants: 5 to 8 inches.
Light: Tolerates partial shade.
Temperature: Grows best in cool weather and produces better with a 10°F to 15°F difference between day and night temperatures.
Water: Kohlrabi should have even moisture or it becomes woody.
Soil: Fertile, well-drained soil that is high in organic matter.
Pests and diseases: Caterpillars, cutworms and aphids.
Cultural hints: Instead of planting all at once, plant a few every couple of weeks. Kohlrabi should be carefully cultivated to keep the weed competition down, but be careful since the roots are shallow. The "turnip" will grow as large as a tennis ball, but it tends to be quite woody at that size. They are much more edible when they are the size of a golf ball.

See the step-by-step discussion of cabbage for more information about growing kohlrabi.

HARVESTING, EATING, STORING

Pick them before the stems are 2½ inches in diameter. The leaves are in much better shape at that time, too. Eat the leaves first as greens and then pull up the swollen stem. Mature kohlrabi should be peeled before slicing. Served raw, steamed or boiled, kohlrabi tastes like a delicate flavored turnip. Give the extras to your friends. Kohlrabi are great conversation pieces and they lose a lot of their appeal as they age.

BY THE WAY...

In German, *kohl* means cabbage and *rabi* means turnip — a clue to the taste and texture of kohlrabi.

Leek

Common name: leek
Botanical name: *Allium porrum*
Origin: Mediterranean, Egypt

DESCRIPTION

The leek is a hardy biennial grown as an annual. It is a member of the onion family but has a stalk rather than a bulb and flat, staplike leaves instead of hollow ones.
Varieties: Titan (120 days).
Grown from: Seeds (11,000 per ounce) or transplants.
Time from planting to harvest: 120 to 130 days from seeds, less from transplants.
Parts eaten: The stems and leaves.
Yield from a 10-foot row: 16 to 20 sticks.

GROWING LEEKS

Space between plants: 6 to 9 inches apart, planted in double rows.
Light: Full sun.
Temperature: Leeks are tolerant but the best yields come when the temperature is below 75°F.
Water: Give them plenty of water to keep them growing.
Soil: Rich, well-worked, well-drained soil.
Pests and diseases: Onion thrips may be a problem in dry weather.
Cultural hints: In order to grow a large, white, succulent "stick" (stalk), you have to blanch the lower part of the stem by hilling the soil up on the stalk or growing the leek in a hole. To plant transplants, make holes 6 inches deep, about 6 to 9 inches apart in well-worked soil. Double rows save space. To make them, stagger the plants with their leaves growing parallel to the rows so they will not grow into the pathway. Drop the leeks in the holes, but do not fill in with soil. Over a period of time, watering will slowly collapse the soil around the leeks and settle them in.

See the step-by-step discussion of onions for more information about growing leek.

HARVESTING, EATING, STORING

Halfway through the summer you can start harvesting the leaves. This trimming will encourage greater growth of the leek stick. But leave at least half of the leaf as you cut. Use

Leek seedling

Leek

Lettuce

Common names: lettuce, crisphead lettuce, butterhead lettuce, stem lettuce (celtuce), leaf lettuce, cos, romaine
Botanical name: *Lactuca sativa*
Origin: Near East

DESCRIPTION

Hardy, fast-growing annual with either loose or compactly growing leaves, lettuce range in color from very light green through reddish brown. When it bolts (goes to seed), the flower stalks are 2 to 3 feet tall with small yellowish flowers on the bud.
Varieties: Crisphead lettuce: Great Lakes (90 days). Butterhead lettuce: Summer Bibb (62 days), Buttercrunch (75 days). Leaf lettuce: Black-Seeded Simpson (45 days), Ruby (45 days). Cos or romaine: Parris Island Cos (73 days). Stem lettuce: Celtuce (80 days).
Grown from: Seeds (25,000 per ounce). Lettuce that forms a head is sometimes grown from transplants.
Time from planting to harvest: 30 to 90 days.

the leaves for flavoring soups. Leeks are milder tasting than onions. Leave the extra sticks "stored" in the ground until you need them.

BY THE WAY...

The Welsh traditionally wear a leek on St. David's day, March 1, to commemorate King Cadwallader's victory over the Saxons in A.D. 640, when the Welsh snitched leeks and wore them as ID's. The more decorous now wear a daffodil instead.

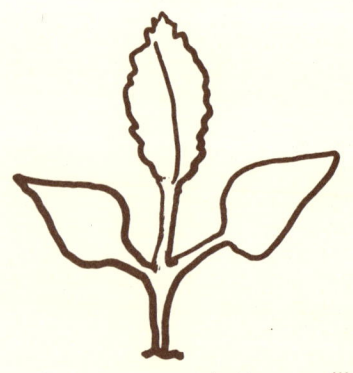

Lettuce seedling

162

Head lettuce

Parts eaten: The whole plant.
Yield from a 10-foot row: 5 to 10 pounds.

GROWING LETTUCE

Space between plants: Thin leaf lettuces to 8 to 10 inches apart. Leave 12 inches between head lettuces.
Light: Lettuce tolerates partial shade.
Temperature: Lettuce needs cool weather. Hot weather and long days cause it to bolt. Leaf lettuce usually matures the fastest, making it ideal for areas with a short, cool spring.
Water: Keep the soil moist, but not soaked. Seedlings should be kept moist.

Soil: Well-worked soil that is slightly acid and high in organic matter. It should also have good drainage and moisture retention.
Pests and diseases: Cutworms, slugs, snails, and aphids.
Cultural hints: Successive crops can be sown if you live where the weather is cool and the days are short. Take care when watering not to splash muddy water on the plants. A light mulch will help cut down on necessary washing before eating.

See the step-by-step discussion of lettuce for more growing information.

HARVESTING, EATING, STORING

As the lettuce grows, pick the outer

Leaf lettuce

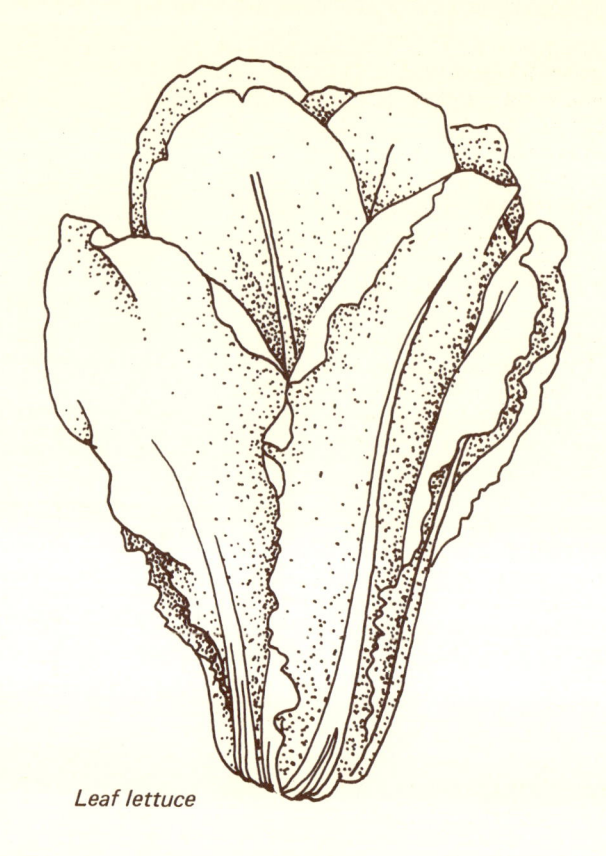

leaves or pick the whole plant at once. Chill the lettuce before serving, especially if you harvest during the heat of the day when the leaves are a little limp. Use the thinnings in soups or salads.

While the lettuce can be stored for short periods in the refrigerator, it cannot be held for long periods or frozen. Share the bounty with your friends.

BY THE WAY...

King Nebuchadnezzar enjoyed lettuce from his gardens in ancient Babylon. The Romans used lettuce as a sedative when they were overstimulated.

Marjoram

Common names: marjoram, sweet marjoram
Botanical name: *Marjorana hortensis*
Origin: Mediterranean

DESCRIPTION

A tender branching perennial, usually grown as an annual, marjoram grows 10 to 15 inches tall. It has greyish opposite leaves and lavender or whitish flowers growing up most of the stem.
Varieties: Plant whatever variety is available.

Grown from: Seeds.
Time from planting to harvest: 70 days.
Parts eaten: The leaves and tender stems.
Yield from a 10-foot row: Enough for the neighborhood.

GROWING MARJORAM

Space between plants: 6 inches.
Light: Tolerates partial shade.
Temperature: Marjoram is sensitive to frost. When first planted out it may need protection from the hot sun until it is acclimated.
Water: The less water the better the flavor.
Soil: Marjoram thrives in poor soil with good drainage. If you fertilize, the marjoram will grow lots of leaves but have little flavor.
Pests and diseases: Nothing bothers marjoram.
Cultural hints: The slower the growth, the better the flavor.

See the step-by-step discussion of herbs for more information about growing majoram.

HARVESTING, EATING STORING

Marjoram to be used fresh can be pinched off as needed. To dry marjoram, cut off the branches when the flowers begin to appear. Tie them in bunches and dry them in a protected place. Crumble the leaves into glass jars with tight tops.

Use marjoram to flavor casseroles, stews, meats, chicken, tomato and egg dishes. Marjoram is a traditional component of bouquet garni.

BY THE WAY...

Marjoram means Joy of the Mountain. Venus was reputed to be the first to grow this herb.

Marjoram

Marjoram seedling

Muskmelon

Common names: muskmelon, cantaloupe, cantaloup
Botanical name: *Cucumis melo*
Origin: South Asia, tropical Africa

DESCRIPTION

The muskmelon is a long-trailing annual that belongs to the cucumber and watermelon family. The netted melon or muskmelon is usually called a cantaloupe. It should not be confused with the real cantaloupe, which is a warty or rock melon.
Varieties: Check with your garden center or local extension office for the varieties that grow best in your area.
Grown from: Seeds (1,300 per ounce).
Time from planting to harvest: 60 to 110 days, depending on type.
Parts eaten: The fruit.
Yield from a 10-foot row: In a good

Muskmelon

year, you might harvest as many as 10 fruits.

GROWING MUSKMELONS

Space between plants: Grow muskmelons in hills (2 or 3 in each hill). Space the hills 4 to 6 feet apart. Or grow them on fences leaving 3 feet between the plants.
Light: Full sun is vital.
Temperature: Melons are sensitive to cold and should not be planted until the ground is warm.
Water: They need a lot of water while the vines are growing. Continue watering until the melons are almost mature, then quit watering while the fruit ripens.
Soil: Muskmelons thrive in well-drained soil that is high in organic matter.
Pests and diseases: Cucumber beetles, aphids, pickle worms (in the South), wilt, blight, mildew and root knot.
Cultural hints: Keep competitive plants weeded out. Cultivate the soil carefully until the vines cover the ground. The roots are very shallow and extend quite a distance, so take care. Plant 6 to 8 seeds in each hill, remove the weakest plants just after sprouting when the "true" second leaves show. Thin out to the best 2 or 3 seedlings after the plants have 3 or 4 of their true leaves. Where cucumber beetles, other insects, or weather are a problem, wait a bit before making the final selection.

See the step-by-step discussion of cucumbers for more information about growing muskmelon.

HARVESTING, EATING, STORING

Leave melons on the vine till they are ripe, since there is no increase in sugar after harvesting. Mature melons slip easily off the stem. A half-ripe melon needs more

Muskmelon seedling

pressure to remove than a ripe melon and often comes off with half the stem attached. Share the extras with friends; melons do not keep for long periods in the refrigerator.

BY THE WAY...

The word cantaloupe means "song of the wolf" and was the name of an Italian castle.

In 1885, when William S. Ross brought 2 barrels of muskmelons into the South Water Market in Chicago, everyone laughed at the little melons. Ross, however, laughed all the way to the bank!

The United States Department of Agriculture spells cantaloup without the final e.

Mustard

Common names: mustard, Chinese mustard, leaf mustard, mustard spinach, greens
Botanical name: *Brassica juncea*
Origin: Asia

DESCRIPTION

Mustard is a hardy annual with a rosette of large light or dark green crinkled leaves that grow up to 3 feet in length.

Varieties: Tendergreen (spinach mustard, 30 days), Green Wave (45 days).
Grown from: Seeds (15,000 per ounce).
Time from planting to harvest: 25 to 45 days.
Parts eaten: The leaves and leaf stalks are eaten. The seeds can be ground and used as a condiment.
Yield from a 10-foot row: 5 pounds.

GROWING MUSTARD

Space between plants: 6 inches apart in rows or bands.
Light: Partial shade.
Temperature: Mustard is a cool-weather plant. It goes to seed quickly in hot weather.
Water: Water before the soil dries out to keep the leaves growing quickly.
Soil: Mustard needs fertile, well-drained soil, with a high organic content.
Pests and diseases: Mustard is fairly disease-resistant although aphids may bother it.
Cultural hints: Sow the seeds as soon as the ground can be worked in the spring. Thin out the seedlings to about 6 inches between plants. Eat the seedlings you thin out in soups or mixed greens. As soon as the plants start to go to seed, pull them up or they will produce a great number of seeds and sow themselves all over the garden. Mustard can be planted again when the weather begins to cool off.

Mustard

Mustard seedling

Okra seedling

See the step-by-step discussion of cabbage for more information about growing mustard.

HARVESTING, EATING, STORING

Pull up the whole plant. For continuous harvest, plant a few seeds at regular intervals, rather than an entire row at once. Cook mustard like greens or serve it in salads.

BY THE WAY...

If you had lived in ancient Rome, you would have eaten mustard to cure your lethargy and any pains you suffered.

Okra

Common names: okra, lady's fingers, gumbo
Botanical name: *Hibiscus esculentus*
Origin: Africa

DESCRIPTION

Okra, a member of the cotton and hibiscus family, is an erect, tender annual with hairy stems and large maplelike leaves. It grows from 3 to 6 feet tall. Its large flowers look like yellow hibiscus blossoms with red or purplish centers. The pods when mature are 6 to 10 inches long and filled with buckshotlike seeds.
Varieties: Emerald (56 days), Clemson Spineless (58 days).
Grown from: Seeds (500 per ounce).
Time from planting to harvest: 50 to 65 days.
Parts eaten: The immature pods.
Yield from a 10-foot row: 6 pounds of okra, depending on the variety grown and the maturity of pods.

GROWING OKRA

Space between plants: When the plants are 6 inches tall, thin them to 1 foot apart for dwarf okra and 3 feet apart for the tall varieties.
Light: Full sun.
Temperature: In parts of the country with very hot summers okra should be grown early or late. It is very sensitive to cold. The yield decreases with temperatures under 70°F and at altitudes over 3,000 feet.
Water: Keep on the dry side. It rots easily if it gets too wet or cold.
Soil: Okra will grow in almost any warm, well-drained soil.
Pests and diseases: Leaf-eating insects, especially those that love cotton, will stop and visit. But generally okra does quite well in the home garden as long as the weather is not too cold or too hot.
Cultural hints: Before planting work the soil deeply. Do not plant

the seeds until the danger of frost is over. Keep any competing plants out of the patch. When the plants begin to set their pods, harvest them at least every other day. Pods grow quickly and unless the older ones are cut off, the plant will stop producing new ones. Okra will grow for a year if not killed by frost and if old pods are not left on the plant.

HARVESTING, EATING, STORING

Keep picking the pods while they are quite small. When they are about 2 inches long they are less gluey. Many people are disappointed because their first mouthful often tastes like buckshot in mucilage. A taste for okra is perhaps an inherited one. Try it in gumbo, mixed with tomatoes, or sauteed.

BY THE WAY...

Okra grows wild in Ethiopia and Sudan. It was brought to the U.S. by slaves. You can let the pods mature and then use them in winter flower arrangements. The pods and the stalks are quite dramatic.

Onion

Common name: onion
Botanical name: *Allium cepa*
Origin: Southwest Asia

DESCRIPTION

Onions are hardy biennial vegetables usually grown as annuals. They have hollow leaves, the bases of which enlarge to form a bulb. The flower stalk is also hollow, taller than the leaves, and topped with a cluster of white or lavender flowers. The bulbs vary in color from white through yellow to red.
Varieties: All varieties can be eaten as green onions, though spring onions, bunching onions, scallions, and green onions are grown especially for their tops. Green onions take the least time to grow. Bermuda and Spanish onions are milder than American onions. American and Spanish onions generally take longer to mature than the Bermuda onions. Check with your local extension service for varieties recommended in your area.
Grown from: Seeds (9,500 per ounce), transplants, and sets.

Okra

Time from planting to harvest: 85 to 120 days for mature onions to develop from seeds, less for green onions. If you start them from sets or transplants, you can have green onions in 3 weeks. Under ideal conditions, sets or transplants may produce mature onions in 110 days, but most home gardens are not ideal and onions may take longer to mature.

Parts eaten: Leaves and bulbs

Yield from a 10-foot row: 8 to 10 pounds of onions, plus leaves.

GROWING ONIONS

Space between plants: 2 to 4 inches.

Light: Green onions will tolerate partial shade. Mature bulbs need full sun. Day length is very important in growing onions.

Temperature: Seeds will germinate in 19 weeks at 32°F and in 1 week at 60°F. Onions grow best when the average temperature runs between 55°F and 75°F. They prefer the temperature to be cool during their early growing season and warmer during their later development.

Water: Keep the soil moist until the plants have started to mature, then the soil should be permitted to dry out.

Soil: Very fertile, well-drained soil is best for onions. If you can get well-rotted manure, use it.

Pests and diseases: Onion thrips and maggots, bulb and root rots, downy mildew, and smut.

Cultural hints: Since onions can be grown from seeds, transplants, and sets the grower has a number of decisions to make. Seeds are available in more varieties, are less expensive, and less dependable. Transplants and sets cost about the same and are usually available in fewer varieties, but the transplants are more certain of producing onions and the sets are fun, producing edible plants almost instantly.

See the step-by-step discussion of onion for more growing information.

Onion

171

Onion seedling

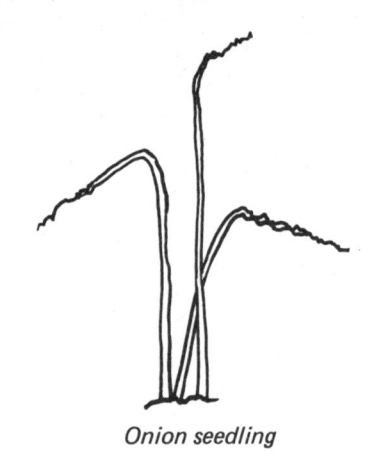

HARVESTING, EATING, STORING

Harvest some leaves for flavoring throughout the season. Pull up the plants when their tops are dry. Let the bulbs dry before storing them. Cut off the tops a thumb's-width from the top of the bulb. If cut too short, the bulb may rot. Or braid the leaves into a long tress for storing in a cool dry place — not in the refrigerator. Use mild onion roots and young tops in salads and use sharp-flavored onions for cooking.

BY THE WAY...

A legendary cure for warts involves rubbing the wart with an onion half, tying the onion halves back together and burying them. When the onion decays in the ground, the wart will disappear.

Parsley

Common name: parsley
Botanical name: *Petroselinum crispum*
Origin: Mediterranean

DESCRIPTION

Parsley is a hardy biennial that is treated as an annual. It has finely divided, fernlike leaves that are either flat or curly. The leaves grow in a rosette from a single taproot that in some varieties is quite large and is eaten like parsnips. Parsley has flat-topped clusters of greenish-yellow flowers, similar to those of dill.
Varieties: Moss Curled (70 days), Perfection (75 days), Hamburg or Parsnip-Rooted parsley (90 days).
Grown from: Seeds (18,000 per ounce).
Time from planting to harvest: 70 to 90 days.
Parts eaten: The leaves and occasionally the roots.
Yield from a 10-foot row: Enough for the neighborhood.

GROWING PARSLEY

Space between plants: 6 to 8 inches.
Light: Parsley grows well in partial shade. It also does well indoors on a bright windowsill.
Temperature: Parsley can survive cold weather. Hot weather encourages the formation of flower stalks.
Water: Water before the soil dries out. Parsley needs a regular supply of water to keep growing new leaves.
Soil: Parsley needs well-drained, well-worked soil with moderate organic content.
Pests and diseases: If you are lucky you may get a parsley butterfly caterpillar (yellow and black striped). The caterpillar can be put in a screen-covered cage with fresh parsley leaves and watched while it changes into a chrysalis and finally emerges as a beautiful black and yellow swallow-tail butterfly.

Cultural hints: The seeds sometimes take a very long time to germinate. The suggestion often seen about soaking the seeds in water overnight can be messy when you want to spread the seeds out to sow. It is easier to plant parsley in the growing season. When the flower stalk appears — it shoots up taller than the leaves and the leaves on it are much smaller — cut it off so that you can continue harvesting the leaves.

See the step-by-step discussion of herbs for more information about growing parsley.

HARVESTING, EATING, STORING

Cut the outside leaves all the way down to the base of the plant. Freeze or dry extra parsley.

BY THE WAY...

The Romans wore parsley wreaths to keep from becoming intoxicated. In the 20th century, when the world discovered chlorophyll, parsley took people's breath away.

Parsley seedling

Parsley

Parsnip

Common name: parsnip
Botanical name: *Pastinaca sativa*
Origin: Europe

DESCRIPTION

Parsnips are biennials grown as annuals and belong to the same family as celery, carrots, and parsley. A rosette of celerylike leaves grows from the top of the whitish, fleshy root. Parsnips taste like sweet celery hearts.
Varieties: Hollow Crown Improved (95 days), All American (105 days), Harris Model (120 days).
Grown from: Seeds (12,000 per ounce).
Time from planting to harvest: 94 to 120 days.
Parts eaten: The roots and sometimes the leaves.
Yield from a 10-foot row: 22 to 40 roots.

173

GROWING PARSNIPS

Space between plants: 6 to 10 inches.
Light: Tolerates partial shade.
Temperature: Parsnips prefer a long, cool growing season. They can take freezing.

Parsnip seedling

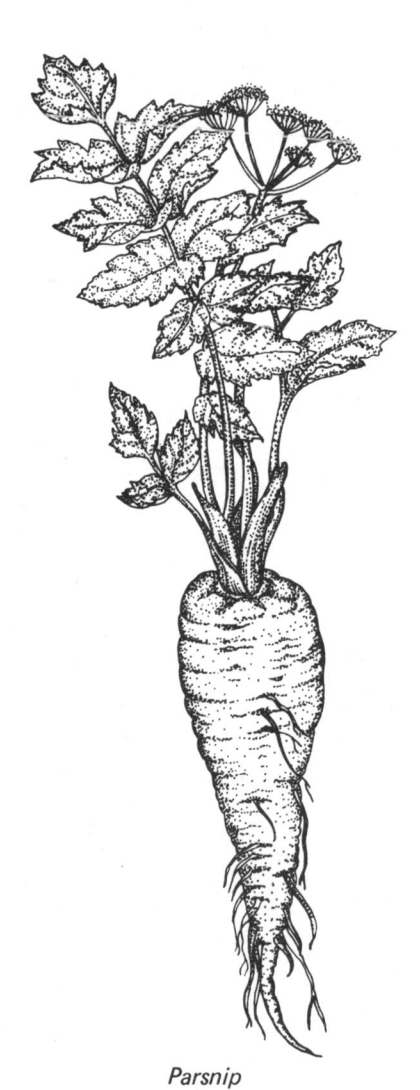

Parsnip

Water: Water when the soil starts to dry out.
Soil: Parsnips prefer rich, loamy soil, not too recently fertilized, or the roots will get stringy. To prevent forking (the root forks, or divides, when it meets an obstruction), plant the parsnips in deep, finely worked soil. If you want to grow showpiece parsnips, plant them in 2 feet of finely worked fertile soil.
Pests and diseases: Parsnips have few enemies but root maggots may be troublesome.
Cultural hints: Parsnips need a long growing season. They will tolerate cold at both the start and the end of their growing season. Like celeriac, parsnips are delicate when young and resent transplanting.

See the step-by-step discussion of root crops for more information about growing parsnip.

HARVESTING, EATING, STORING

Leave the parsnips in the soil until you need them. The roots are not harmed by the ground's freezing. In fact, some people think this makes them taste better. The low temperatures convert the roots starch to sugar. Parsnips can be cooked like carrots. If the roots are very large, remove the tough core after they have been cooked.

BY THE WAY...

Roman Emperor Tiberius demanded annual supplies of parsnips from Germany. Parsnips were the potato of medieval and Renaissance Europe.

Pea, Black-Eyed

Common names: peas, black-eyed peas, cowpeas, chowder peas, southern peas, black-eyed beans, China beans
Botanical name: *Vigna sinensis*
Origin: Asia

DESCRIPTION

Black-eyed peas are tender, annual beans. They can be either bushy or climbing plants, depending on the variety. The seeds of the dwarf varieties are usually white with a dark spot (black eye) where they were attached to the pod. Sometimes the spots are brown or purple.
Grown from: Seeds (125 per ounce).
Time from planting to harvest: 70 to 110 days.
Parts eaten: The green pods and the dry beans.

Black-eyed pea

Black-eyed pea seedling

Yield from a 10-foot row: 1 to 2 pounds.

GROWING BLACK-EYED PEAS

Space between plants: Leave 5 to 6 inches between the plants, in rows 3 to 4 feet apart.
Light: These peas tolerate partial shade.
Temperature: Unlike the sweet pea, these peas can take high temperatures, but not cold ones.
Water: Try to keep water off the leaves and flowers. Do not work with the plants when they are wet or you may spread diseases.

Soil: They will grow in very poor soil. In fact, they are often grown to improve soil. A well-drained, well-worked soil, high in organic matter, increases their production.
Pests and diseases: Beetles, aphids, spider mites, leafhoppers, blights, anthracnose, rust, mildews, mosaics and wilts all attack the black-eyed pea.
Cultural hints: The seeds can be sown in rows or broadcasted. The vines can be used for hay or turned under for green fertilizer.

See the step-by-step discussion of beans for more information about growing peas.

HARVESTING, EATING, STORING

Pick pods at whatever stage of maturity you desire — either young and tender, or fully matured. But do not harvest while the plant is wet. The pods can be eaten like snapbeans when they are green, or they can be shelled and used as dry beans later on. The young pods can be frozen and the mature seeds dried.

BY THE WAY...

Black-eyed peas may look like beans and taste like beans, but the U.S. government in 1956 declared them to be peas.

Pea, Sweet

Common names: peas, garden peas, sugar peas, English peas
Botanical name: *Pisum sativum*
Origin: Europe, Near East

DESCRIPTION

Peas are hardy, weak-stemmed, climbing annuals that have leaflike stipules, leaves with 1 to 3 pairs of

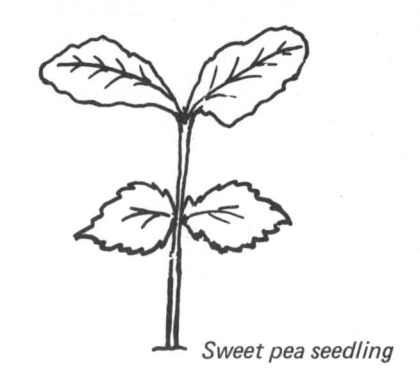

Sweet pea seedling

leaflets, and tendrils that they use for climbing. The flowers are white, streaked or colored. The fruit is a pod containing 4 to 10 smooth or wrinkled seeds.
Varieties: Freezonian (62 days), Little Marvel (62 days), Frosty (64 days), Wando (68 days), Dwarf Gray Sugar (65 days).
Grown from: Seeds (50 to 230 per ounce).
Time from planting to harvest: 55 to 80 days.
Parts eaten: The peas, the pods, and sometimes the peas in their tender pods.
Yield from a 10-foot row: 3 pounds in pods.

GROWING SWEET PEAS

Space between plants: 3 to 5 inches apart, supported by brush, wire or string. They can be planted in double rows, 8 to 12 inches apart. Commercial growers just let them flop on the ground.
Light: Peas tolerate partial shade.
Temperature: A cool-season crop that should mature before the weather gets hot. The ideal growing weather is moist and between 60°F and 65°F.
Water: Peas need ample moisture; the soil should not dry out. Rain dur-

ing the time of flowering can cut down on the crop.

Soil: Peas need good drainage in soil that is high in organic material. They produce earlier in sandy soil, but yield a heavier, later crop if grown in clay soil.

Pests and diseases: Aphids, rabbits and birds are all attracted to peas. People like to eat them right off the vine, too. Peas are affected by rot, wilt, blight, mosaic and mildew — but they can be fairly well controlled by using resistant varieties, treated and disease-free seeds, by rotating the crop, and by keeping the foliage dry.

Cultural hints: If peas have not grown on the soil before, it is a good idea to treat the seeds with a nitrogen-fixing bacteria inoculant. Although soaking seeds can speed up germination, a lot of seed can be ruined by oversoaking and they are harder to plant when they are wet because the seeds tend to break.

HARVESTING, EATING, STORING

Pick the peas when the pods are full and green, before the peas start to harden. Overly mature peas are nowhere near as tasty as young ones. As peas increase in size, the sugar content goes down as the starch content goes up. Sugar will also begin converting to starch as soon as peas are picked. To slow down this process, chill the peas in their pods as they are picked and then shell them immediately before cooking.

Add very little water when you cook fresh peas. Try lining the pot with lettuce leaves and cooking the peas briefly over low heat.

Storing fresh peas is rarely a problem with small gardens; there are never any left to store. If you have more than you need, share the bounty with a friend. Peas freeze well, but the process leaves them tasting no better than store-bought frozen peas.

BY THE WAY...

You can make a wish if you find a pea pod with 9 or more peas in it.

Sweet pea

Peanut

Common name: peanut
Botanical name: *Arachis hypogaea*
Origin: South America

177

Peanut

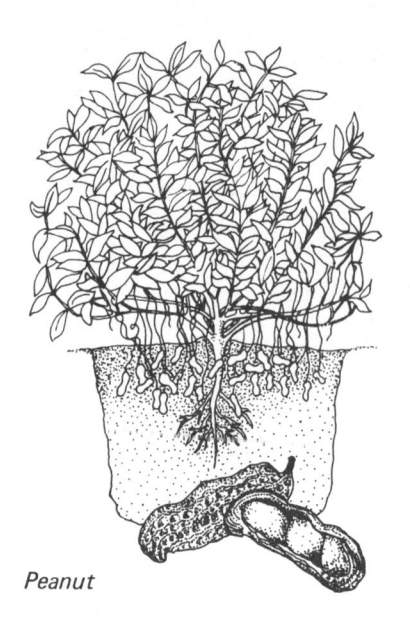

DESCRIPTION

The peanut is a tender annual belonging to the pea family. It grows 6 inches to 2½ feet tall, depending on whether it is the bunch type that grows upright or the runner type that spreads out over the ground. Small clusters of yellow, sweet-pealike flowers grow on stems called pegs. The pegs grow down and push into the soil and the nuts develop 1 to 3 inches underground.

Varieties: Try either Virginia or Spanish peanuts, whichever is available. If you can find raw peanuts at the grocery store, try planting them.

Grown from: Seeds which are raw, shelled — not roasted — peanuts.

Time from planting to harvest: 120 to 150 days.

Parts eaten: The seeds.

Yield from a 10-foot row: Your yield depends on the variety of peanut and the weather at the time of flowering. Usually there are not as many peanuts as you might imagine.

GROWING PEANUTS

Space between plants: Plant the seeds in warm soil 1 to 3 inches deep, 4 to 12 inches apart. Peanuts are often grown in double rows.

Light: Full sun.

Temperature: A frost-free growing season 4 to 5 months long.

Water: Keep soil moisture even until the plants start to flower, then water less. Blind (empty) pods are the result of too much rain or humidity at flowering time.

Soil: Well-worked sandy soil, high in organic matter is preferred. The pegs have difficulty penetrating a heavy clay soil.

Pests and diseases: Peanuts are not plagued by too many pests or diseases.

Cultural hints: If you use a heavy mulch the pregnant peanut pegs will not have to work as hard. Mulching will also make harvesting a lot earier.

Peanuts are not grown commercially north of Washington, D.C., but they can be grown for fun much farther north. If your growing season is short, you can start the peanuts in pots inside and then transplant them outdoors when the weather warms up.

See the step-by-step discussion of beans for more information about growing peanut.

Peanut seedling

Peanut

DESCRIPTION

Hot peppers are tender erect perennials that are grown as annuals. They have several flowers growing in the angle between the leaf and stem. Sweet peppers are erect annuals that have only a single flower growing from the space between the leaf and the stem.

Varieties: Hot pepper transplants, Hungarian Wax (65 days), Jalapeno (73 days). Sweet pepper transplants, Canape Hybrid (62 days), Bell Boy Hybrid (70 days), Yolo Wonder (76 days), Keystone Resistant Giant (85 days).

Grown from: Seeds (4,500 per ounce) or transplants.

Time from planting to harvest: 62 to 85 days from transplants.

HARVESTING, EATING, STORING

Pull up the whole plant and let the pods dry on their vine. Roast the pods in the oven at 300°F for 1 hour. Try homemade peanut butter or peanut soup, if you have a large harvest. To store, keep them in the shell, or shell and store them in airtight containers.

BY THE WAY...

Peanuts are 30 percent protein and 40 to 50 percent oil. George Washington Carver made over 117 separate products out of peanuts.

Pepper

Common names: pepper, bell pepper, hot pepper, sweet pepper
Botanical names: *Capsicum frutescens* (hot pepper), *Capsicum annuum* (sweet and hot peppers)
Origin: New World tropics

Hot pepper

179

Parts eaten: Fruit.
Yield from a 10-foot row: 6 pounds.

GROWING PEPPERS

Space between plants: 18 to 24 inches.
Light: Full sun.
Temperature: Peppers prefer a soil temperature above 65°F. They will drop most of their flowers when the day temperature gets above 90°F and the night temperature above 75°F. Hot peppers can take hot weather better than sweet peppers. Optimum temperatures are between 70°F and 85°F for the hot peppers, 70°F and 75°F for sweet peppers.
Water: The pepper needs less water than its relative the tomato. Too much water can lower the soil temperature and encourage rot.
Soil: A soil that holds water but drains well and is high in organic matter is best for peppers.
Pests and diseases: Aphids, cutworms, flea beetles and hornworms will compete for your peppers. Ripe rot, blossom end rot, anthracnose and mildew are some common pepper diseases.
Cultural hints: If you smoke, wash your hands before working with peppers or you may spread a viral disease called tobacco mosaic.

See the step-by-step discussion of pepper for more growing information.

HARVESTING, EATING, STORING

If you want to grow sweet red peppers, leave your sweet green peppers on the vine until they ripen and turn red. Cut the peppers off the vine; if you pull them off half the plant may come up with the fruit. Hot peppers can irritate skin, so you may want to wear gloves when you pick them. When you are preparing raw hot peppers, cut and wash them under running water and wash your hands well when you are finished. Avoid rubbing your eyes while handling hot peppers.

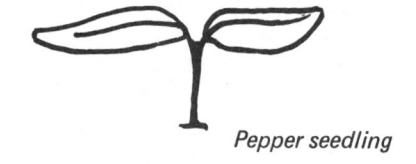

Stuffed, raw, pickled, or roasted, sweet and hot peppers add lively flavor to any meal. There are lots of ways to store them too. They can be pickled whole or in pieces. They can be chopped and frozen or dried. Or whole peppers can be strung up to dry.

BY THE WAY...

Milk is more soothing than water for washing the hot pepper's sting from your skin.

Pepper seedling

Sweet pepper

Sweet potato

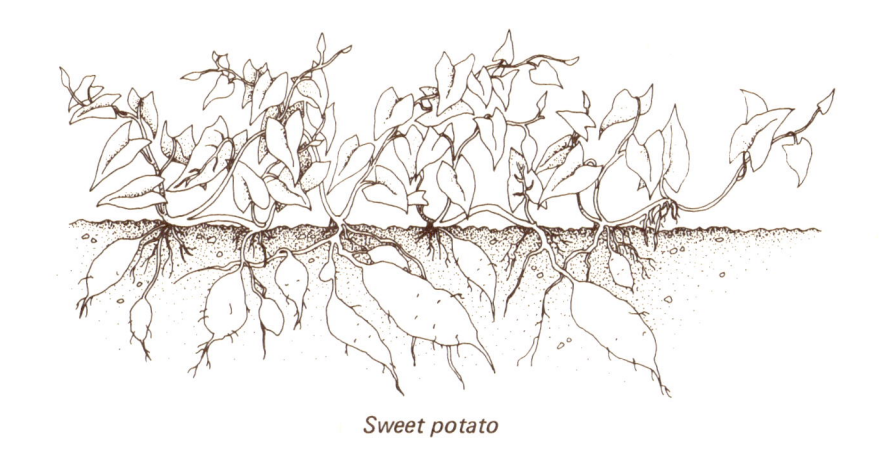

Potato, Sweet

Common names: potato, sweet potato, yam
Botanical name: *Ipomoea batatas*
Origin: tropical America and Caribbean

DESCRIPTION

A tender vine or semi-erect perennial plant, the sweet potato is related to the morning glory. It has small white, pink, or red-purple flowers and swollen, fleshy tubers that range in color from creamy-yellow to deep red-orange. There are "dry" and "moist" kinds of sweet potatoes. Dry and moist refer to softness when eating; some dry varieties have a higher moisture content than some moist ones. The moist varieties are often called yams.
Varieties: Centennial (150 days).
Grown from: Rooted sprouts, called slips, taken from an old tuber.
Time from planting to harvest: 100 to 150 days.
Parts eaten: The tubers.
Yield from a 10-foot row: 4 to 8 pounds.

GROWING SWEET POTATOES

Space between plants: Set the slips on top of ridges 8 inches high and 12 inches wide. Space the ridges about 12 inches apart in rows about 3 feet apart.
Light: For good tuber production sweet potatoes need full sun. In partial shade, the vine will be handsome but not very productive.
Temperature: Sweet potatoes are extremely sensitive to frost. They need warm moist weather. It never gets too hot for *Ipomoea batatas*.
Water: Although they will survive dry seasons, the yield is much higher if they get 1 inch of water every week until a couple weeks before harvesting.
Soil: Sweet potatoes prefer moderately fertile, sandy, organic soil that has been well worked to assure looseness. Rocks and brickbats can cause deformity of the tubers. Rich soils produce luxuriant vines and small tubers.
Pests and diseases: Insects and diseases are not much of a problem in the North. In the South, the sweet potato weevil and wireworms are common pests. Fungous diseases

and root knot caused by nematodes can be problems. For control measures, check with your local extension agent.

Cultural hints: Plant sweet potatoes at least 1 month after the last frost so that the ground is good and warm. Keep the weeds under control until the vines have grown enough to shade them out. Tubers are damaged by freezing or cold soils, so dig them early rather than late.

HARVESTING, EATING, STORING

Dig up the tubers before the first frost. Be careful when you dig — these potatoes are thin-skinned and bruise easily. If you have not eaten them all by Thanksgiving you can keep them for 6 months at 55°F to 60°F with 85 percent humidity.

BY THE WAY...

Try serving sweet potato as a dessert, either mashed in pumpkinlike pie or candied in sugar syrup.

Potato, White

Common names: potato, white potato, Irish potato
Botanical name: *Solanum tuberosum*
Origin: Chile, Peru, Mexico

DESCRIPTION

The potato is a perennial grown as an annual. A weak-stemmed plant with hairy, dark green compound leaves that look a little like tomato leaves, it produces underground stem tubers when mature. Related to the tomato, the eggplant and the pepper, the potato originated at high altitudes and still prefers cool nights.

Varieties: Irish Cobbler (75 days), Norland (75 days), Norchip (90 days), Red La Soda (110 to 120 days).
Grown from: Seeds are whole small potatoes or pieces of larger potatoes. If you want to experiment, you can create your own "seed" by cutting up store-bought potatoes, leaving at least 1 eye per piece, and then planting the pieces. But before you go to all this trouble, try to find out if the potatoes have been treated to retard sprouting. If they have been treated, you will be wasting your time trying to grow them.
Time from planting to harvest: 75 to 130 days.
Parts eaten: The underground stem tubers.
Yield from a 10-foot row: 8 to 10 pounds. Each plant will have 3 to 6 regular potatoes and probably a number of small ones.

GROWING POTATOES

Space between plants: 9 to 12 inches in rows 2 to 3 feet apart.
Light: Full sun.
Temperature: A cool-weather plant, the potato is grown in the summer in

White potato seedling

the North, and in the fall, winter, and spring in the South. The ideal potato-growing temperature is 60°F to 70°F. Hot weather cuts down the production of tubers.

Water: For the best production try to maintain even soil moisture, watering before the soil dries out. Thick mulch will conserve soil moisture, keep down weeds, and keep the soil cool.

Soil: Potatoes need well-drained, fertile soil, high in organic matter with a pH of 5.0 to 5.5. Adding lime to improve the soil and reduce acidity usually increases the size of the crop but also increases the incidence of scab.

Pests and diseases: Colorado potato bugs, leafhoppers, flea beetles, aphids and blights attack the potato. Scab may also show up. It causes a curly roughness of the skin but does not affect the eating quality of the potato. Plant resistant varieties for the best results, especially for large plantings. Use seed certified as true to type and free of disease.

Cultural hints: Fertilize the soil before planting the seed. Plant either in a trench or on top of the ground and cover with a thick mulch, such as 12 inches of straw or hay. Keep the weeds down and keep the developing tubers covered with soil or mulch.

HARVESTING, EATING, STORING

Potatoes are fun to grow to see how they work and the young new potatoes are delicious. Dig up new potatoes after the plant blooms, or after the leaves start to yellow if it does not bloom. These little walnut-sized spuds are delicious when boiled in their jackets. For potatoes that taste like store-bought ones, dig 2 weeks after the vine dies.

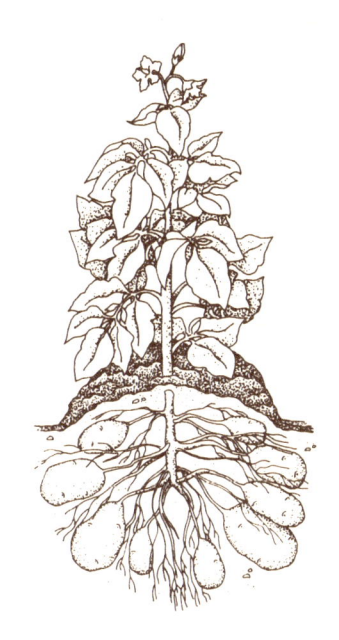

White potato

To store potatoes, put them in crates and cover with polyethylene. Cure them in a dark place for 10 days at 60°F to 65°F with relative humidity of 85 percent. You may have to wet the floor and add a heater to achieve those conditions, but be careful not to wet the tubers. After the curing period, keep potatoes at 40°F to 45°F with relative humidity of 85 percent and good air circulation.

BY THE WAY...

To encourage the growing of potatoes, Louis XVI wore potato flowers in his buttonhole and Marie Antoinette wore a wreath of potato flowers in her hair to a ball. But the people didn't get interested in potatoes until an armed guard was assigned to watch the royal potato patch.

Pumpkin

Pumpkin

Common name: pumpkin
Botanical names: *Cucurbita maxima, Cucurbita moschata, Cucurbita pepo*
Origin: tropical America

DESCRIPTION

Pumpkins are tender annuals with large leaves on branching vines that can grow 20 feet long. The male and female flowers are large, sometimes 8 inches in diameter, and the fruit can weigh as much as 100 pounds. The name pumpkin is also given to a number of other squashes and gourds — anything that is orange and hard.
Varieties: Cinderella (95 days), Cheyenne Bush (100 days), Connecticut Field or Big Tom (115 days), Jack-O-Lantern (115 days), Big Max (120 days).
Grown from: Seeds (100 per ounce) planted in hills.
Time from planting to harvest: 95 to 120 days.
Parts eaten: The male flowers, the fruit and the seeds.
Yield from a 10-foot row: 1 to 3 pumpkins. When you are talking pumpkins 10x10 feet is a very small space.

GROWING PUMPKINS

Space between plants: Since many vines grow quite long, the plants should be spaced 5 to 8 feet apart. If you have a space problem, pumpkins can be grown on a fence or trellis.
Light: Pumpkins tolerate partial shade.
Temperature: Pumpkins are sensitive to cold soil and frost. Plant the seeds after the soil has warmed up.
Water: Pumpkins need plenty of water to keep the vines and fruit growing.
Soil: Pumpkins prefer well-drained soil, high in organic matter. Too much fertilizer tends to encourage the growth of the vines rather than the production of pumpkins.
Pests and diseases: Stem borers, mildew, anthracnose, and bacterial wilt. Wilt may be due to a stem borer rather than bacteria. If the vine wilts

from a definite point onward, look for a very thin wall or hole near the point where the wilting starts. The culprit may still be there. Make a slit lengthwise in the stem, remove the borer and dispose of it. Cover the stem with soil.

Cultural hints: Plant 6 to 8 seeds in a hill; thin to 3 to 5 plants. Do not take out the extra plants too soon. Wait to see which ones the cutworms decide to eat. When the plants have 4 to 6 leaves, remove all but 1 plant. One early fruit can suppress the production of any more pumpkins. If you are a gambler, remove the first pumpkin. Eat it like squash and hope that 2 or 3 more fruits set.

See the step-by-step discussion of squash for more information about growing pumpkins.

HARVESTING, EATING, STORING

Leave the pumpkins on the vine as long as possible before a frost, but not too long — they become very squishy when they freeze. Cut off the pumpkin with 1 or 2 inches of stem. You can cook a pumpkin that was used as a jack-o'-lantern, if fur has not started to grow inside.

Store pumpkins at 50°F to 60°F. Stored pumpkins will shrink as much as 20 percent in weight. They will still make good pies, but they look sad if kept too long.

Pumpkin seedling

BY THE WAY...

The harvest poem reference, "when the frost is on the pumpkin," means the first light frost, not a hard freeze. The first pumpkin pies were made by pouring milk into a pumpkin and baking it.

Radish

Common name: radish
Botanical names: *Raphanus sativus* (spring radish) *Raphanus sativus longipinnatus* (winter radish)
Origin: temperate Asia

DESCRIPTION

The radishes are hardy annuals or biennials that produce white, red, or black roots and stems under a rosette of lobed leaves.
Varieties: For growing, pick out whatever size, shape and color you find attractive. For eating, plant spring radishes such as Cherry Belle (22 days), or Burpee White (25 days); or plant winter varieties such as Black Spanish (55 days), or White Chinese (60 days).
Grown from: Seeds (2,000 per ounce).
Time from planting to harvest: Spring radishes, 20 to 30 days; winter radishes, 50 to 60 days.
Parts eaten: Root.
Yield from a 10-foot row: 60 to 120 spring radishes; 25 to 30 winter radishes.

GROWING RADISHES

Space between plants: For spring radishes, plant seeds ½ inch apart. For winter radishes, plant seeds 1 inch apart. Thin to 4 to 6 or more inches apart, depending on the variety.

Radish

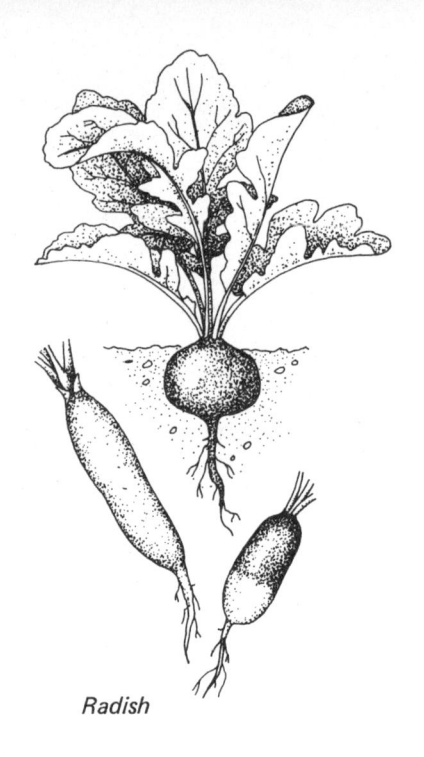

Light: Tolerate partial shade.
Temperature: Radishes are cool-season crops and can take temperatures below freezing. Their going to seed in the summer is more often a question of day length than temperature. Cover plants with boxes in midsummer so they only get an 8-hour day and they will grow radishes; a 12-hour day produces flowers and seeds.
Water: Enough water to keep the radishes growing quickly. If the water supply is low, the roots become woody.
Soil: Well-worked, well-drained soil.
Pests and diseases: Aphids and root maggots are occasional problems, but radishes are not bothered much by any pests or diseases. The greatest mortality comes from weak-hearted gardeners who are too chicken to thin the radishes out, allowing them to choke each other to death.
Cultural hints: Radishes germinate quickly and are often used with slower growing seeds to mark the rows. Spring radishes produce a crop so fast that in the excitement very few people ask about the quality of the crop. They can also be grown in 6-inch pots in a bright, cool window. They will grow in sand if watered with liquid, all-purpose fertilizer diluted to ¼ strength.

See the step-by-step discussion of root crops for more information about growing radishes.

HARVESTING, EATING, STORING

Pull up the whole plant when the radish appears to be the right size. Do not wait too long or the centers of spring radishes become pithy. Radishes can be sculptured into rosettes or just sliced up in a salad. They are quite low in calories and make good cookie substitutes when you have to nibble. Try pickling the excess crop by mincing them and then marinating with vinegar.

BY THE WAY...

More youngsters get hooked on gardening after growing radishes than any other eatable. A bunch of radishes, well washed, makes a great posy to give away.

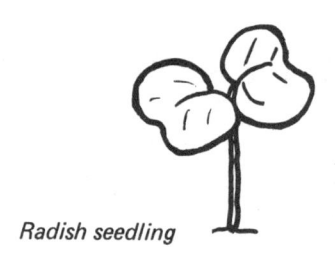

Radish seedling

Rhubarb

Common names: rhubarb, pie plant
Botanical name: *Rheum rhaponticum*
Origin: southern Siberia

DESCRIPTION

A hardy perennial, the rhubarb grows 2 to 4 feet tall with large leaves on strong stalks. The leaf stalks are green or red and grow up from a rhizome or underground stem. The flowers are small and grow on top of a flower stalk which should be removed when it first appears, unless seed production is more important than stalks.
Varieties: Canada Red, MacDonald, Valentine, Victoria (green stalks).
Grown from: It can be grown from seed, but divisions are preferred since plants do not come true when grown from seed.
Time from planting to harvest: You will have to wait 2 to 3 years while the roots establish themselves. You can sneak a single leaf stalk the first year, if it has 4 or more leaves. Control yourself for the next couple years, then enjoy.
Parts eaten: The stalk. The leaf can make you very sick.
Yield from a 10-foot row: 9 to 10 pounds from mature plants.

GROWING RHUBARB

Space between plants: About 3 feet.
Light: Light shade or full sun.
Temperature: Rhubarb is very hardy and prefers cool weather. In areas where the weather is warm or hot, the leaf stalks are thin and spindly.
Water: Rhubarb does best with even soil moisture. Water it

Rhubarb seedling

thoroughly before the soil dries out, but do not create soggy soil.
Soil: Rhubarb prefers well-drained, very rich soil, so add 1 pound of all-purpose fertilizer per plant each year. Since they thrive in soil that is high in organic matter, try to use composted manure, if you can get it.
Pests and diseases: Though there are no pests to worry about, some old clumps may develop crown rot which can be avoided by dividing the clumps before they get too large.
Cultural hints: Soil should be dug up and mixed with fertilizer and organic material so it will be loose and permit water and roots to travel freely. Put the root divisions in the prepared ground so that the tips are slightly below the surface. Keep grass and other competitors away from these plants. Mulch the rhubarb especially in winter. To get earlier and longer leaf stalks, cover the plants with bottomless boxes in the early spring. Remove the flower stalks when they appear — they distract the plant. Divide the plant every 3 to 4 years.

HARVESTING, EATING, STORING

Twist off the leaf stalk at the soil line. To keep the plant going strong, do not cut more than $1/3$ of the leaves in any year. Freeze or make preserves from any extra rhubarb.

Rhubarb

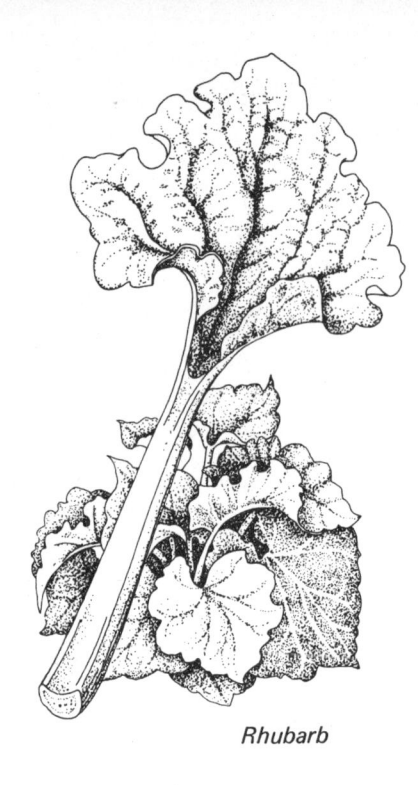

BY THE WAY...

Rhubard can be forced, made to produce before its natural time. Dig up roots that are at least 2 years old. Pile them on the ground so they will be frozen with the first hard frost. After the freeze, put them into pots or boxes. To keep the roots moist, use sand both inside and outside the container. Store them in a cold place but not where the temperature could fall more than a couple of degrees below freezing. Moved to a dark cellar at 60°F, the stalks will grow tall with very small, pale, folded-up leaves. Rhubarb can also be forced in a cold frame later in the year. These stalks will be greener, more nutritious, and the leaves will be almost normal size.

Common name: rosemary
Botanical name: *Rosmarinus officinalis*
Origin: Mediterranean

DESCRIPTION

Rosemary is a half-hardy, evergreen, perennial shrub with narrow, aromatic, grey-green leaves. It can grow 6 feet tall. The flowers are small, light blue or white.
Grown from: Seeds or cuttings.
Time from planting to harvest: 60 days from seeds. Use your judgment in harvesting.
Part eaten: Leaves and sprigs.
Yield from a 10-foot row: Enough for the neighborhood.

GROWING ROSEMARY

Space between plants: From 4 inches to 6 feet, depending on the size of the plant.
Light: Full sun.
Temperature: Rosemary can take temperatures a bit below freezing. It will survive more cold on sandy, well-drained soil, but is not really hardy north of Washington, D.C.
Water: If the weather is dry, water regularly to keep the soil moist. Once the roots dry out the plant does too.

Rosemary seedling

Rosemary

Then the leaves, which look like short pine needles, can be put in a tight-capped jar. Stews, soups, beef and chicken are often flavored with rosemary. When used with other herbs, rosemary tends to dominate.

BY THE WAY...

Rosemary is one of the traditional strewing herbs; in the language of flowers it says, "Remember." It was once believed that rosemary wouldn't grow unless the mistress was master. Add a sprig of rosemary to a New Year's gift pomander.

Rutabaga

Common names: rutabaga, Swedish turnip, Swede, Russian turnip, yellow turnip
Botanical name: *Brassica napobrassica*
Origin: Northern Europe

DESCRIPTION

Rutabaga is a hardy biennial grown as an annual. It has a rosette of smooth, greyish-green leaves that grow from the swollen stem and a root which can be yellow, purple or white. The rutabaga can be distinguished from the turnip by the leaf scars on its top.
Varieties: American Purple Top (90 days), Laurentian (90 days).

Soil: Rosemary likes sandy, well-drained soil, low in fertility. Rich soils produce beautiful plants but the fragrance and the flavor are not as strong.
Pests and diseases: None to worry about.
Cultural hints: Sometimes all the seeds will germinate; at other times very few or none at all appear. Start seeds in a nursery flat or pot and then transplant them. Plants can be propagated from cuttings pulled off the stem, planted in sandy soil and kept moist. Rosemary makes a great pot plant.
See the step-by-step discussion of herbs for more information about growing rosemary.

HARVESTING, EATING, STORING

Harvest rosemary as needed. It can be used fresh or the branches can be hung to dry in a protected place.

Rutabaga seedling

Rutabaga

Grown from: Seeds (12,000 per ounce).
Time from planting to harvest: 90 to 100 days.
Parts eaten: The root.
Yield from a 10-foot row: If the weather is right, you may have over 10 pounds of rutabagas.

GROWING RUTABAGAS

Space between plants: Thin the seedlings 4 to 6 inches apart in rows.
Light: Rutabagas will tolerate light shade.
Temperature: This vegetable prefers cool weather. In hot weather it produces lots of leaves, but the roots will be small and stringy.

Water: Water thoroughly before the ground dries out. Water frequently enough to keep the roots growing without stopping. When the growth slows down, the root gets tough.
Soil: Rutabagas grow best in well-drained soil, high in organic matter. Although rutabagas are less likely to split or fork than carrots, they need well-worked soil, with all the rocks and rubble removed.
Pests and diseases: Aphids can sometimes look worse than they are. The rutabaga has no serious disease problems.
Cultural hints: Rutabagas grow better in cool weather. They like a definite difference between day and night temperatures. Plant them in late summer in the North, and in the fall in the South or where the weather gets very hot. In places where the summer is not hot, start them early in the spring and marvel at how large they grow. If you intend to grow enormous rutabagas, increase the distance between them to 1 foot.

See the step-by-step discussion of root crops for more information about growing rutabagas.

HARVESTING, EATING, STORING

Rutabagas can be left in the ground. Cover them with a heavy mulch of leaves where the weather gets very cold. If you have a cold storage areas, dig up the rutabagas, clean them and dip them in paraffin to keep them from drying out. Keep them cool without freezing. Serve them as you would turnips.

BY THE WAY . . .

As vegetables go, rutabagas are a fairly modern invention. They were created less than 200 years ago by crossing a cabbage with a turnip (probably Swedish).

Sage

Common name: sage
Botanical name: *Salvia officinalis*
Origin: Mediterranean

DESCRIPTION

A hardy, perennial shrub, sage grows to 2 feet high. The leaves are oval, sometimes 5 inches long. Grey leaves are more common but several varieties have variegated leaf color. The flowers are bluish-lavender and grow on spikelike stems. The plant gets quite woody.
Varieties: Most garden shops and catalog lists offer only the grey varieties. Shop herb specialists for less common varieties of sage.
Grown from: Seeds, cuttings or divisions.
Time from planting to harvest: 75 days.
Parts eaten: Leaves.
Yield from a 10-foot row: Enough for the neighborhood.

GROWING SAGE

Space between plants: 15 inches to 3 feet.
Light: Full sun. The plant will survive in partial shade but the flavor won't.
Temperature: Sage is not very particular.

Sage

Sage seedling

Water: Keep sage plants on the dry side.
Soil: Sage thrives in poor soil with good drainage.
Pests and diseases: None, but it may rot if kept too damp or shady.
Cultural hints: Start seeds in a nursery flat or pot and then transplant outside, or plant the seeds directly where they are to grow. A most accommodating plant, sage can be reproduced by layering, division, or cuttings almost any time.

See the step-by-step discussion of herbs for more information about growing sage.

HARVESTING, EATING, STORING

Pick as desired, but do not cut back more than half the plant if you want it to keep producing. Sage and onions make a good flavor team. To dry sage, cut branches and hang them in a protected place. When dry, remove the leaves from the stem and put them in a jar with a tight-fitting lid.

BY THE WAY...

Sage water is supposed to improve the memory and keep hair from falling out.

Salsify

Common names: salsify, oyster plant
Botanical name: *Tragopogon porrifolius*
Origin: Southern Europe

DESCRIPTION

Salsify is a hardy biennial grown as an annual. It belongs to the same family as dandelion and chicory. Its flowers look like lavender chicory blossoms. The eatable taproot is very long.
Grown from: Seeds (1,800 per ounce).
Time from planting to harvest: 120 days.
Parts eaten: Roots.
Yield from a 10-foot row: 20 to 40 roots.

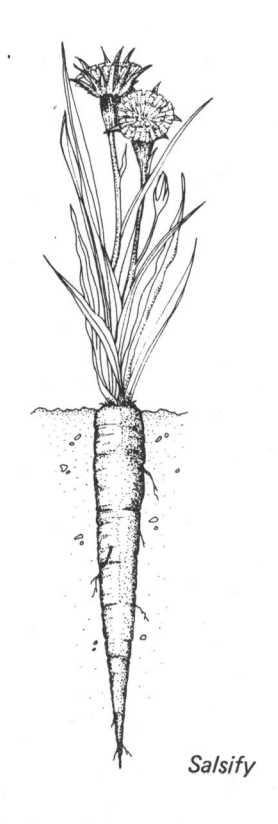

GROWING SALSIFY

Space between plants: 3 to 6 inches.
Light: Full sun.
Temperature: Tolerates cold temperatures and does well anywhere dandelions grow.
Water: Keep evenly moist to prevent roots from getting stringy.
Soil: Plant salsify in deep, well-worked soil that is rich but not recently manured or fertilized. Rocks and lumps will cause roots to fork (split). Soil that is too fertile will cause roots to divide and grow off in all directions.
Pests and diseases: None.
Cultural hints: The growing is easy but the eating is not. Salsify takes some work to prepare it for the table.

See the step-by-step discussion of root crops for more information about growing salsify.

HARVESTING, EATING, STORING

Salsify roots can take freezing, so leave them in the ground until you want them. The longer they are out of the ground, the less they taste like oysters. The roots should not be peeled before cooking or they might "bleed." Just scrub them clean and then steam them for 1 hour. Then squeeze off the skin, cut slices ⅓- to ½-inch thick. Dip the slices in batter or breadcrumbs and fry. Serve with

Salsify

Salsify seedling

tartar sauce. People who have never had oysters cannot tell them apart.

BY THE WAY...

This salsify should not be confused with black salsify which is *Scorzonera hispanica* or Spanish salsify which is *Scolymus hispanicus*.

Soybean

Common name: soybeans
Botanical name: *Glycine max*
Origin: East Asia

DESCRIPTION

The soybean is a tender, free-branching annual that belongs to the pea and bean family. Though it can grow 5 feet tall, it is usually only 2 to 3½ feet tall. The stems and leaves are hairy; the flowers are white with lavender. The pods are 1 to 3½ inches long and grow in clusters. The soybean is extremely high in protein and calcium.
Grown from: Seeds.
Time from planting to harvest: 45 to 65 days.
Parts eaten: The beans.

Yield from a 10-foot row: 1 to 2 pounds.

GROWING SOYBEANS

Space between plants: 6 to 15 inches apart in rows 24 to 30 inches apart.
Light: Soybeans have to grow in full sun.
Temperature: Soybeans need warm weather and are sensitive to cold.
Water: Although soybeans need regular waterings while they are growing, they are drought-resistant toward maturity. Cold and lots of rain when soybeans are in flower can reduce the crop because the insect pollinators stay home.
Soil: Soybeans require fertile, well-drained, inoculated soil.
Pests and diseases: Insects (ex-

Soybean

Soybean seedling

cept Japanese beetle) and diseases are no real problem. Rabbits, raccoons and woodchucks love soybeans and can be strong competitors for the crop.
Cultural hints: Soybeans need to be grown in soil that contains nitrogen-fixing bacteria. Nitrogen-fixing bacteria inoculants can be bought at seed stores or through seed catalogs and dusted on the seed if beans have not been grown before.

See the step-by-step discussion of beans for more information about growing soybeans.

HARVESTING, EATING, STORING

Pick the pods when they are fully grown and the beans are mature but not hard. Dropping the pod into boiling water for a minute or two makes shelling easier. Soybeans may be dried or frozen. The dried ones may be cooked like beans. You can also grow bean sprouts from the dried seeds, but if you intend to sprout them, do not freeze them.

BY THE WAY ...

The ancient Chinese considered the soybean their most important crop. The United States now produces about 75 percent of the world's soybeans.

Spinach

Common name: spinach
Botanical name: *Spinacia oleracea*
Origin: Asia

DESCRIPTION

Spinach is a hardy annual with a rosette of dark green leaves. The leaves may be crinkled (savoy leaf) or flat. Spinach is related to beets and chard.
Varieties: Bloomsdale Longstanding (43 days), America (52 days).
Grown from: Seeds (2,800 per ounce).
Time from planting to harvest: 40 to 52 days.
Parts eaten: Leaves.
Yield from a 10-foot row: 5 pounds.

GROWING SPINACH

Space between plants: Spinach seeds can be broadcasted or sown in rows. Thin the plants to 3 to 6 inches apart — 3 inches if the whole plant is going to be harvested at one time, 6 inches if only the outside leaves are going to be picked.
Light: Spinach will tolerate partial shade.
Temperature: Spinach does not

Spinach seedling

Spinach

mind cold weather, but it goes to seed in warm weather, especially when the days are long. Ideal spinach weather is 50°F to 60°F. It grows well in the winter in the South and in early spring and late summer in the North.
Water: Spinach does best when soil is uniformly moist.
Soil: If the soil is too rich, spinach goes to seed quickly. Like beets, it sulks if the soil is too acidic. If the soil is sandy, the sand gets in the folds of the leaves. The soil should have good drainage and high organic content.
Pests and diseases: Aphids and leafminers are the main pests. Plant resistant varieties and make sure that the soil is well drained to control diseases.
Cultural hints: Spinach does not like competition, but because it is shallow-rooted you will have to take care when eliminating the weeds. Although spinach needs moisture, too much water will decrease the production. Try not to splash soil on the leaves when watering.

HARVESTING, EATING, STORING

Either pick the outside leaves periodically, or pull up the whole plant at one time. Be sure to wash spinach thoroughly to eliminate the grit that sometimes sticks to the crinkled leaves. Fresh, tender leaves are especially good in salads. Spinach can be frozen, though it loses its fresh appeal.

BY THE WAY...

The iron in spinach is as absorbable by the body as that from tin cans.

Spinach, New Zealand

Common name: New Zealand spinach
Botanical name: *Tetragonia expansa*
Origin: New Zealand

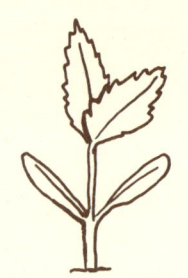

New Zealand spinach seedling

DESCRIPTION

New Zealand spinach is a tender annual with weak, spreading stems 2 to 4 feet long, sometimes longer. It is covered with dark green leaves, 2 to 4 inches long.
Grown from: Seeds (350 per ounce).
Time from planting to harvest: 55 to 65 days.
Parts eaten: Leaves.
Yield from a 10-foot row: 5 pounds.

GROWING NEW ZEALAND SPINACH

Space between plants: Thin plants to 18 inches apart; leave 2 feet between rows.
Light: It will tolerate partial shade.
Temperature: New Zealand spinach cannot take a freeze or weather that is too hot. It grows best at 60°F to 75°F but it tolerates heat better than regular spinach.
Water: A regular supply of water is necessary to produce lots of leaves.
Soil: This spinach likes well-drained, moisture-holding soil, high in organic matter.
Pests and diseases: Nothing too serious.
Cultural hints: Each seed head contains a number of seeds. The seeds are slow to germinate. Plant the seeds outside when the soil has warmed up or start them inside and transplant outdoors when all danger of frost is past. Grow New Zealand spinach to follow spinach which is much less resistant to heat. Keep the tip ends cut off to encourage more growth.

HARVESTING, EATING, STORING

Keep cutting the tender tips off all the ends of the stems. Harvesting can continue until frost. The leaves and tips can be prepared like spinach. Freeze any excess crop.

New Zealand spinach

BY THE WAY...

This eatable grows wild on the sandy beaches of New Zealand.

Squash

Common name: squash
Botanical names: *Cucurbita maxima, Cucurbita moschata, Cucurbita pepo*
Origin: mostly American tropics

DESCRIPTION

Squash are weak-stemmed tender annuals with large cucumberlike leaves. Separate male and female flowers are born on the same plant. Some varieties have a bushy growth habit while others tend to vine. The summer squashes have thin, tender skin and are generally eaten immature. Winter squashes have a hard skin and are usually eaten when mature.
Varieties: Summer varieties include Aristrocrat (50 days), Early Prolific Straightneck (50 days), Zucchini Hybrids (50 days). Winter varieties include Acorn (80 days), Table Queen (85 days), Butternut (95 days), Buttercup (100 days).
Grown from: Seeds (100 to 300 per ounce).
Time from planting to harvest: Summer squash, 50 to 55 days; winter squash, 80 to 100 days or more.
Parts eaten: Fruit, male blossoms.
Yield from a 10-foot row: Depends on the variety and successful fertilization. A happy zucchini can overwhelm you with its production.

Zucchini squash

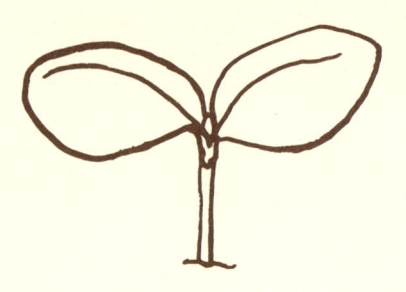

Squash seedling

GROWING SQUASH

Space between plants: Plant in hills 4 to 6 feet apart. (Hill planting means arranging the seeds in a circle, not at the top or bottom of a mound.)
Light: Full sun.
Temperature: Mostly natives of the American tropics, squashes are warm-weather eatables and are very sensitive to cold and frost.
Water: Keep the soil evenly moist. Squashes can use a lot of water in hot weather. There is less trouble with mildew if the leaves are kept dry.
Soil: Well-worked soil with good drainage.
Pests and diseases: Squash bugs and borers, cucumber beetles, whiteflies, bacterial wilt, mosaic and mildew.
Cultural hints: Do not plant the seed until the soil has warmed up. The minimum temperature for germination is 60°F. If starting the seedlings indoors, grow them in containers that can be planted since squash seedlings do not like to be disturbed after they have started. The vining types can be trained up a fence to save space. In insect-free situations, the female flowers should be hand-pollinated.

See the step-by-step discussion of squash for more growing information.

HARVESTING, EATING, STORING

Summer squashes are delicious when very young and removing the fruits encourages the plants to produce more. Test at various sizes. Winter squashes should not be harvested until the skin cannot be dented by the fingernail. However, they should be harvested before a frost hits. The male blossoms can be dipped in egg batter and fried.

Extra summer squashes can be frozen. Winter squashes should be stored at 70°F for a couple weeks, then put into a well-ventilated place with a temperature of about 50°F. Do not stack more than 2 deep.

BY THE WAY . . .

The word squash is an abbreviation of the Narraganset Indian word *asquutasquash* which comes from *adq,* meaning raw, uncooked, and *ash,* a plural ending as in succotash.

Strawberry

Common name: strawberry
Botanical names: hybrids of *Fragaria virginiana* and *Fragaria chiloensis*
Origin: North and South America

DESCRIPTION

Strawberries are low-growing, hardy perennials with rosettes, or crowns, of 3-part, dark green leaves. The flowers are white and grow in clusters at the ends of the stems. The seeds grow on the skin of the fruit which is usually red.
Varieties: Varieties are available for special areas and conditions of soil, climate and day length. Check with

Strawberry

your local extension service for recommendations.
Grown from: Transplants. Plant only certified plants; they will be disease-free and produce better fruit.
Time from planting to harvest: 1 year.
Parts eaten: The fruit.
Yield from a 10-foot row: Production varies greatly, depending on soil, climate, pests and diseases.

GROWING STRAWBERRIES

Space between plants: Plant strawberries in double-, or triple-row hill systems or in matted-row systems. Leave 1 to 1½ feet between plants.
Light: Full sun.
Temperature: Mulch in winter to protect the plants.
Water: Strawberries are shallow-rooted and need an even water supply to keep growing and producing. Water the soil, not the leaves and fruit. Use a mulch to conserve soil moisture and keep the fruit clean.
Soil: Plant strawberries in well-drained soil, high in organic matter. Do not grow strawberries where sod was grown the year before; there may be grubs and root weevils in the ground. Start a new strawberry bed each year and change the location every 4 years.
Pests and diseases: Slugs and snails, leaf splotch, blotch, scorch, molds, rots, nematodes, viruses and fungi.
Cultural hints: Strawberry plants should be planted with their crowns level with the soil, neither too deep nor to shallow. The roots should be spread out carefully. Use a mulch to keep down weeds and decrease fruit rot. Pick the blooms off the first

season to encourage strong plants.
See the step-by-step discussion of strawberries for more growing information.

HARVESTING, EATING, STORING

Keep the fruit harvested as it ripens. Enjoy the berries fresh from the patch. Berries will keep longer if you pick them in the morning when they are cool. Store the berries in a cool place until used. Make jam or jelly if you cannot eat or give away all the fresh berries — an unlikely situation.

BY THE WAY...

The coronets of English dukes, marquis and earls all bear golden strawberry leaves.

Tarragon

Common name: tarragon
Botanical name: *Artemisia dracunulus*
Origin: Caspian Sea, Siberia

DESCRIPTION

A hardy perennial that grows 2 to 4 feet tall with slender stems and thin narrow leaves that taste a bit like licorice.
Grown from: Plant divisions and seeds, although when grown from

Tarragon seedling

Tarragon

seeds tarragon may lack flavor.
Time from planting to harvest: 60 days.
Parts eaten: Stems and leaves.
Yield from a 10-foot row: Enough for the whole neighborhood.

GROWING TARRAGON

Space between plants: 12 inches.
Light: Full sun. Plants will survive in the shade but have no flavor.
Temperature: Tarragon is hardy in well-drained, sandy soils but will often winter kill if soil is compacted or wet.
Water: Grow on the dry side to encourage flavor.
Soil: Well-drained with low fertility.
Pests and diseases: None.
Cultural hints: Tarragon is very slow coming up so mark the spot to avoid digging it up by mistake in the spring. In areas where the ground freezes and thaws during the winter,

mulch after the ground freezes so the plant is not pushed up out of the ground. Since one plant can provide enough leaves for an average family, a strong-flavored plant is worth the investment.

See the step-by-step discussion of herbs for more information about growing tarragon.

HARVESTING, EATING, STORING

Pick tarragon as needed. It can be dried, frozen, or slipped into bottles of good cider vinegar or wine vinegar and, voila! tarragon vinegar. Since the flavor of tarragon is so distinctive, use it with a light touch. The leaves are often used to decorate cold dishes glazed with aspic.

BY THE WAY...

The word tarragon comes from the Arabic word for dragon. The French word *estragon* (little dragon) might reflect the fierce way tarragon fought pestilence during the Middle Ages or the snakelike appearance of its roots.

Grown from: Seeds, cuttings, or divisions.
Time from planting to harvest: 60 days from seed.
Parts eaten: Leaves and sprigs.
Yield from a 10-foot row: Enough for the whole neighborhood.

GROWING THYME

Space between plants: 1 to 3 feet.
Light: Full sun.
Temperature: Prefers a mild climate but can survive temperatures below freezing. Can survive colder temperatures when grown in well-drained soil.
Water: Seldom needs added water. Grow in the dry side.
Soil: Well-drained soil, preferably low in fertility. Rich soils produce plants that are larger but less fragrant and flavorful.

Thyme

Common name: thyme
Botanical name: *Thymus vulgaris*
Origin: Mediterranean

DESCRIPTION

Thyme is a fragrant, small perennial evergreen shrub with 6- to 8-inch stems that often spread out over the ground. A member of the mint family, it has square stems with small opposite leaves. The small, mintlike flowers are pale lavender.
Varieties: Over 200 species and many hybrids.

Thyme

Thyme seedling

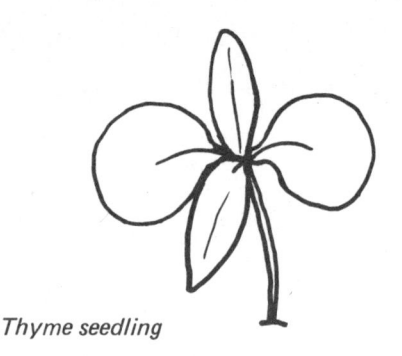

Pests and diseases: Nothing to worry about.
Cultural hints: Plants should be renewed every few years. They tend to become woody. Weeding is important. Thyme lasts longer and tastes better when grown in a sunny, well-drained spot.

See the step-by-step discussion of herbs for more information about growing thyme.

HARVESTING, EATING, STORING

Pick thyme as needed. For drying, harvest when the plants begin to bloom. Cut off the tops of the branches with 4 to 5 inches of flowering stems. Hang the sprigs in a dry, protected place for best color and flavor. Shade drying keeps the color brighter. After drying, crumble and put into tightly-capped jars.

BY THE WAY...

The Greeks and Romans thought that using thyme would give people courage and strength. The highest compliment was to tell a man that he smelled of thyme. In the Middle Ages ladies embroidered sprigs of thyme on the scarves they gave their knights. Linnaeus, the father of modern botany, recommended thyme as a cure for hangovers.

Tomato

Common names: tomato, love apple
Botanical name: *Lycopersicon esculentum*
Origin: tropical America

DESCRIPTION

Tomatoes are tender perennials grown as annuals. They have weak stems and alternate lobed and toothed leaves that have a distinctive odor. The yellow flowers grow in clusters. Depending on the variety, the fruit varies in size and color — red, yellow, orange, white.
Varieties: The varieties of tomatoes would fill a book. You will have more success if you plant the varieties recommended for your area by your local garden center or extension service.
Grown from: Transplants or seeds (11,000 to 12,000 per ounce).
Time from planting to harvest: 40 to 180 days from transplants. Transplants usually produce earlier than tomatoes grown from seed.
Parts eaten: The fruit.
Yield from a 10-foot row: 10 to 45 pounds.

GROWING TOMATOES

Space between plants: 18 to 48 inches.
Light: Full sun.
Temperature: Tomatoes grow best when the day temperature is between 65°F and 85°F. They stop growing if it goes over 95°F. If the night temperature goes above 85°F, the fruit will not turn red. The flowers will not set fruit if the temperature goes below 55°F at night.
Water: Tomatoes need lots of water, but they do not like to swim. Water thoroughly before the soil dries out.

Tomato

Soil: Tomatoes need warm, well-drained, fertile soil. Although they will produce earlier on sandy soils, they will have a larger yield in clay soils.

Pests and diseases: The tomato fruitworm (also known as the corn earworm) and the hornworm are the worst offenders. Nematodes are a problem in the South. Fusarium wilt, verticillium wilt, blights and blossom end rot are common diseases.

Cultural hints: For the best results, start with stocky transplants that are 6 to 10 inches tall with well-developed roots. In a small area where each plant is precious, it is best to start with individually-grown plants. Cultivate to eliminate the soil's crust and the weeds. Staked tomatoes produce about half as much per plant as tomatoes that sprawl on the ground, but often they are cleaner. Caging plants is a good compromise.

Sometimes a tomatoe plant curls its leaves as a survival tactic on hot days and during a long period of no rain.

Since tomatoes are warm-weather plants you will not be getting the jump on your neighbors by planting tomatoes when the weather is still cool.

If you are a smoker, wash your hands before working with tomatoes or you may transmit tobacco virus.

See the step-by-step discussion of tomatoes for more information.

HARVESTING, EATING, STORING

Remove the fruit from the vine when the color is to your taste. When the temperature is high during the day, the fruit may get soft but not red. Take hard green fruit inside at the end of the season and they will turn red. Can or pickle your extra crop. Green tomato pickles are delicious.

BY THE WAY...

Lycopersicon esculentum, the botanical name for tomatoes, means tasty wolf peach. When shopping for tomato varieties to grow, look for VFN after the name. This means the plant is resistant to verticillium wilt, fusarium wilt, and nematodes.

Tomato seedling

Turnip

Common name: turnip
Botanical name: *Brassica rapa*
Origin: northeastern Europe, Siberia

DESCRIPTION

The turnip, a hardy biennial grown as an annual, sports a rosette of hairy, bright green leaves growing from a "root." The turnip "root" is not really a root, but a swelling at the base of the stem.

Varieties: Shogin or Foliage Turnip (30 days), Tokyo Cross or Tokyo Market (35 days), Just Right (40 days) and Purple Top White Globe (57 days).
Grown from: Seeds (13,000 to 15,000 per ounce).
Time from planting to harvest: 30 to 60 days.
Parts eaten: Leaves and roots.
Yield from a 10-foot row: 5 pounds of leaves and 10 pounds of roots.

GROWING TURNIPS

Space between plants: Thin the seedlings to 4 to 6 inches apart in rows 12 to 15 inches apart. Turnips can also be grown in a block by broadcasting the seeds.

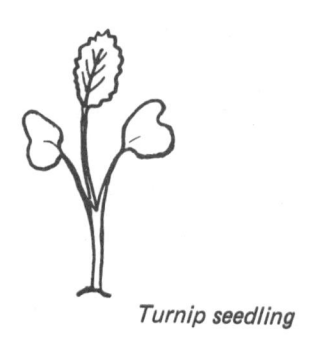

Turnip

Turnip seedling

Light: Turnips tolerate partial shade.
Temperature: Turnips are a cool-weather crop, grown in the fall, winter and spring in the South and grown in the spring and fall in the North. They go to seed in warm weather.
Water: Water is important to keeping the turnip growing as fast as possible. Water before the soil dries out. If the growth is slow the root gets very strong flavored and woody and the plant will often send up a seed stalk.
Soil: Turnips need moisture-holding soil that is high in organic matter and drains well.

Pests and diseases: Aphids and flea beetles are fond of turnip greens. No serious diseases.
Cultural hints: Sow seeds where the turnips are to grow since they do not transplant well. Transplanting often triggers the growth of a seed stalk. Take advantage of cool weather for planting. Too much nitrogen in the soil encourages leaf and seed stalk production rather than root production.

See the step-by-step discussion of root crops for more information about growing turnips.

HARVESTING, EATING, STORING

You can eat the tops as you thin the seedlings, or when the root is ready to be pulled. Harvest the roots when they are 1 to 2 inches across. To store turnips, leave the roots in the ground and cover them with leaves to protect them from freezing. Or you can dip them in wax to protect from dehydration and store them just above freezing.

BY THE WAY . . .

When small, turnips make a great substitute for radishes. They are also easier to carve than radishes, if you feel the urge to sculpt roses or daisies for decorative garnishes.

Watermelon

Common name: watermelon
Botanical name: *Citrullus vulgaris*
Origin: tropical Africa

DESCRIPTION

The watermelon is a spreading, tender, annual vine related to the cucumber. It produces round, oval or oblong fruits that weigh 5 to 100 pounds and have pink, red, yellow or

Watermelon seedling

greyish-white flesh. Male and female flowers appear on the same vine.
Varieties: The new smaller watermelon varieties are more suited to a limited garden patch than the large varieties. Small watermelons include Petite Sweet (75 days), New Hampshire Midget (77 days) and Sugar Baby (79 days). Standard size watermelons include Charleston Gray (90 days) and Crimson Sweet (90 days).
Grown from: Seeds (225 to 500 per ounce).
Time from planting to harvest: 65 to 100 days.
Parts eaten: The fruit pulp. The rind is used for preserves.
Yield from a 10-foot row: If you are lucky, 3 melons.

GROWING WATERMELONS

Space between plants: 4 to 8 feet, depending on the variety. Watermelons can be grown on a fence to save space. The stems are strong enough to hold dangling melons.
Light: Watermelons require full sun.
Temperature: Warm soil and warm days. Weather below 50°F at night will ruin the flavor of the fruit.
Water: Watermelons are 95 percent water, so make sure they have

Watermelon

enough. Do not let the soil dry out. Use a mulch to keep the soil moisture up and the fruit, if on ground, clean.
Soil: Watermelons prefer well-drained soil that will hold moisture well. Too much nitrogen will encourage leaves rather than fruit.
Pests and diseases: Cucumber beetles can be picked off. Avoid anthracnose and wilt by using resistant varieties.
Cultural hints: In places with a short growing season, start seedlings inside in individual pots. Outdoors, plant seeds in hills, 4 to 5 seeds in each hill. Place each hill on a hole that has had 2 bushels of manure or compost mixed in it. Eliminate all but 1 or 2 seedlings when they develop their true leaves.

If 1 melon gets an early start on a vine it can suppress all further activity until it is mature. Some people suggest pinching out this first melon to encourage more melons, but sometimes no more melons will set.

See the step-by-step discussion of squash for more information about growing watermelon.

HARVESTING, EATING, STORING

If melons are lying on the ground, pick them when the bottoms are yellow and they sound dull and hollow when rapped with knuckles. You can store a melon for a week or so in your refrigerator. It takes up to 12 hours to thoroughly chill a large melon.

BY THE WAY...

Watermelon was Dr. Livingston's favorite African fruit. It is also highly regarded by the African Elephant Congress.

Favorite Crops Step By Step

Bean

Beans are beautiful. They are one of the products Columbus and his men snapped up when they thought they had found India. In countries that take their vegetable protein seriously, markets sometimes carry 40 different varieties of dried beans and five or six varieties of immature beans.

All the American members of the legume family (the lima beans and the snap beans) believe in central heating — they like it warm. The black-eyed pea, the mung bean, the soybean and the four-angled bean like warm weather, too. The sweet or English peas and the broad beans, however, have lots of character — they disdain warm climates, preferring brisk cold showers and all that sort of thing.

Snap beans are easy to grow as long as you do things their way. They even have a mutual exchange going with soil microorganisms called nitrogen-fixing bacteria that helps them produce their own fertilizer. They are also one of the sun-loving crops that will produce (not as well, perhaps) in partial shade. For the specific varieties that will thrive in your area, contact your extension service — they can give you personalized information.

If space is limited, grow bush beans in a large pot. Beans can even be grown on a sunny windowsill. For small outdoor gardens, grow the beans in block beds rather than rows. You can save a lot of space by cutting down the amount of walking path. Pole beans can be grown along a fence, up the side of a lattice, up a wigwam, up a sunny wall — or from a window box.

Growing Beans

 1. Best bed. Beans like a warm and cosy bed — no lumps. Locate the bed in the sun or partial shade (partial shade — partial crop).
 2. Planting. Make rows for bush beans and hills for pole beans. Plant the seeds two inches apart — that way you will have enough seedlings to share with the birds, the cutworms and the things that go crunch in the night. When the beans are growing well, thin the plants to four to six inches apart. Use scissors and cut off the seedlings at ground level. Be polite, you do not want to disturb the others in the bed. Beans do not mind being crowded a little. If you plant them in a 3x10-foot bed you will have more beans than if you plant them in single rows.
 3. Food and drink. Before planting, mix a pound of 5-10-10 fertilizer for each 3x10-foot space. Keep the soil moist until the beans have pushed up through their blanket. Water regularly if there is no rain, but remember that water on the leaves can sometimes ruin the plant's complexion and water on the flowers will frustrate the fruiting.

Plant 1" to 2" deep in hills

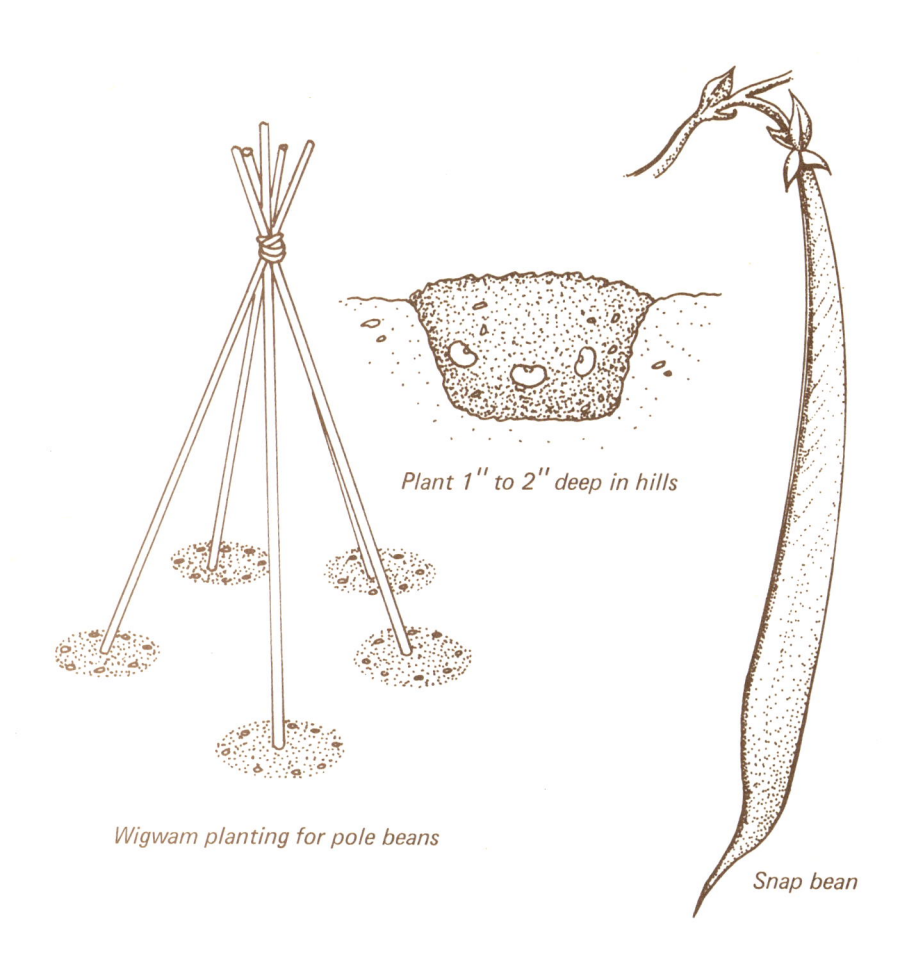

Wigwam planting for pole beans

Snap bean

4. Special care. Do not bother bean plants when they are wet or covered with heavy dew. Handling them or brushing against them when they are wet spreads fungous spores. Eliminate competition in a gentle but determined manner. Start after weeds early and keep their heads chopped off. Beans are shallow-rooted, so do not cultivate too deeply and be careful when you pull out weeds.

5. Harvesting. Pick the beans when they are to your taste. For continuous production, pick them before the seed matures. If you want dry beans, let them grow until the pods are brown and dry.

6. Pests and diseases. Mexican bean beetle, bean leaf beetle, aphids, and a host of other pests that occasionally stop by can usually be ignored. Anthracnose, bacterial blight, rust, mildew and mosaic may be controlled by planting disease-free seeds and resistant varieties. Keep the plants dry, and, if possible, rotate the crops with other plant families.

Questions and Possible Answers

Why didn't seeds come up?
  Soil too cold or wet and the seeds rotted.
  Birds or other creatures ate them.
  Soil crust was too hard.
  Planted too deep.

Why were young plants tortured and deformed?
  Soil crust was too hard.
  Soil dried out while the beans were sprouting.

Why were there no beans?
  Weather too cold (average temperature below 50°F).
  Weather too hot (average temperature above 80°F).
  All leaves and no beans indicates too much nitrogen.

Cabbage

Broccoli, Brussels sprouts, cabbage, cauliflower, collards, kale, and kohlrabi are all members of the Cole family *(Brassica oleracea)*. Their flowers look alike; their seeds are impossible to tell apart; they are all cool-season crops; and, they usually transplant very well. Eventually, those that "got a head" were called cabbages.

The oldest members of the clan are the kales and the collards. The word "kale" is used for the plants with curly leaves, and the word "collard" for plants with smooth leaves. However, greens cut from cabbages before they head are often called collards.

Broccoli and cauliflower are easy to tell apart, until you meet a white-flowered heading broccoli or a green cauliflower. Since they both also come in purple even the U.S. government sometimes cannot distinguish them. Cauliflowers are prima donnas and need a lot of care and attention. Mark Twain defined cauliflower as a cabbage with a college education.

Brussels sprouts are those cute miniature cabbages that often stay in the refrigerator until they turn yellow because people are not quite sure what to do with them.

Kohlrabi, which look like turnips growing on top of the ground, are delicious in their tender youth. When they reach their full size and wooden maturity, their best use is as conversation pieces.

When compared with other Coles, cabbages sometimes look like

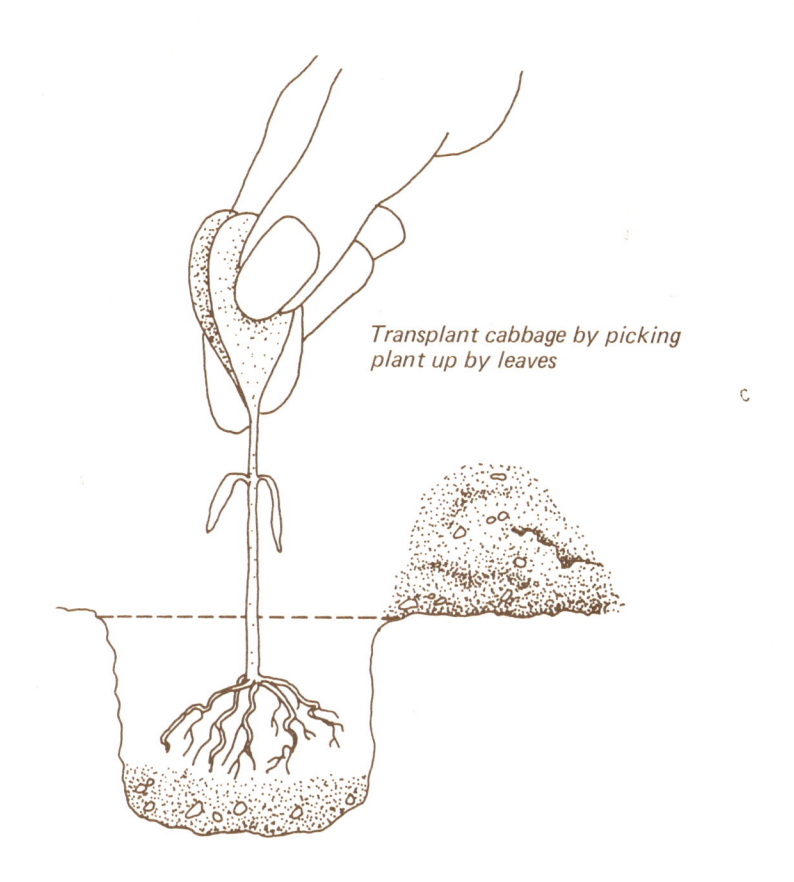

Transplant cabbage by picking plant up by leaves

overstuffed fatties whose success has gone to their round, pointy, or flat head (depending on the variety). Cabbages come in a choice of colors: green, greener, and magenta, which is called red by people who do not know purple when they see it.

Cabbages have four stages of growth: 1) rapid growth of leaves; 2) formation of the head; 3) a resting period while the embryonic blossoms are being formed; 4) development of the stalk, flowers, and seeds. The head formation stage is essential for the production of the eatable, but not at all necessary for the survival of the plant. Cabbages that are held in check by severe frost, lack of moisture, or too much heat will bolt, which means that they will go directly to seed without bothering to form a head at all. And even if cabbage does make a head, if the weather gets too hot once it reaches that stage the head can split.

In small spaces, grow cabbages as an accent point in each corner of a flower bed or as a border. Grow a single cabbage in an eight-inch flowerpot. Try flowering cabbage or a small early variety.

Growing Cabbage

1. Best bed. Cabbages like cool and moist beds located in full sun. Mulch if necessary to keep the soil cool.

2. Planting. Plan for only a few heads at a time, or plant transplants and seeds at the same time for succession crops. You will have succession crops, too, if you plant early varieties and later mid-season varieties at the same time. Use either seeds or transplants, depending on the length of your cool growing season. Plant the seeds three inches apart and then thin the seedlings to 18 to 24 inches or more (depending on the variety) when you can lift the plant by picking it up with its own true leaves. If they all look healthy, transplant or give away the extras. Pinching the stem can cause permanent damage to the cabbage — it is perfectly all right to use a spatula or trowel to lift as you pull. Transplants should be planted carefully, spreading out the roots in a comfortable hole.

3. Food and drink. Cabbages are big eaters. Both compost and commercial fertilizers should be used when preparing the soil before planting. Light fertilizer feedings can be made every three weeks to encourage rapid growth. Too much fertilizer can cause the heads to split. Water liberally, but cut down a bit when the cabbages approach maturity to prevent splitting.

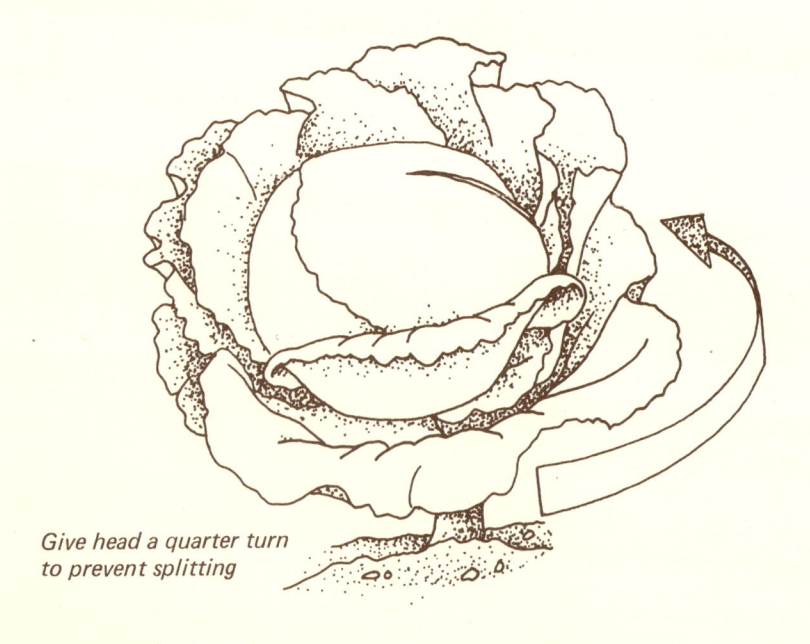

Give head a quarter turn to prevent splitting

4. Special care. Police the area and keep the competition down. Cabbage roots are near the surface, so cultivate carefully. Splitting can be held down by cutting the roots or giving the head a quarter to half a turn.

5. Harvesting. Cut off the head leaving the stem with a couple of leaves. Often a few small heads will grow on the remaining stalk.

6. Pests and diseases. Cabbage worms, cabbage aphids, harlequin bugs, black rot, root knot, yellows, clubroot, black leg are all traditional Cole enemies. If you cannot deal with a problem, contact your cooperative extension service for solutions.

Questions and Possible Answers

Why did the head split?
    It was growing too fast.
    It had too much water.
    It had too much fertilizer.
    It became bored waiting around and was looking for excitement.

Reduce water intake and cut roots to prevent head from splitting

What made it bolt?

Too much cold.
Very small plants with leaves 1" to 1½" wide can stand low temperature for six months before going to seed. Larger plants with leaves 2" to 3" wide will go to seed if it is 40°F to 50°F for 2 to 4 weeks.
The plants were injured in transplanting.
The weather was too hot.

Why did the cabbage turn yellow and die?

It contracted black rot (yellowing with black veins).
It had a case of the yellows (yellowing and leaves falling off).

Corn

The creators assembled and held council in the night. They searched, discussed and reflected and thought and at dawn they decided what must go into the flesh of man – the making of our first mothers and fathers. From yellow corn and white corn they made their flesh. Only corn meal dough went into the flesh of our forefathers...
From the Maya *Popol Vuh (Book of the People)*

Corn was as important to the earliest Americans as it is to us. Today it is impossible to be more than three feet away from a product made from corn unless you are skinny dipping in the middle of a lake. Paper, plastics, plate glass, pipes, jelly beans and bourbon are all made with corn.

Corn, sometimes called man's greatest agricultural achievement, is a completely domesticated plant. It is unable to grow on its own and has to be planted, cultivated and harvested by people. It also likes the same temperature as people like and will slow down and quit if the average temperature gets much below 60°F.

Because of the space it occupies, corn is impractical in a small garden, but there is no other eatable in the United States that so quickly signifies "Here is a garden." So perhaps you might try growing corn in a washtub. Usually the results are better if you grow a small variety, and you water and feed more frequently. Or grow plants in groups of three as accents.

Try growing corn in a washtub

Growing Corn

1. Best bed. Corn needs a bed that is warm and cosy, located in full sun.

2. Planting. Wait until the soil temperature reaches 60°F. Plant in rows (short rows in a block, rather than one long row) or hills. Planting in clumps or blocks insures pollination. In either case, plant the seeds two to four inches apart. Plant one for the blackbird, one for the crow, one for the cutworm, and two to grow. Of course, if the competition does not show and all the seeds come up, you will have to compost the excess. For a continuous supply, plant the same variety every two weeks (or when the previous planting shows three leaves) or plant early, mid-season, and late varieties at the same time.

When the corn is about six inches high increase the distance between the plants to 10 to 24 inches, depending on the variety. Corn

Protect ears with bags after pollination

can be grown closer together, but then the roots are more crowded and it takes more care in watering and feeding.

3. Food and drink. Fertilize at planting time. Use a couple of small fish per hill (classic style) or a third of a pound of 5-10-10 fertilizer on each side of a 10-foot row. Place the fertilizer an inch below and two inches away from where you plan to put the seed. Feed again when the corn is eight inches high, and again when it is 18 inches high. Watering is very important. Corn often grows so fast in hot weather that the leaves wilt because the roots cannot keep up with the leaves. The soil moisture should be kept even.

4. Special care. Keep the competition down. Weed early and keep the weeds cut back. Corn has very shallow roots and a vigorous attack on the weeds may destroy the corn. Eliminate the extra corn plants. Crowding stimulates lots of silage, but no cobs.

Protect the ears with bags after pollination if you are having trouble with birds. Do not bother with bags if you have raccoons, since they can remove them as well as people can.

5. Harvesting. Harvest when the juice of the kernel is milky. If the juice is watery, it is too early and the kernels are still very small. If the juice is pasty, the kernels will be starchy and not as sweet. Dry silks and the "feel" of the ear are also indications of approaching maturity. Eating maturity is not seed maturity.

Have the water boiling when you go out to pick the corn. The sugars start turning to starch as soon as the corn is picked.

6. Pests and diseases. Corn earworm, corn-borers, raccoons, birds, two-legged borrowers, smut, wilt and blight are some of corn's commoner afflictions. Smut and fungous diseases are the most serious since their spores stay alive in the soil for years. Contact your cooperative extension service for special instructions for your area.

Questions and Possible Answers

Why didn't seeds come up?	Soil too cold (seeds take 3 weeks to germinate at 50°F, 3 days at 95°F).
	Seeds rotted in cold, wet soil.
	Birds or other creatures ate them.
	Seed too old (viability of corn seed uncertain after first year). Test germination.
Why was there no corn?	Weather too cold (average temperature below 60°F).
	Not enough soil moisture.
	Rained during pollination period and pollen stuck to the tassel.

Cucumber

Are cucumbers cool because the heat has been removed from them? Gulliver, in the report of his voyage to Brobdingnag, told of a project for extracting sunbeams from cucumbers, sealing them in jars, and letting them out to warm the air on raw summer days. Or are they cool and aloof because of their low calorie count and their aristocratic past? The Emperor Tiberius was so kooky about cucumbers that the first greenhouses (sheets of mica in window sashes) were developed to keep the plants growing on happily indoors when it was too cold to take them outside. Or are cucumbers cool because of the way they feel when you crunch them or use them for face cream? Whatever the reason, salads and sandwiches are always dressed up when cucumbers are added.

Growing Cucumbers

1. Best bed. Cucumbers want a warm bed (soil temperature 70°F), well made, located in full sun. If you are short on bed space you

Cucumbers

Female cucumber blossom

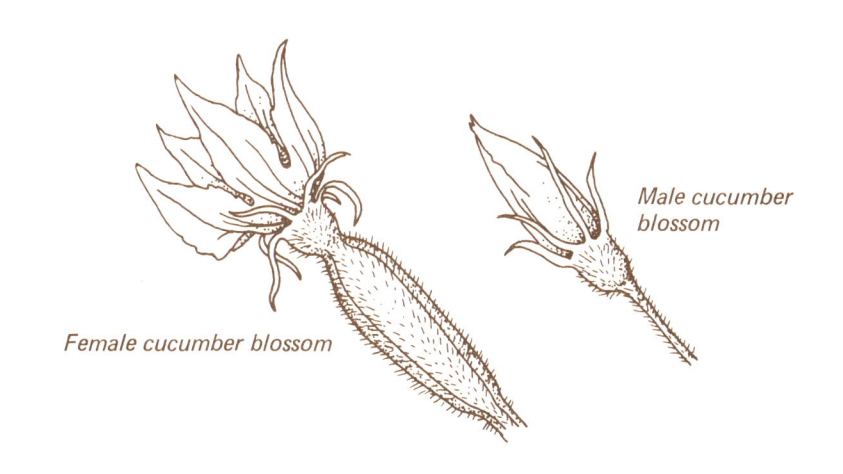

Male cucumber blossom

can grow cucumbers in a large pot, a tire planter, or a hanging basket. Train them up on a fence or grow on a roof or over an arbor.

2. Planting. Plant hills of six to eight seeds which you thin later, if catastrophe has not done it first. Set the hills three feet apart with rows five feet apart. Plant the seeds 12 inches apart, if you are growing the cucumbers on a fence. Cucumbers respond to a rich, well-worked soil, high in organic matter. For super cukes, dig out the soil to two feet, put in one foot of vintage manure (cow, pig, or horse) mixed half and half with compost, or one part chicken, duck, or turkey manure mixed with three parts compost. Fill the rest of the hole with soil and compost or peat moss mixed with a cup of 5-10-10 fertilizer for each ten-foot row.

3. Food and drink. Cucumbers need a lot of water, but they do not like wet feet. The soil should be well-drained. When outdoor temperatures are 70°F or below, cold water may lower the soil temperature and retard growth. Water should be applied on the ground and not on the leaves. The plants will sometimes wilt in very hot weather because their roots cannot keep up with the evaporation from their leaves. Check, though, to see that the soil is moist below the surface. Their season's food supply should be packed in before planting.

4. Special care. Keep the weeds down and the watering up. In insect-free areas, nature will need a little help in carrying pollen from male to female flowers. Use a soft-bristled brush to pollinate female flowers.

5. Harvesting. Keep all cucumbers cut off as soon as they are ready. Stunted and deformed fruit should be removed, too, since any maturing fruit will stop the flowering of the plant.

6. Pests and diseases. Cucumbers are affected by aphids, cucumber beetles (striped and 12-spotted), spider mites, mildew and mosaic. Contact your cooperative extension service for control recommendations.

Questions and Possible Answers

Why didn't seeds come up?	Soil too cold. They rotted. Something ate them.
Why were plants cut off in their prime?	Cutworms did it. Damping off disease, a rot caused by too much water and cool weather.
No cukes. Why?	Flowers were not pollinated. All the flowers were male. All female flowers not pollinated. Cucumber left to grow on vine suppressed flowering.
Why were cukes lopsided or deformed?	Weather was rainy during pollination. Flowers were imperfectly pollinated.

Grape

All grapes originated in France, right? Wrong. Grapes grew in such wild abundance along the northeast coast of the North American continent that the Vikings named the country Vinland when they touched shore long before Columbus.

Concord, Delaware, Fredonia and Niagara are native American grapes that are suitable for home-growing and eating out-of-hand. Even a small garden that gets at least a half-day of sun can grow a vine or two, with the aid of a trellis or fence. A trellis, fence or old-fashioned arbor gives the grapes a durable support and saves space, keeps the grapes off the ground and minimizes maintenance. A single vine can be grown in a large pot or container, providing the drainage is good and the vine is well cared for. Grapes in containers should have support against a fence or wall. If a potted vine is grown against a wall, a trellis eight inches away from the wall will allow air circulation.

Grapes take more care than many garden eatables because they must be carefully pruned. Pruning should be done when the vine is dormant in late winter or very early spring. Prune to keep the vines as short as possible. Production will improve if you keep pruning back to the main trunk each year or so. No more that two grape clusters should grow on a shoot. You will find that it is easier to tie the canes before the buds start to grow because the fat buds snap off easily.

Growing Grapes

1. Best bed. Grapes require a sunny bed, one with excellent drainage. The soil should be high in organic matter to conserve soil moisture.

2. Planting. Plant premium one-year-old or two-year-old grape plants. (Two-year-old plants cost more and do not do that much better.) Plant them about two inches deeper than they grew in the nursery and about eight feet apart. Do not crowd the roots. Plant them so they are between, but not against, posts. Roots may be injured when it is necessary to replace posts, and the wood preservative used on posts may be toxic to the plants. Also, it is easier to work with vines without posts in the way. After planting you can sprinkle a half cup of 5-10-10 fertilizer in a circle around the base of the vine. Do not put fertilizer in the hole.

3. Food and drink. Fertilizer requirements vary with the kinds of soil. If any fertilizer is used, it should be applied in early spring, since fertilizing in summer and early fall stimulates growth that may not mature before winter. A good supply of soil moisture is important in the production of grapes. Lack of water when the berries are growing rapidly can delay maturity and keep them from growing to full size.

4. Special care. Grapes do well on a fence, trellis or arbor. Construct the support with durable materials. As the newly-planted vines grow the first season they should be tied up, and after their first winter

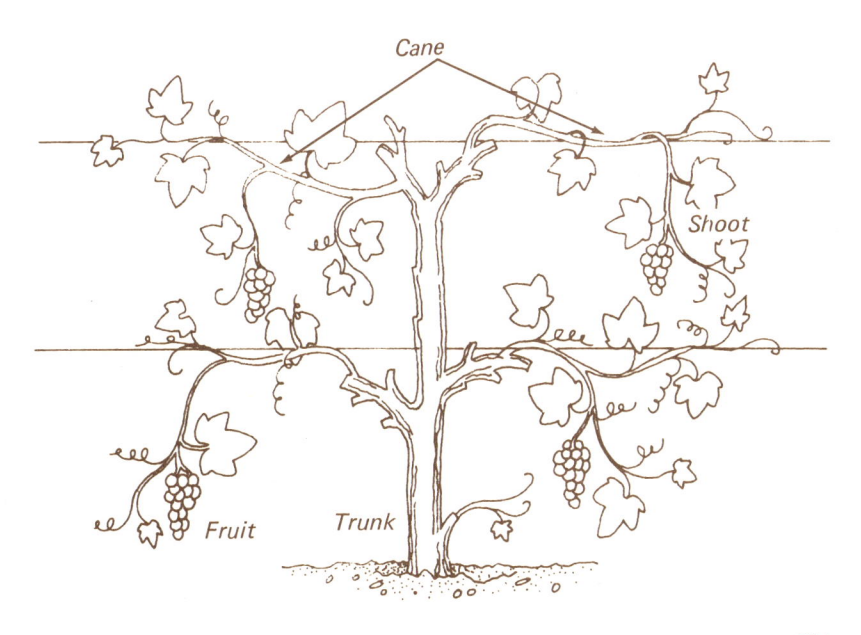

Before pruning   *After pruning*

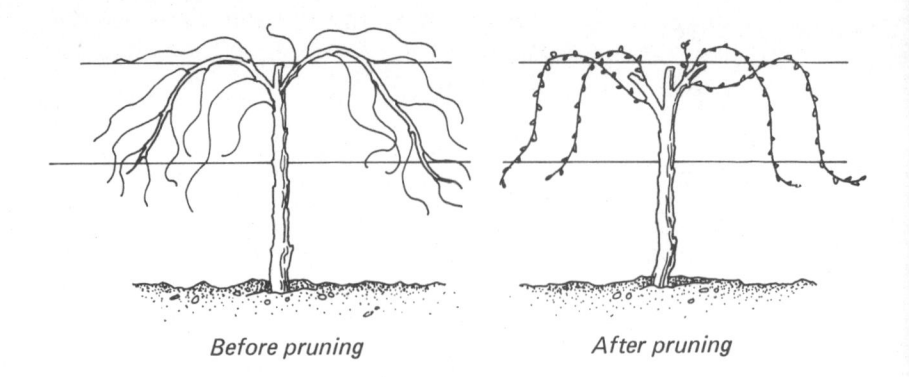

the strongest shoot should be kept to serve as the trunk of the vine. All the other shoots should be removed. Pruning should be done after the worst of the winter has passed. Vines may "bleed" (lose a lot of sap), but it does not hurt them.

During the second summer the shoot will continue to grow and it should be tied to the top of the trellis or other support that provides as much light and air as possible. The second winter the vines remaining should be pruned to encourage new shoots. Select two canes to grow at each level and remove the rest. Shorten remaining canes to five buds and tie them to the support before the buds start to grow. Fat buds snap off easily.

Leave only one cane to grow in each direction along the support and two to four more canes, each cut back to two to three buds, as renewal spurs that will produce the canes for the next year's crop. Do not have more than two grape clusters to a shoot.

The number of buds to leave on the long canes depends on how much growth the vine produced the previous year. The growth gives an indication of the grapes health and vigor. An easy system of deciding how many buds to leave is to weigh the prunings. Gather them up and weigh them on a small spring balance and then shorten the canes to the number of buds in the following table.

Weight of pruning (one year's worth):	Number of buds to leave:
less than one pound	less than 30
one pound	30
two	40
three	50
four	60
five	70
six	80
more than six pounds	80 plus

For example, on a vine with four canes from which you remove two pounds of prunings you would leave 10 buds per cane or 40 buds total.

Fruit grows only from buds on wood that the vine produced the previous year. Do not leave more than two grape clusters to a shoot. Letting the vine go unpruned will greatly reduce the yield and the quality of the fruit.

5. Harvesting. Let the grapes stay on the vines until they are completely ripe; they will not get any sweeter after being picked. Color is no indication of ripeness. They can be a good color and still quite sour. A taste test is the best test. Or watch the birds. They will harvest them for you if you are a day late. Check the color of the seeds: green seeds, sour grapes; brown seeds, ripe grapes. If you have trouble with birds and other pests, you can enclose the bunches in paper bags since they do not need the direct sun as long as the leaves are getting plenty of light.

Grapes on a trellis

6. Pests and diseases. Pests and diseases are more of a problem to commercial growers than to individuals growing a few vines. Commercial growers cannot go out and remove bad berries from a bunch. The fungous diseases such as black rot, and downy and powdery mildews can be controlled by spraying, and lessened by keeping the infected leaves and fruit cleaned up and cleared out of the area. Fungi and rots spread quickly in damp, humid weather. A number of insects can attack the leaves and the fruit. A reduction in the amount of foliage has a direct effect on fruit production, so foliage diseases should be controlled. Each area has its own problems and control solutions. For information on identification and control, consult your cooperative extension service.

Questions and Possible Answers

Why were there no grapes?	Not enough light.
	Too much vine and old wood.
	Poor pollination.
Why were grapes deformed?	Too many in a bunch.
Why did vines grow scant, small, poor quality grapes?	Vine not pruned back to main trunk so bunches were greater distance from roots.
Why were grapes sour?	Picked too early.
	Grew too high.

Herbs

Herbs are fragrant plants with medicinal, aromatic, or culinary uses. With herbs, as with any other gardening, it is important to plan before you plant. Do you want to grow herbs for fragrance, flavor, or pharmaceutical use? Or do you want them just for show? If you want a formal knot garden you will have to concentrate on plants that have little fragrance or smell like horse liniment because these are the ones that look best clipped and keep their shape without a battalion of gardeners. Those that will take discipline are the grey and green lavender-cottons *(Santolina chamaecyparissus* and *Santolina virens),* germander *(Teucrium chamaedrys),* and lavender *(Lavandula officinalis).* These all make excellent border plants that can be clipped for decorative knot gardens.

    Herbs grown for fragrance or for eating can be kept in neat beds with two or three plants of each kind next to each other and all the herbs together in one block. Herbs look well in containers on a patio or tucked in among other plants in a flower or vegetable garden. A "tussy

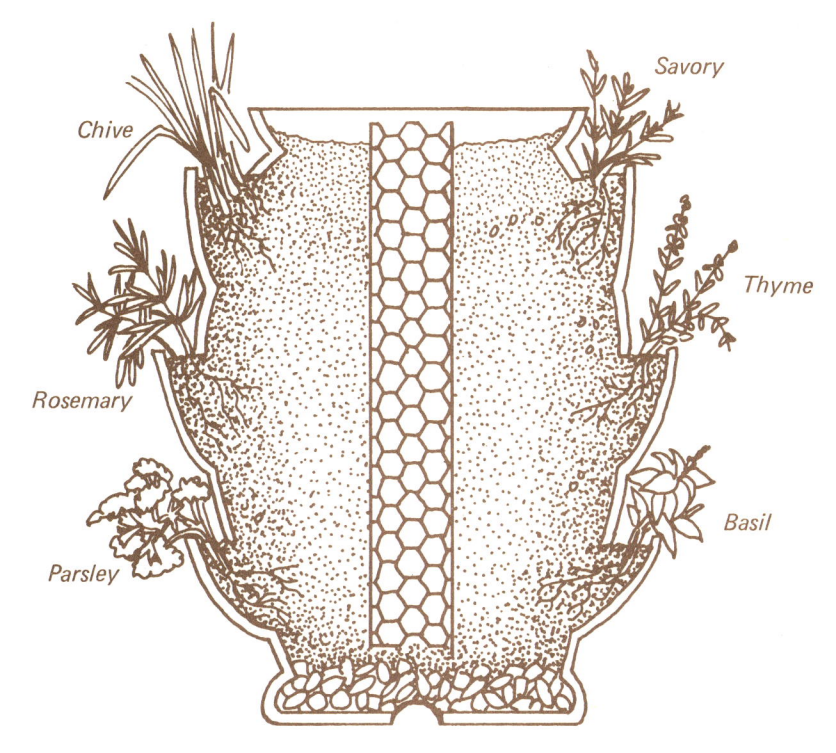

Herbs in strawberry jar

mussy" made with a sprig of rosemary for remembrance, a bit of lavender for love, and some leaves of scented geraniums — perhaps lemon, rose, and apple — will feed the romantic spirit of almost everyone.

Chives and garlic are usually thought of as herbs, but onions are regarded as vegetables. Parsley and dill are herbs, but carrots are a vegetable. Herbs are eatables where a little goes a long way. They have a strong fragrance and should be used with a light hand to enhance other eatables. Fresh herbs are more subtle and less strong than dry herbs. A rule of thumb is to use a tablespoon of fresh herbs for each teaspoon of dry. Dried herbs should be kept in tightly-sealed containers and away from heat. Many times dry herbs when they are over a year old should be in a museum rather than a kitchen.

Fines herbes are a mixture of four or five finely minced herbs which always include chives and either parsley or chervil.

Bouquet garni is a bundle of herbs usually made up of thyme, parsley, and a medium bay leaf — plus other herbs, depending on the food to be seasoned. It is either tied up or put in a clean bag and dropped in at the end of the cooking period and then removed before serving. The flavor becomes harsh if herbs are cooked too long.

If there is not enough room in your garden — or if you have no garden at all — grow herbs in a narrow planter on a windowsill. They can thrive under fluorescent lights. Or, grow them in a hanging basket in a bright natural light. A number of plants can be grown together in a strawberry jar. A strawberry jar filled with herbs is great on a terrace outside, and it can even grow in a sunny window if you put it on a lazy susan so each side can have time in the sun. Thyme can be planted in the cracks in the sidewalk, and it is more exciting to step on than chickweed. Parsley can be used to edge rose beds and chives look great as accents in perennial borders. Enough herbs for the summer and most of the winter can be grown in a bed the size of a washtub or in a tire planter.

Herbs do better indoors if it is not too hot and they do not dry out. They are not among the forgiving indoor plants and once they have dried out they are gone. On the other hand they hate to be wet. Basil, chives, marjoram, parsley, and rosemary do well inside. Dill and fennel can get stringy and tall. Sage, tarragon, and thyme soon look quite unhappy under regular indoor conditions. Except for basil, they all take quite some time to sprout from seed. If you are planning to grow herbs inside, it is best to start with plants which you buy or pot up in late summer to bring indoors. Let newly potted herbs rest outdoors a while, until they get over the transplanting shock before they have to be cooped up.

Underground herb gardens can be fun in areas where the winters are long and dreary. Herbs in rather large containers can be brought into a basement and kept very well under fluorescent lights. In fact, with a few comfortable chaises and a good imagination you may be able to forget the snow and cold outside as you occasionally brush your hand over a rosemary or pick off a piece of basil, and if you add a sun lamp you can close your eyes and imagine you are on the Costa del Sol.

Growing Herbs

1. Best bed. Herbs need a bed in the full sun. Some herbs like a warm bed and some prefer a cool one.

2. Planting. Start with seeds or transplants. Plant the perennials where they will not have to be moved. Resist overplanting; a pinch can flavor a whole pot. Three of each plant can give leeway for accidents and provide a good feeling of providence as well as material for drying for winter use. If plants are to be brought inside at the end of the season, keep them in pots or pot them up a month before freezing since plants cannot take being dug up and brought inside at the same time.

3. Food and drink. Go easy on the food. Herbs do best when growing under adversity and a hot sun. Fertilizer produces lush growth but poor flavor or fragrance. Water is important; the drainage should be excellent, but the plants should not be permitted to dry out.

4. Special care. Most herbs are able to hold their own with other plants. In fact, a number of them can grow so well that they are often considered weeds. Pull out the largest competition.

5. Harvesting. You can mulch in the fall and harvest the hardy ones most all winter long. Clip the plants as needed. Flavor is usually not as good after the plant blooms since it has finished its work and is on its way downhill. If you are harvesting herbs for winter use, cut as the plant begins to bloom. Hang bunches in a shaded spot and let them dry. When thoroughly dry, crumble and put the herbs in a container with a tight-fitting lid.

6. Pests and diseases. Other than an occasional caterpillar, there is nothing much to worry about. Most of the herbs will even take moderate amounts of being stepped on.

Questions and Possible Answers

Why did herb lack flavor?	Too much fertilizer. Flavorless or poor-flavored variety. Not enough sun or light. Too much water. The less water, the better the flavor.
It died. Why?	Not enough water. Even though herbs prefer excellent drainage and relatively dry soil, if watering is neglected too long, especially when they are growing indoors, they will die. It was an annual. It was too cold. Some herbs are hardy perennials. Others are hardy annuals, while still others are tender and can't take freezing.
Why did mints spread all over?	The roots were not drastically confined. Mints should be grown in a pot or container, or planted in a bottomless tin can.

Lettuce

"Lettuce Entertain You" is the name of a restaurant company that caters to salad lovers who expect things to be tossed about a bit. But very few of them would follow the lead of Venus who, on the death of Adonis, tossed herself on a bed of lettuce to lull her grief and still her desires.

The most common lettuce found in supermarkets, the iceberg or head lettuce, is the most difficult to grow at home. On the other hand, the butterhead or bibb lettuces, which are often so extravagantly expensive in the store, are easier to grow. Butterhead lettuces have loose heads and delicate crunchy leaves that refuse to travel well. Stem lettuce (celtuce) might fool you into thinking you are eating hearts of palm and they make a crunchy celerylike addition to a salad, without any strings attached. Cos or romaine lettuce forms a loose long head and is part way between a butterhead and leaf lettuce in flavor. Leaf lettuce grows fast and can provide bulk and color to salads. It is also delightfully easy to grow.

Leaf lettuce and butterhead lettuce make attractive borders or accents in a flower garden. Butterhead or leaf lettuce can be grown as single plants in four-inch pots, or they can be grown as fillers in a window box. You can grow lettuces as part of all the makings for a salad in an old tire. That way an entire salad garden can be grown on a balcony or paved terrace.

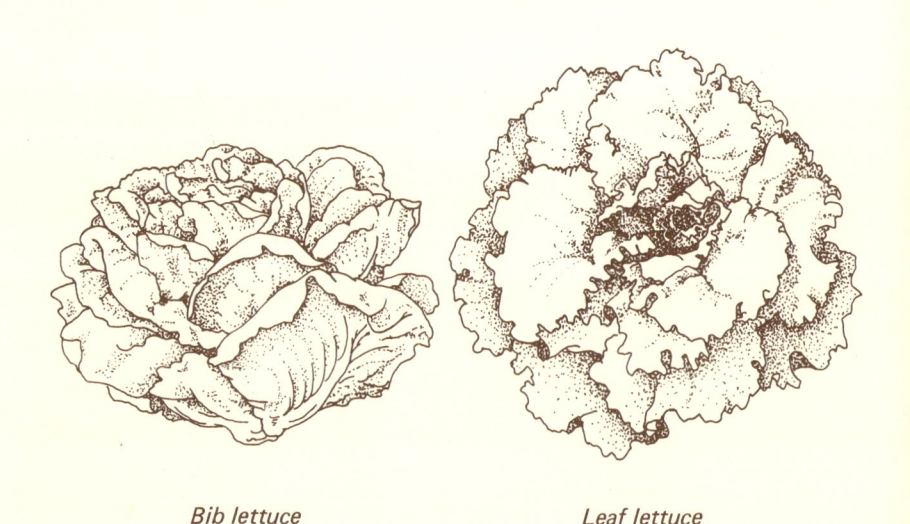

Bib lettuce   *Leaf lettuce*

Celtuce

Head lettuce

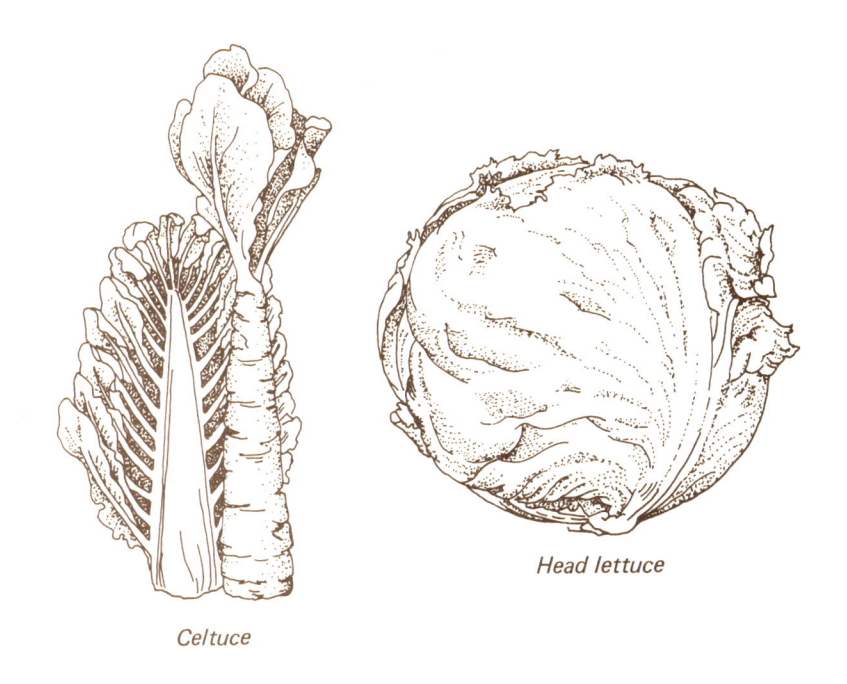

Growing Lettuce

1. Best bed. Lettuce is a cool-weather crop and its bed should be well-worked, with good drainage and moisture retention.

2. Planting. Plant in cool weather, hot weather and long days cause lettuce to go to seed (bolt). Sow seeds a quarter-inch deep in rows or blocks. Transplants of head lettuce should be planted 12 inches apart. You can sow successive crops in "cool weather-short day" locations.

3. Food and drink. If you fertilize at all, do it before planting. Lettuce is shallow-rooted and should not dry out. Keep the soil evenly moist, but not soggy. Heading lettuce needs careful watering when the head is forming. When watering, take care not to splash muddy water on the plants — the cleaner the plants, the easier they are to prepare for eating.

4. Special care. Thin the lettuce. Heading lettuce will not head and all lettuce may bolt if crowded. A light mulch helps cut down muddy soil getting on the leaves.

5. Harvesting. As the lettuce grows, pick the outer leaves, or wait and harvest the whole plant.

6. Pests and diseases. Cutworms, slugs and snails can be troublesome.

Questions and Possible Answers

Why didn't lettuce develop a head?	It was not the variety that makes a head. The plants were too close together. Not enough moisture. The temperature got too hot (air above 80°F). Rabbits ate it before it got to that stage.
Why was lettuce bitter?	Not enough moisture. Weather too hot. Left too long before harvesting. Too crowded in the bed — they like a little privacy.
Why did lettuce bolt?	Plants were too crowded. Weather was too hot. Left too long before harvesting.

Onion

Nobody feels neutral about onions. Chives, garlic, leeks and onions all have their loyal adherents and vehement detractors. There are still people who feel that putting onion juice on a bald head will bring back the hair.

In the United States, onions are divided into American, which are strong-flavored, and foreign (Bermuda and Spanish), which are mild. Spring onions, bunching onions, scallions, and green onions all are young onions eaten for their green leaves. Green onions are one of the easiest and most fun eatables to grow. If you do not care for green onions you can always give them away. Dry onion bulbs are among the more frustrating plants for a home garden. Although there are some onions that are not supposed to make a bulb and are grown solely as green onions, all onions can be pulled and eaten green.

Most onions are sensitive to day length. The American and Spanish onions need long days to produce their bulbs and the Bermudas prefer short days. Onions are also sensitive to temperature, generally requiring cool weather to produce their tops and warm weather to produce their bulbs. The strength of the onion's flavor is not just a matter of variety, the soil and the growing conditions are important as well. Since soil and growing conditions vary greatly throughout the U.S., you should check with a garden center or cooperative extension service for specific varieties to grow in your area.

In addition to the many varieties, onions are available in three forms — as seeds, as transplants and as sets. Sets are onions with a case of arrested development — their growth was stopped when they were quite small. They are the easiest to plant and the quickest to produce a green onion, but not the most reliable for bulb production. They are available in the least number of varieties and sometimes will shoot right on to the flowering stage without producing a bulb. Transplants are available in more varieties than sets and are usually more reliable about producing bulbs. Seeds are the least expensive and are available in the greatest variety, but they take such a long time to grow that the forces of nature often kill them before they produce anything.

In limited space you can grow onions between other vegetables, such as tomatoes or cabbages, or tuck them in among flowers. They do not take much room, are unobtrusive and may even repel bugs. They can also be grown in containers. An eight-inch flowerpot can hold eight to ten green onions.

Growing Onions

1. Best bed. Onions appreciate a well-made, well-worked bed with all the lumps removed for at least six inches deep. The soil should be fertile and contain organic matter. Locate onion bulbs in full sun. Green onions can be placed in a partially shady spot.

2. Planting. In the North, onions can be planted as soon as the severe frosts are over. In the South, they can be planted in the fall or

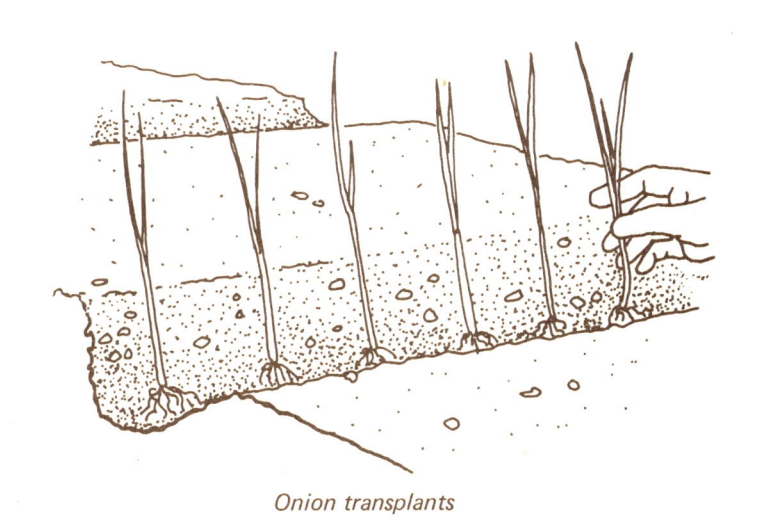

Onion transplants

winter. The time of planting depends on the day length and temperature requirements of the individual variety.

When you plant seeds, make sure the surface is smooth and does not dry out. When you plant transplants and sets, remember that less is more. Large transplants and large sets (over ¾ inch in diameter) will often go directly to seed and should be planted and grown only for green or pulling onions. Smaller transplants or sets should be grown for bulbs.

Onion transplants do best when they are about the size of a pencil. When you buy a bundle of onion transplants, divide it into three piles — those that are pencil sized and those that are larger and smaller. Plant the large ones for green onions, plant the pencil sized ones for green onions or bulbs and throw the small ones into the soup. The final size of the onion is affected by the amount of room it has to grow.

3. Food and drink. Onions grow best in a fertile soil that is well-drained and rich in organic matter. If manure is available, use it or work a 5-10-10 fertilizer into the soil before planting. The soil should not dry out until the plants have started to mature (the leaves start getting yellow and brown and droop over), then it should be allowed to get as dry as possible.

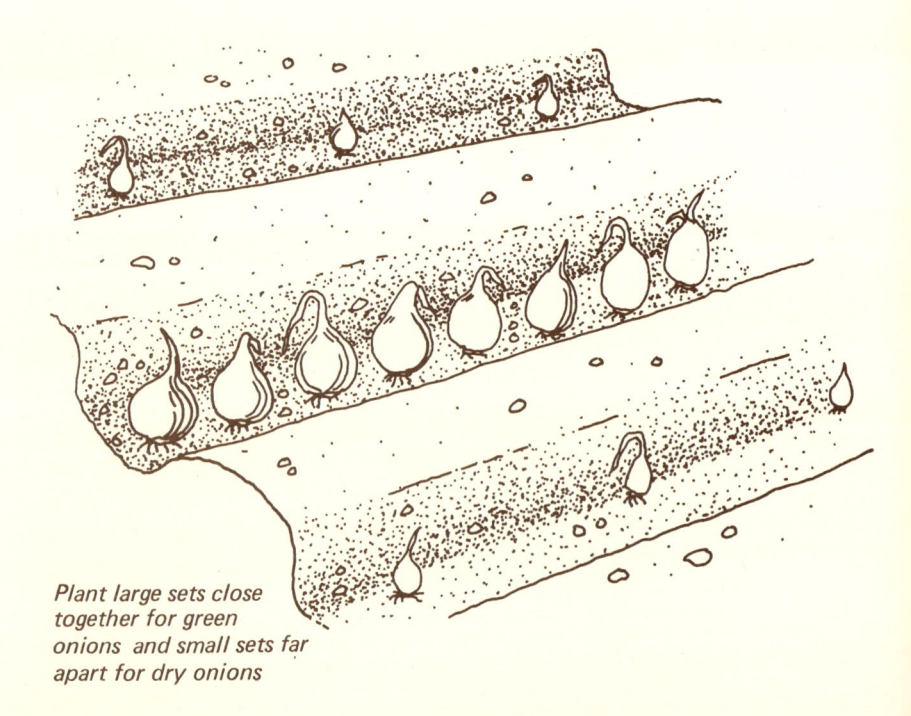

Plant large sets close together for green onions and small sets far apart for dry onions

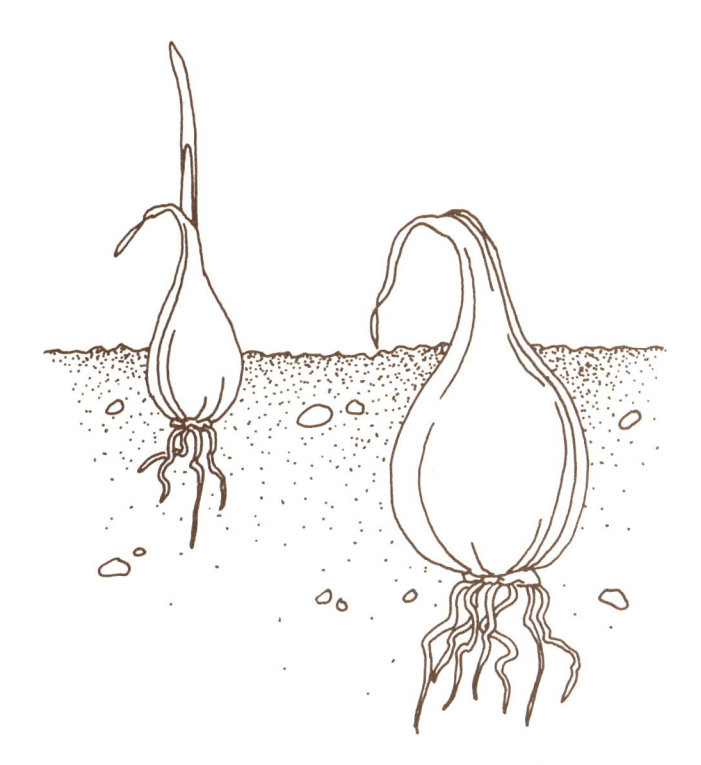

Plant small sets shallower than large sets

4. Special care. Onions are not good fighters; you will have to keep the weeds from crowding in and taking all their food and drink. Keep the weeds cut off from the very beginning since they are very hard to remove when they snuggle up to the onions. If onions grow in a crowded bed they will mature when very small.

5. Harvesting. Harvest the green onions when the bulb is full but not much larger in diameter than the leaves. Harvest the dry onion bulbs after the leaves have dried. Lift them completely out of the soil; if the roots touch the soil they may start growing again and get soft and watery. Let the bulbs air dry for several days. Then they can be braided into a long braid to hang from the rafters, or you can cut off the tops and store the bulbs in a cool dry place with good air circulation. Leave ½ inch, about the thickness of a thumb, of stem on the bulb. The tops should not be cut off too short or the onion may rot.

6. Pests and diseases. Onion thrips and maggots, bulb and root rots, smut and downy mildew are the onion's enemies. For serious problems, contact your cooperative extension service for the best means of control in your area.

Questions and Possible Answers

Why didn't onions produce bulbs?	The day length was either too short or too long.
	The temperature was too low after the green onion stage. At 50-60°F, 10 percent will bolt, and between 70°F and 80°F none of them will bolt.
	Not enough sun. Green onions will produce their greens in partial shade, but onions need full sun to grow bulbs.
Why did onions taste weak?	Depends on the variety. Generally, Spanish and Bermudas are milder.
	Affected by soil condition and weather during growing season.
Why did bulbs split?	The sets or transplants were too large. When planting, separate by size. Then plant the large ones for green onions and the smaller ones for bulbs.

Pepper

When Columbus was looking for the black pepper (the dried berries of the *Piper nigrum* vine), he found the fruit of the *Capsicums,* not related in any way to the peppers he had started out to find. But that did not stop him from using the name.

The American peppers are members of a famous plant family that includes tomatoes, potatoes, eggplants, tobacco. They range in size from the large sweet bullnose or mango peppers to the tiny, fiery bird or devil peppers. Peppers also grow in many shapes: round, long, flat, and twisted. Some like them hot, some like them sweet. The large sweet ones are used raw, cooked, or pickled, and the hot ones are used as an unmistakable flavoring or relish. In Jamaica, there are some peppers so hot that people claim a single drop of sauce will burn a hole in the tablecloth. People eat hot peppers in hot countries to cool off because peppers raise the body temperature and make the surrounding air seem cool by comparison. Read the plant catalog carefully when you make a selection to be sure the variety you order suits your palate. Talk to your garden center or cooperative extension service to find the varieties that will do best in your area.

Try growing peppers in a large pot or container. Individual plants can be grown in a cubic foot of soil. A single chili (hot pepper) plant is very decorative, and can fill many families' hot pepper requirements for a whole year.

Growing Peppers

1. Best bed. Grow peppers in a warm bed (60°F at night), located

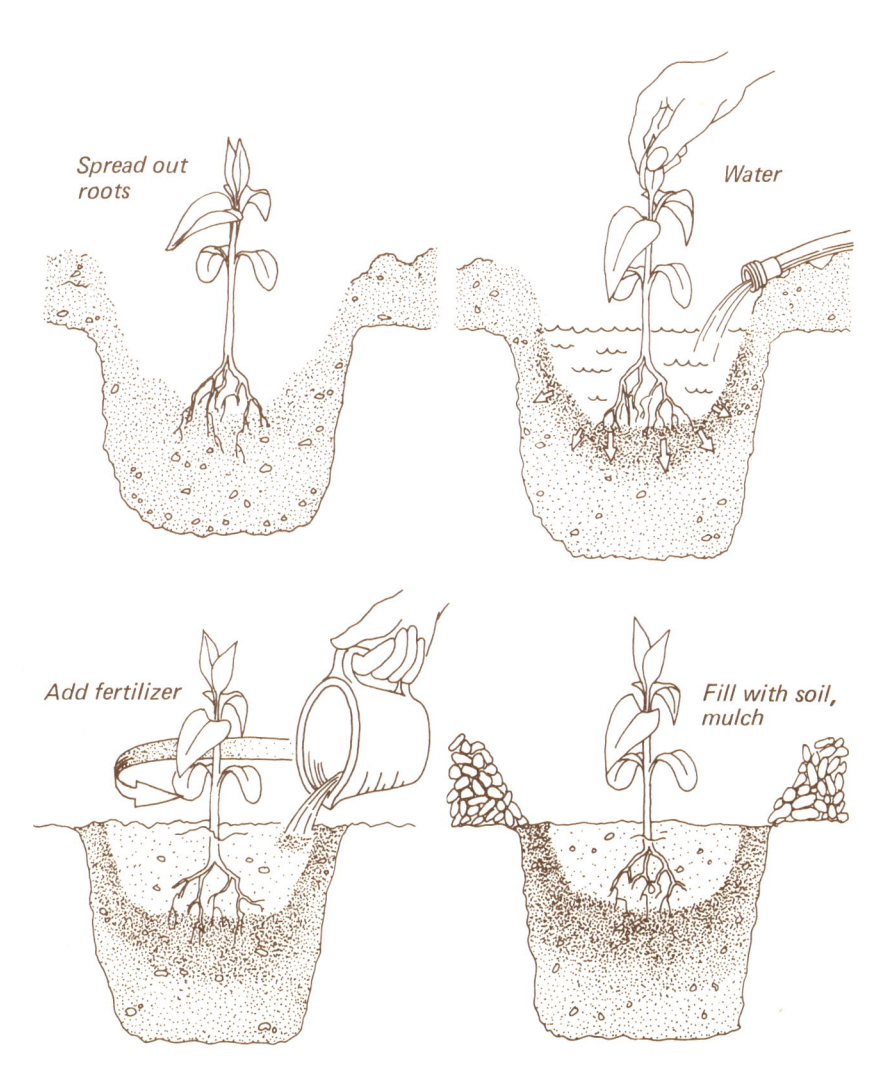

Spread out roots

Water

Add fertilizer

Fill with soil, mulch

235

in full sun. Do not plant until the soil warms up or the plant will just sulk and may never come out of its depression.

2. Planting. Start with transplants. Set the plants 18 to 24 inches apart. If possible, plant in the late afternoon. If sun is very hot, shade the plant to protect it for the first few days.

3. Food and drink. Use one cup of starter solution per plant when transplanting. You can make a starter solution by mixing one tablespoon of all water soluble, high-phosphorus (10-50-10) fertilizer in a gallon of water. Or you can mix a cup of 5-10-10 fertilizer in the soil where you will put each plant. You can fertilize again when the plants begin to bloom. Keep the soil evenly moist, but not wet.

4. Special care. Peppers are shallow-rooted, so cultivate them gently to eliminate weeds without discouraging the pepper's growth. Use a mulch to keep the soil moisture even.

5. Harvesting. Do not harvest too early. Wait until the pepper is about full size. Use scissors or a knife to cut the fruit off. The plant is rather woody and brittle. Half the plant may break if you try to snap off the pepper by hand. Peppers keep better if there is about a half inch of stem left on them.

6. Pests and diseases. Peppers are usually not bothered much by pests and disease if you keep the area clean, plant resistant varieties, mulch to maintain even soil moisture, and keep an eye open for transient insects.

Questions and Possible Answers

Why did the blossoms drop off?	Too cold, night temperature below 60°F.
	Too hot, night temperature above 75°F or day temperature above 90°F. Hot varieties can take warmer weather better than sweet peppers.
	Not enough water.
Why did plants wilt?	Lacked water.
	Certain varieties wilt in reaction to stress such as hot, dry weather.
	It may be diseased. During hot weather (80°F-95°F) peppers may suffer from fusarium wilts.
	During cool weather (under 75°F peppers can develop verticillium wilt.

Why did bottoms of the fruit rot?	Calcium deficiency.
	Uneven soil moisture.
Why were there no peppers?	Location too shady.
	Growing season too short.
	Nights too cold (below 60°F).
	Too much water.
	Too much fertilizer.

Root Crops

Root crops are some of the oldest vegetables. Until the 20th century they were almost the only fresh vegetables available in the winter.

Except for sweet potatoes and peanuts, most underground root eatables are cool-weather crops and tolerate cold weather. Although several root vegetables, such as beets, celeriac and turnips, are grown for their greens, most root crops are grown for their enlarged "root." Beets, carrots, celeriac, parsnips, radishes, rutabagas, salsify and turnips all have similar growing needs and, with the exception of the radish, which can be either annual or biennial, all are biennials. They all do best in well-worked, well-drained soil without lumps, rocks and rough stuff. Hard soil and hard objects in the soil cause the roots to split, fork or become deformed. Root crops do best on a slightly acid soil, although beets are not happy if the pH goes below 6.0.

Root crops are among the easiest eatables to grow and there are very few pests or diseases that bother them — and when they do it is usually not fatal. The greatest problem in growing root crops is giving

Thin radishes so that roots have room to develop

them enough room. It seems such a waste to pull all those good plants out, but they compete with each other for available moisture and light and none of them will develop if they are not thinned. Think of thinning as an early harvest and put the chosen ones, well washed, into a salad or soup. Root crops prefer full sun, but they will tolerate partial shade. With the exceptions of rutabagas and parsnips, which have very long growing seasons, successive crops should be planted in short rows rather than putting the seeds in the ground all at one time.

If space is a problem, beets, carrots, celeriac, radishes and turnips can be grown in large pots or in boxes. Since most of their important growth is underground, they should have eight to ten inches of soil. They will all grow some sort of root in six inches of soil. Radishes will grow in four inches of soil, if the soil does not dry out. Pick the shorter more compact varieties of root crops for better results in confined spaces. Radishes can be grown inside if there is a cool spot that receives good light. Since the tops of the root crops do not grow too large, these vegetables are quite decorative tucked into odd spots in flower beds.

Growing Root Crops

    1. Best bed. A cool one. Although they prefer full sun, they will tolerate partial shade.
    2. Planting. Start with seeds sown ½ inch apart and covered with sand, peat moss or vermiculite if the soil tends to crust. Add a few radishes when sowing slower-growing seeds to mark the rows. Radishes will also help keep the soil from crusting.
    3. Food and drink. Work in ½ cup of 5-10-10 fertilizer per ten feet of row when preparing the soil. Make sure enough moisture is available to keep them growing fast. Rapid growth is essential for

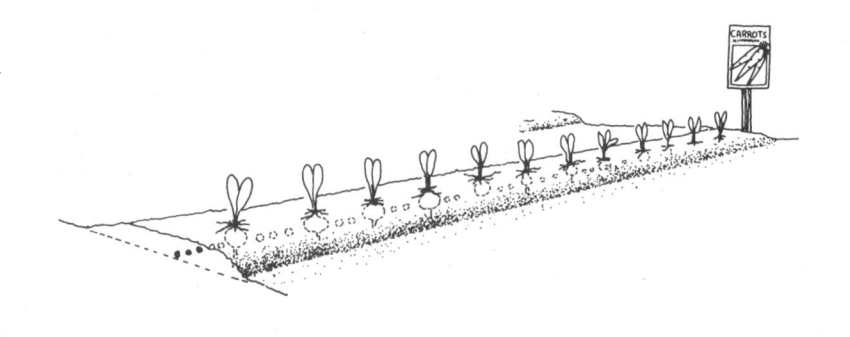

Mark rows of slower-growing seeds with fast-growing radishes

Carrots come in many shapes and sizes

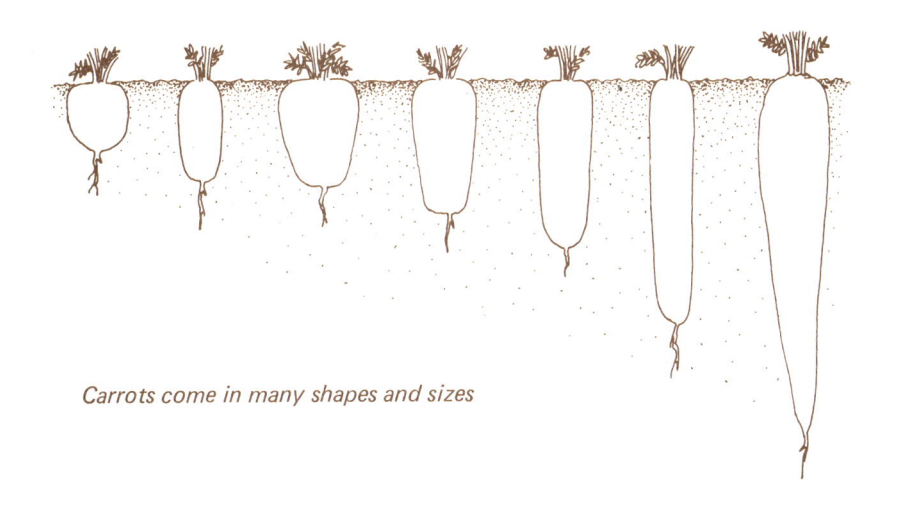

tender root crops and a lack of moisture will make the roots strong and woody. If there is no rain for a week give them a good soaking. After they have been thinned for the last time, a couple inches of organic mulch will help control weeds and will keep the soil moisture even.

4. Special care. Get rid of the competition from each other, as well as competition from outsiders.

5. Harvesting. Root crops can be harvested from 20 days (radishes) to 120 days (parsnips). Root crops are usually best when harvested before they are as large as they can grow. Size in itself is not the only consideration, nor are looks. For example, Winter Keeper beets are large, lumpy, rough-looking and delicious, while some beautifully symmetrical smoothies taste as if they were made of wood. Harvesting is something of a matter of taste. Parsnips are said to be better if they have been left in the ground until frozen. Cover parsnips with a mulch after the first hard frost so they can be dug as needed.

6. Pests and diseases. Root crops are not much bothered by pests and diseases. Occasionally, they are visited by aphids and root maggots, but if they are not thinned, they are their own worst enemy.

Questions and Possible Answers

Why didn't seeds come up?   Soil too cold.
　　　　　　　　　　　　　　　Soil crust too hard.
　　　　　　　　　　　　　　　Seed not viable (seeds of root crops usually last a long time).

Why were plants all tops?   Crowded too close together.
　　　　　　　　　　　　　　　Not enough moisture.

Forked carrot

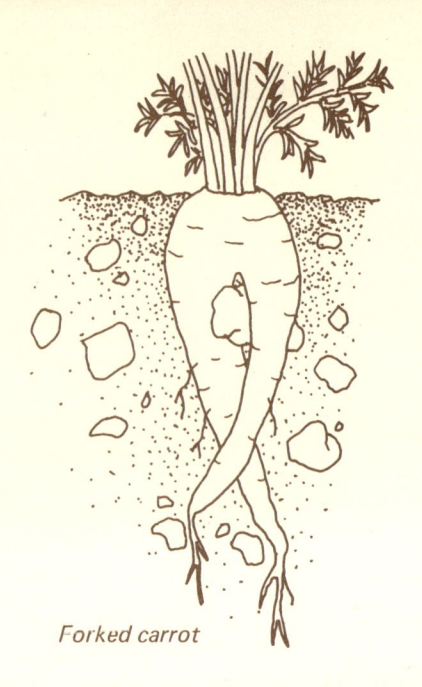

Why were roots deformed?   Soil too hard.
                           Too many rocks.
Why were roots woody?   Not enough moisture.
                           Too much competition.

Squash

The gourd family probably has the greatest diversity of shapes and sizes of any family except the cabbages. Cucumbers and melons are family members, as are squashes, pumpkins and gourds. The importance of the gourds was recognized by Henri Christophe (he fought in the American Revolution under La Fayette and then was a leader of the slave revolt in Haiti in the early 19th Century). One of his first official acts as King Henri I was to have the Haitian army bring in every gourd they could find (over a quarter of a million), and he then used them as a medium of exchange. Haitian currency today is made of paper, but it is still called *gourde,* which is also Louisiana slang for a dollar.

The genus *Cucurbita* includes certain gourds, pumpkins, and **squashes.** Most are trailing or climbing plants with large yellow flowers (male and female) that appear on the same vine and have mature fruit with a thick skin and definite seed cavity. Summer squash, winter squash, and pumpkins are not definite botanical names. "Pumpkin," which any child can tell you is a large round eatable used for Jack-o'-lanterns and pies, is applied to long-keeping varieties of *Cucurbita moschata, Cucurbita pepo,* and a few varieties of *Cucurbita maxima.* Summer squashes are eaten when they are immature; winter squashes are eaten when mature.

Sex is more important to some plants than to others. For all the members of the gourd family, including the squashes, pumpkins, cucumbers, and melons, it makes a big difference which blossom you pick and eat. The female flowers always look a little pregnant and usually grow on short stems in the axils of the leaves, while the male flowers have no bulge and are often on longer, thinner stems. Since the female flowers are pollinated by insects, you may have to give nature a nudge if you are gardening on the 79th floor, if you were too heavy-handed with the insecticide, or if you are growing plants in a sunny spot inside. All you have to do is take a soft watercolor brush — sable is nice, but any full soft brush will do — and rub it first on the pollen of the male flower and then dust it about the inside of the female flower. After you have played matchmaker, you can take the male blossoms, dip them in egg batter, and sauté them.

Squashes, like St. Bernards, are hard to confine. A bush-type zucchini will grow well in a tire planter if kept well-watered and fertilized. A vining squash can be trained up a fence. The fruit does not have to be supported. When grown on a fence the fruit will support itself.

Female squash blossom

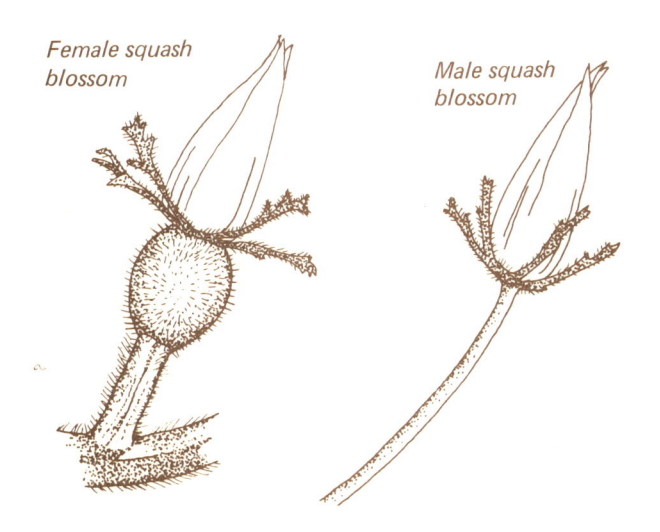

Male squash blossom

Growing Squash

1. Best bed. Squashes like a warm bed, at least 60°F at night. They need full sun.

2. Planting. Start your squash with seeds. Transplants are possible if they are grown in plantable pots so the roots are not disturbed when they are set in the soil. Plant squashes in hills of six to eight seeds. Space the hills four to six feet apart. For hills, arrange the seeds in a circle. Let one or two strong plants remain in each hill. (Hill planting does not mean at the top or bottom of a mound.) As the squashes grow, thin them out when they have three or four true leaves.

3. Food and drink. Squash do well in a soil that is high in organic matter — they grow beautifully on a compost pile and respond well to a half pound of 5-10-10 fertilizer mixed thoroughly in each ten feet of row. Keep the soil evenly moist but not wet and try to keep water off the leaves.

4. Special care. Squashes are shallow-rooted, so cultivate carefully. Use a mulch to keep soil moisture even. Aluminum foil mulch confuses squash and cucumber bugs so that they scamper off in all directions. Make sure that female flowers are pollinated by insects or pollinate them with a clean watercolor brush.

5. Harvesting. Continue harvesting summer squashes when they are young and tender; the more you pick the more will grow. If the

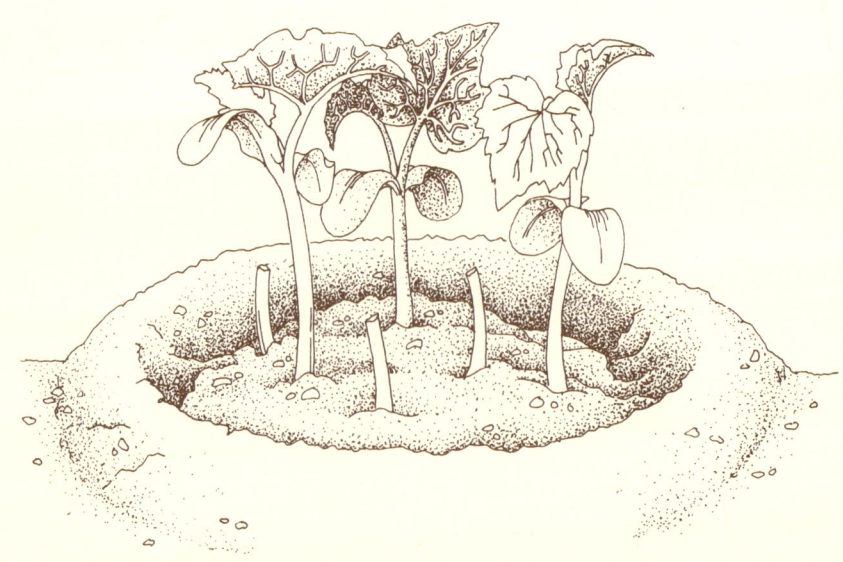

Hill planting of squash thinned to the three strongest plants

fruit is left on the vine until it gets very large it will suppress blooming. With winter squash, leave them on the vine until the skin cannot be dented with thumbnail (you can write your name on them). Harvest before a frost. Store winter squash at 70°F for a couple of weeks and then keep in a well-ventilated place with the temperature about 50°F.

6. Pests and diseases. Squash bugs, borers and cucumber beetles are the worst insect pests. Bacterial wilt, mosaic and mildew can be bothersome in wet humid weather. Trouble can be minimized by keeping the leaves dry when watering.

Questions and Possible Answers

Why didn't seed come up?	Soil too cold.
	Weather too cold.
	Seed too old.
	Birds or squirrels ate it.
Why was there no fruit?	Nights too cold.
	No insects.
	All male blossoms.
	The female flowers were picked for eating.
Why did vine collapse and wilt?	If the whole vine wilted, lacked water.
	If part of it wilted, there may be squash borer. Or perhaps somebody stepped on part of the vine.
	Bacterial wilt disease carried by cucumber beetle did plant in.

Strawberry

"Doubtless God could have made a better berry, but doubtless God never did."

Dr. Butler

Strawberries never made it big until the meadow strawberry *(Fragaria virginiana)*, a sweet thing with a lovely fragrance from eastern North America, met the beach strawberry *(Fragaria chiloensis)*, a large, sturdy, yellow-fleshed fruit from the southern coast of Chile, at the beginning of the 18th century in Europe. Their descendents were the origins of many of the cultivated varieties around today. Strawberries were very high class, and the coronets of English dukes, marquises,

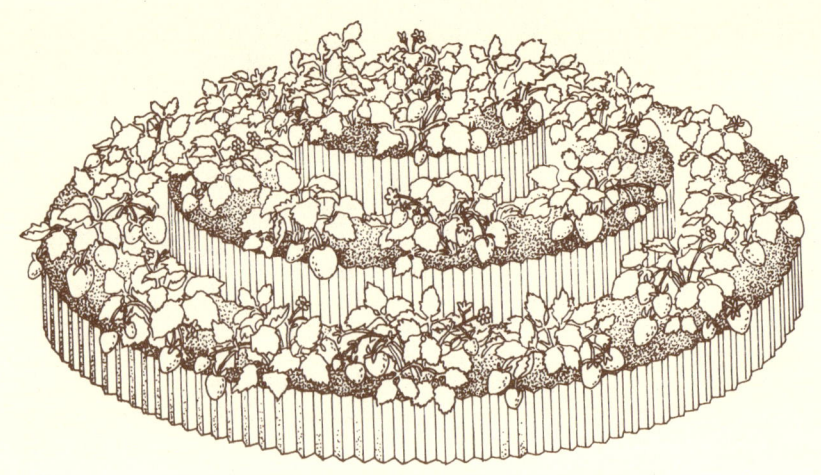

Strawberries planted in a pyramid of lawn edging

and earls still bear golden strawberry leaves. Fresh strawberries, even today in the era of fresh-frozen everything, still make an occasion seem special.

Varieties are available for special areas and conditions of soil, climate, and day length. In small spaces strawberries can be grown in a strawberry jar, hanging baskets or pyramids. There will not be too much fruit, but the shiny dark green leaves, white flowers, and occasional berry look lovely and make a great conversation piece. Check with your local extension service for recommendations.

Growing Strawberries

1. Best bed. Strawberries must have well-drained soil, high in organic matter. Locate their bed in full sun.

2. Planting. There are basically two ways to lay out a strawberry bed: the matted-row system and the double- or triple-row hill system. With matted rows, the strawberry plants are spaced about 18 inches apart in rows four feet apart and are allowed to spread by means of runners from the parent plant. Eventually, the plants of all sizes will cover the ground. About the only work involved in this system is picking off the flowers as they appear the first year in order to produce stronger plants. Double- and triple-row hill systems are more work but they take less garden space and result in more productive plants. As in the matted row, strawberry plants are spaced about 18 inches apart but the rows need be only 30 inches apart. The flowers are also picked off the first season. With hill systems, however, the stronger runners are moved into parallel rows of their own while the weaker runners and any runners that appear after the middle of June (assuming the plants were set out in early spring) are removed.

Strawberries can also be grown in hanging baskets, strawberry jars, or pyramids made with circles of lawn edging that are stacked and filled with soil. When growing strawberries in containers, each plant should be put in separately. All runners must be cut off and so should all the flowers of the first season. The plants will be weakened and will not produce as well if runners and flowers are allowed to grow. You cannot cheat and get away with it.

Plant only certified plants; virus-free plants produce more and larger fruit. Plants should have light-colored roots; black-rooted plants are old, tired plants that grow very poorly. Plants should be set in at the right depth, not too deep and not too shallow, and the roots should be spread out like a fan and not twisted or bent. Press the soil firmly around the plant. The plant is planted firmly enought if, when you jerk a leaf it comes off and the plant stays planted.

Since you don't let strawberry plants bear the first year, start new plants each year so that you will have a harvest every season. This way after plants have produced two years they can be removed as the newer ones will be giving you fruit. Try to keep rotating the crop by planting in a different spot each time you make a new planting. Try to put new strawberry plants where strawberries have not grown for four years, or where tomatoes, peppers, eggplants, or potatoes have not grown for three years. Sometimes, in a small space, it is easier to bring in new soil rather than find a new spot. If possible, do not grow them where there was sod the year before, because that ground may still be hosting a lot of grubs and root weevils.

3. **Food and drink.** Work a pound of 10-10-10 or 12-12-12 fertilizer into 100 square feet before planting, or work in a well-rotted

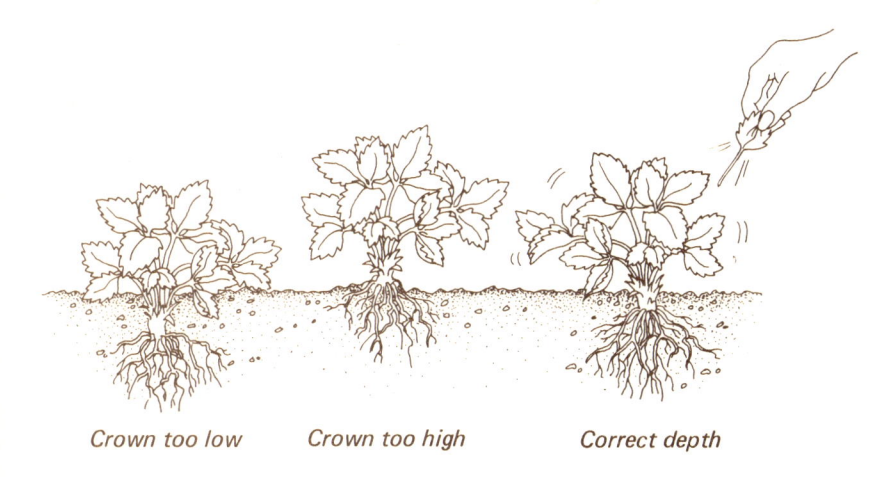

Crown too low   *Crown too high*   *Correct depth*

Matted row of strawberry plants

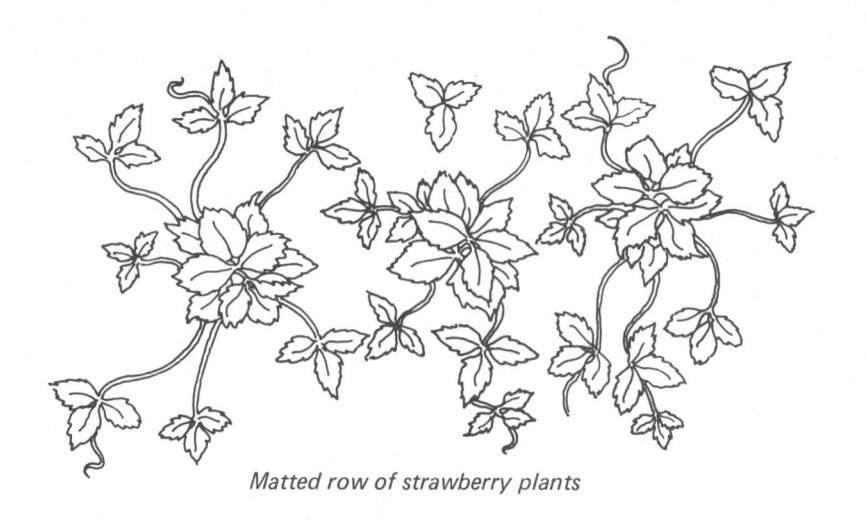

manure. Fertilizing the first season means better fruit the second. Do not apply nitrogen fertilizer the next year before flowering because it encourages excessive foliage and there will be no fruit or soft fruit that rots easily.

Strawberries are shallow-rooted and need water to keep growing and producing. If possible, keep the water down on the ground and not on the leaves and fruit. Use mulch to conserve soil moisture, keep down weeds, and decrease fruit rot.

4. Special care. Cultivate plants to keep them weeded, but do it gently since strawberries are shallow-rooted. Pick off all the flower clusters the first few months after planting to increase plant vigor and encourage runner production. If growing everbearing varieties, remove the runners as they appear.

Apply mulch to protect strawberries from winter injury when the temperature gets to about 20°F. If this straw mulch is applied too early the plant may suffocate if there is warm weather, and if it is applied too late there may be damage to the plants. The mulch will delay the warming of the soil in the spring and, in cold areas of the country it may hold the berry production back, lessening the risk of spring frost damage.

5. Harvesting. The length of the season depends on the variety and the weather. The picking season is short if the weather is hot, and long if the weather is cool and the plants have plenty of moisture. The ripe berries should be removed every day or every other day, depending on how fast they are ripening. All ripe slug-chewed, bird-stabbed, or rotting berries should be removed, too, and thrown on the compost pile. Letting them stay on the plant cuts down on berry production and increases the chance of rotting. The berries will keep longer if you pick them in the morning when they are cool and keep them in a cool place until used.

6. Pests and diseases. Strawberries are susceptible to attack by many two-legged, four-legged and many-legged pests. The one-footed pests, slugs and snails, are also very fond of the leaves and fruit. Watch carefully, use a net, and if necessary pray or spray.

Diseases can be reduced by buying certified plants, rotating strawberry plantings, and keeping the plants from growing too closely together. A spray program often helps. Watch out for leaf splotch, blotch, scorch, molds and rots, nematodes, viruses, and fungi. Contact your local extension service for advice about controlling diseases in your area.

Strawberries planted in a strawberry jar

Questions and Possible Answers

Why were there no berries?	Blossoms may have been injured by frost. You did not use a variety suited to your climate, soil conditions, and day length.
Why were there not as many berries as last year?	Production per plant is generally less each year. Plants crowding each other. Warmer weather.
Why was there an unusual number of weeds?	Turning ground over brings new seeds to surface. Seeds in the mulch.

Tomato

For production, satisfaction and color there is nothing in the home gardening line to match the tomato. Botanically, tomatoes are fruits. Technically, tomatoes are berries. But by law and custom they are vegetables.

Discovered with America, the tomato fascinated the Europeans. They took these new plants home, grew them in their flower gardens, and whispered behind their hands about them — anything that looks that good must be bad for you. Many people felt they were poisonous and that eating might kill you or cause you to succumb to a fate worse than death. George Washington Carver ate raw tomatoes in front of horrified people in the South to convince them that they could eat this vitamin-rich fruit and live to tell about it. In the North, tomatoes were carefully peeled and treated with plenty of vinegar, just to make sure.

Tomatoes can be divided into two main groups, determinate and indeterminate, according to growth habits. On the determinate tomato (bush tomato), when the end buds set fruit the plant stops growing at about three feet high. It seldom needs staking. On the indeterminate tomato (vine tomato), the end buds do not set fruit; the plant can grow almost indefinitely if not stopped by frost. Most of the varieties that are staked or caged are indeterminate tomatoes.

Tomatoes are also classified by the size and shape of their fruit (currant, cherry, plum, pear, etc.), and by their color (red, pink, orange, yellow, and cream).

Night temperatures are especially important for tomatoes. They will not set fruit when the night temperature is below 55°F or above 75°F. Nor will they set fruit in rainy or very humid weather. Sometimes

Caged tomato

Break off rim of peat pot

when the plants have plenty of water and fertilizer they have such a good time growing leaves and branches that they never get around to the business of producing tomatoes. In the last case, if you give the plant a shock by pruning it back and cutting down on water, it might start producing.

During the hot days of summer the leaves sometimes wilt because they use more water than their roots can supply. Plants growing in containers can exhaust the moisture available and the leaves will wilt. However, the plants will revive when they are watered. The leaves on some varieties tend to curl much more than others.

Although tomatoes are usually set out as transplants, it is sometimes easier and just as successful, to plant the seeds directly in the ground where the plants are to grow. This grows a plant with a strong taproot; it will produce fruit almost at the same time as the transplanted tomato. Often, even in the North, tomato plants will volunteer from seeds dropped the previous year, and when the soil warms up they sometimes grow so fast that they catch up with transplanted tomatoes by the middle of the summer. When you are short on garden space, grow tomatoes in a large pot or container. Dwarf tomatoes can be grown in one cubic foot of soil, and standard tomatoes can be grown in two to three cubic feet of soil. The small-fruited tomatoes do very well in hanging baskets, window boxes, or staked along with other vegetables in a planter.

Growing Tomatoes

1. **Best bed.** Tomatoes need a warm bed (55°F at night), in full sun. The soil should be free of lumps and debris, drain well and contain a lot of organic matter.
2. **Planting.** If you start with transplants, remember that the ideal transplant is stocky, not leggy, as wide as it is tall, and should have 4 or 5 leaves. Set the plants 18 to 48 inches apart, depending on variety and on whether you want to cage them, stake them, or let them sprawl.

Naturally sprawling tomatoes require less work. They are less likely to develop blossom end rot and they produce more fruit per plant. In dry areas sprawling on the ground protects the fruit from sunburn. They are harder to cultivate around and need mulching under the fruit to keep them clean and to reduce anthracnose and fruit rots.

Staked tomatoes give you cleaner fruit, less loss from soil rot, less loss from problems that occur in warm humid areas. They require less room for each individual plant, but they produce less fruit per plant, are much more susceptible to blossom end rot, and are more work. Use six-foot stakes (1x2 inches) or reinforcing rods. Put them in when transplanting. Or, you can plant giant sunflowers and use their stems as stakes.

Caged tomatoes require less work than staked tomatoes, but slightly more effort than doing nothing. Caged tomatoes conserve space, keep the fruit cleaner, and are easier to work around in small areas. Use 6x6-inch mesh concrete reinforcing wire. A five-foot width can be cut five feet long and bent into a cylinder by locking the ends. Remove the bottom strand and push the whole cage into the ground six inches deep around the transplanted tomato. If the area is windy or there is a lot of traffic, drive in a supporting stake.

Set plants out on a cloudy day or in the late afternoon. If the sun is very hot, protect the plants with hats made of newspapers. Disturb the roots as little as possible when transplanting. Plants should be gently slipped out of clay and plastic pots, and if they are planted in peat pots or cubes, make sure the tops of the containers are below the soil's surface or the peat will act like a wick and evaporate the soil moisture. If the plants are growing together in a flat, it is a good idea, if possible, to cut the plants apart several days before transplanting them.

Put the plant in the soil so that it is deeper than it was growing before, up to the first leaves. If the stem is very long or spindly, lay it in on a slant so that only the leaves are above soil level. The roots will grow from the submerged stem, making a sturdier plant.

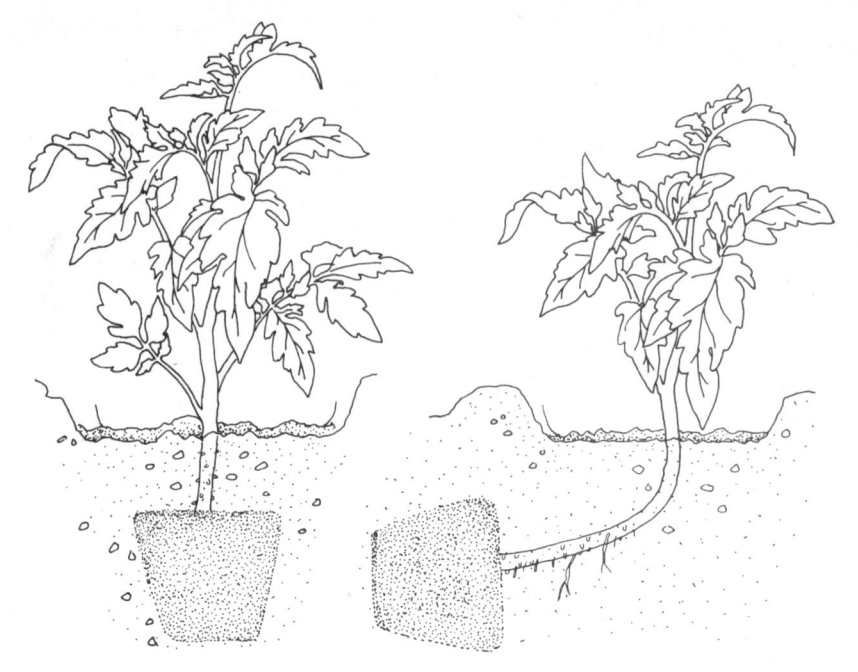

Long-stemmed tomatoes can be planted deeper or on a slant

3. Food and drink. Use a starter solution or mix a cup of 5-10-10 fertilizer in the soil where each plant will go. The tomato is a vegetable that responds to higher fertility with higher fruit production. Keep the soil evenly moist but not wet. Keep water off the leaves.

If you start with seeds, start five to six weeks before time to set the plants outside. Use good seed of a variety that will do well in your area. Contact your garden center or cooperative extension service for a list of tomatoes that thrive in your area. Use disease-free soil mix or vermiculite in containers (pots or trays) that drain well. The planting material must be thoroughly moist before the seeds are sown and it must not dry out. Keep the pots or trays covered with plastic. Tomato seeds germinate best between 75°F and 85°F. When the seedlings sprout, give them as much sun as possible, 12 hours if you can, and keep them growing at 70°F to 75°F during the day with a 10° drop at night.

If the seeds have been started in vermiculite, they should be transplanted into pots filled with a disease-free soil mix when the first true leaves show up. Lift the seedling carefully out of the vermiculite and set it in a small hole in the soil mix. Plant the seedlings so the leaves are about ½ inch from the top of the soil. This two-step method makes it easier to select the sturdiest plants and also avoids damping off, the killing of seedlings by disease organisms which exist in many soils.

Young plants should be gradually introduced to the great outdoors. They should be taken out on a tray for increasing amount of bright sun, and brought in at night to protect them from the cold night air.

4. Harvesting. The time when you harvest the tomatoes depends on their use. To make fried green tomatoes and green tomato pickles pick them green. Tomatoes to be sliced are picked firmer than those to be quartered or stuffed. Mature green tomatoes will ripen in one to three weeks at 70°F. Picked just before frost, green tomatoes can be kept at room temperature where they will ripen slowly. Wrapping is not necessary — in fact, wrapping makes it harder to watch the tomatoes. Since oxygen is important in coloring, wrapping fruit may slow the coloring process.

5. Pests and diseases. If cutworms are a problem, protect the plants with a styrofoam cup collar when they are first set out. The tomato fruitworm and tomato hornworm look fierce and will eat voraciously if you let them, but they can be picked off by hand. Aphids, white flies, and a number of transients can settle on your plants without doing too much damage.

Diseases can be reduced by planting resistant varieties, controlling weeds and insects, keeping the fruit off the ground, protecting the fruit from sunburn (sun scald). Use a mulch to keep the available soil moisture even and to control blossom end rot and cracking.

Questions and Possible Answers

Why did blossoms drop off?   Temperature too cold — night temperature below 55°F.
Temperature too hot — day temperature over 95°F, night temperature over 75°F.
Too much nitrogen fertilizer.
Too little nitrogen fertilizer.

Why did plants wilt?   Needs water.
Certain varieties react to stresses such as hot, dry weather, by wilting.
During hot weather (80°F-95°F), tomatoes may develop fusarium wilts.
During cool weather (under 75°F), tomatoes may develop verticillium wilt.

Why did bottoms of fruit rot?	Calcium deficiency. Drastic fluctuations in soil moisture.
Why did fruit crack?	Too much water. Over-fertilization. Fluctuation in soil moisture. Characteristic of the variety grown.
Why were there no tomatoes?	The location was too shady. Growing season too short. Weather was too cold (temperature below 55°F at night). Hot dry winds caused flowers to drop. Too much rain. Too much fertilizer.

Tree Fruit

Growing good tree fruit such as apples and pears takes discipline and dedication, and even dwarf trees take time and attention to produce blemish-free fruit. Training and pruning must be done each year and insect and disease control must be carried out systematically. The reason people grow fruit trees, in addition to their charisma and lovely spring bloom, is that many fruits that ship well don't taste as if they were worth shipping. Tree fruit must be planted in full sun in reasonably fertile, well-drained soil where they will not be competing with hungry trees or shrub roots or standing all afternoon in the shade of the garage.

Fruit fruit can be dwarfed by several methods. They can have their roots confined in a container. The Japanese sometimes grow bonsai apples *(ringo)* that fruit with as little as a pint of soil. Dwarf trees also can be produced by regular pruning when they are trained on a fence or a trellis (espalier), or by custom crafting them from a variety of dwarfing rootstocks and inter-stems. Much of the early research on custom crafted trees was done at the East Malling Research Station in Kent, England and much of the current American work is being done at Cornell and Michigan State Universities.

Since fruit trees need a lot of attention, dwarf trees offer a number of advantages. They are smaller and will fit in less space. It is not unusual to have a nice little tree which bears normal-size fruit in a five-gallon container. Dwarf trees are easy to prune and dust and

Dwarf apple tree grown like a bonsai

spray. They start to bear fruit earlier. Their roots do not travel as far and they do not cast as much shade as a larger tree. They are easier to train into espaliers and fans and they can also be trained flat against a wall. Trees grown against a wall have the double advantage of being protected and supported as well as being decorative and saving space.

The disadvantages are that they often need staking, the original pruning is important to give them a good start and they may need more maintenance to look well. They also cost more initially and may not live as long as a regular-sized tree.

Apples always say "orchard" and can be planted not only for their fruit but also as a tribute to Johnny Appleseed, and the other pioneers who settled our country. Pears are fussy. They don't do well in many parts of the country and are often troubled with fire blight which can spread to other plantings. Whichever fruit you decide to try, buy your tree from an established source and pay a bit more to get a quality tree. A strong healthy one- or two-year-old tree is much superior to an older tree. Older trees do not acclimate as well. Select varieties that are adapted to your location and find out if they are self-pollinating. Many fruit trees are not self-fertile and need a tree of another variety (or at least a branch grafted in the tree) to provide the pollen for setting the fruit. Others are biennial in their bearing habits. Contact your local extension service for the best varieties for your area.

Growing Tree Fruit

1. Best bed. Tree fruit need a cool bed. They are best planted when they are dormant in late fall or very early spring, but they will not survive where temperatures get below −20°F for any length of time. They do not do well where it never drops below freezing.

2. Planting. Trees can be planted in the fall and in the spring. When you plant in the fall, the plants have probably been in storage a shorter period of time, there may be a larger selection, the plant may settle in before a hard freeze and you may be in better condition and may have more time than you will have in the spring. When you plant in the spring, you avoid the risk that the plants were dug too early (before the leaves had dropped naturally), and you avoid the chal-

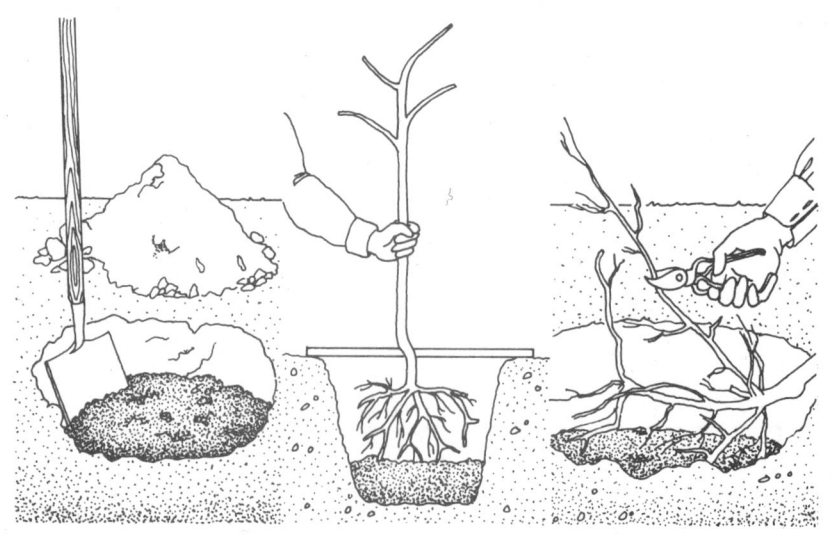

Hole 2" wider than roots   *Prune roots*

lenges of a harsh winter and hungry rodents. On the debit side, there may be a very wet spring, and you may have many other things to do.

Most fruit trees are purchased bare root, not in containers. After getting the tree, unwrap the roots to see that they are moist. If they are dry and brittle, scream and return the tree. Keep the tree cool, but above freezing, and moist until you are ready to plant. Before planting, the roots should be soaked a while or, if the tree looks dry, several hours. If they can not be planted right away, heel them in (lay them on the ground with their roots in a trench and covered with soil).

Plant trees that are going to be grown individually six to ten feet apart. Trees that are being trained against a fence or wall can be planted two feet apart or closer. Dig a hole two feet wider than the spread of the roots and deep enough to plant the tree at the same depth as it was growing in the nursery, without being cramped. Do not plant them with the graft below the soil surface or the tops will root and the tree will grow large. Keep the roots in a bucket of water until planting the tree in the ground. Just before planting check the roots and cut off with a sharp pruning shears any damaged roots or any roots over 18 inches long. Place the tree in the hole and spread out all the roots. Do not cheat and try to cram them in. Start filling the hole and tamp the soil down with your feet. When the hole has been filled to a few inches from the top, fill up the hole with water. The water will help settle the soil around the roots. Wrap the trunk up 18 inches or to the first branches to protect it from sun. Hardware cloth (¼ inch) can

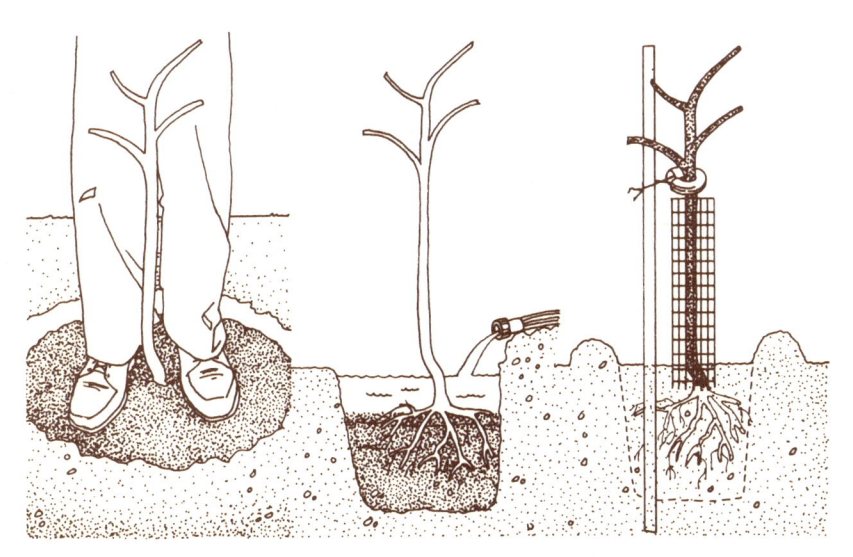

Tramp down the soil *Fill with water* *Protect with hardware cloth*

be cut into a sleeve to protect the tree from rodents and deer. It should extend from just below the first branches to three to four inches below the soil line. Mulch to protect the roots, keep down the weeds, and retain the soil moisture.

3. Food and drink. Give the trees a good drink when you first meet them but do not fertilize when planting. During the first growing season, encourage the root stem and leaf growth by keeping a three-foot area around the tree well cultivated. Watch that the soil does not dry out.

4. Special care. Pruning is important for a good start. Early pruning will give the tree the shape it will have the rest of its life. Annual pruning of a producing tree helps it grow more branches, giving it more and better distributed fruit. It will also keep the tree open to light and air and make it easier to spray. Trees tend to grow bigger, thicker on their protected side and the trees will become unbalanced if they are not trimmed.

Pruning tools include a sharp knife, strong hand shears and a pruning saw with small fine teeth. The saw is used for cutting branches more than a half inch thick. The tools should be kept sharp and clean; when using them, take care not to bruise or tear the bark. When using shears, have the cutting edge as close to the main branch as possible.

Pruning instructions are very simple when read and somewhat confusing when one is facing a tree with shears or a knife. The best thing to do is watch an experienced individual operate — as they say in bridge, "one peek is worth two finesses."

Pruning is done when the tree is dormant in winter, or in early spring before the growth starts. If the newly-planted tree is a single unbranched stem, cut to 30 inches ¼ inch above a bud. If the newly

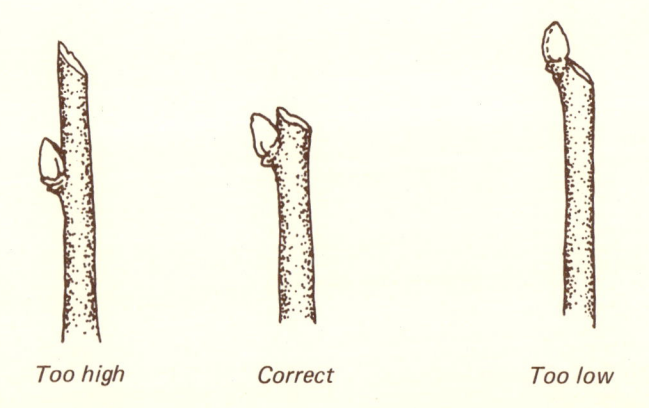

Too high   *Correct*   *Too low*

Proper pruning

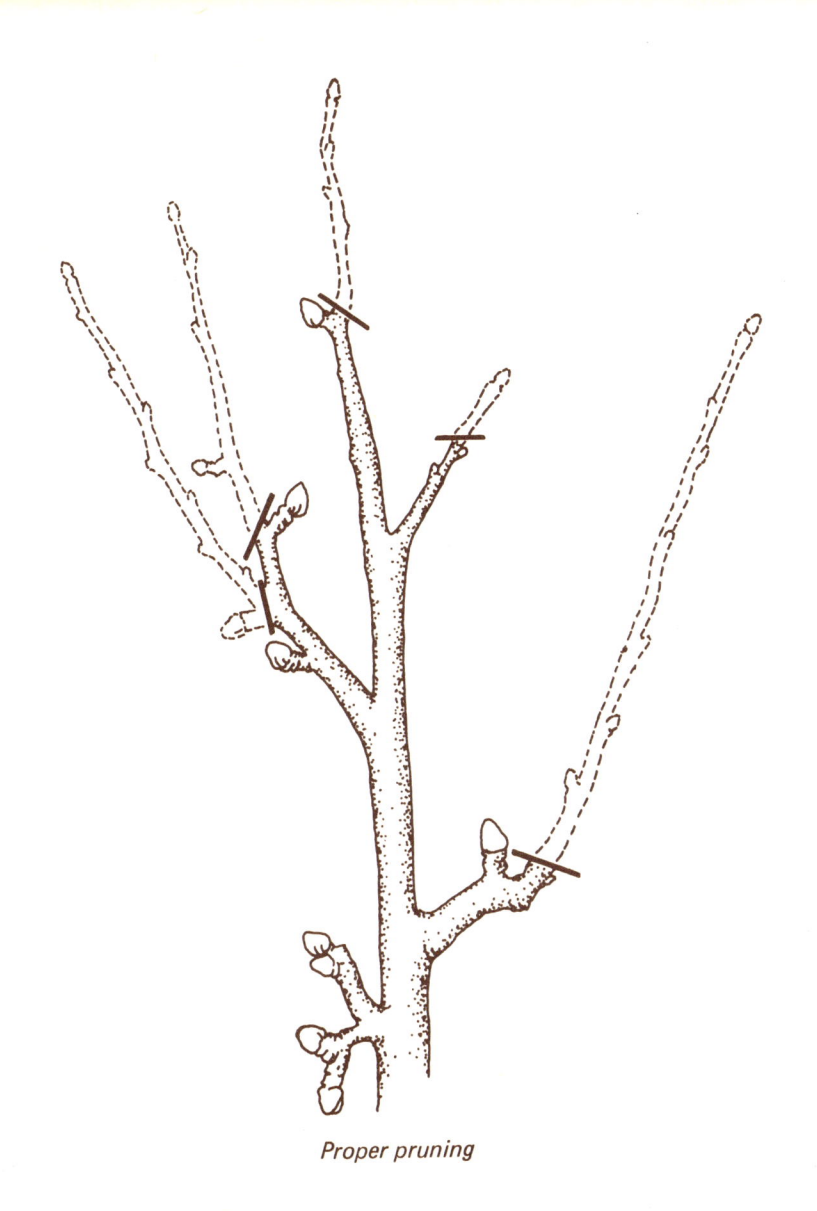

planted tree is branched, remove all branches except the central leader and one or two of the branches with the widest angle to the main stem. The next year, choose one or two more wide angle branches to keep and remove all the rest. This will give the tree its permanent skeleton. From then on, each year: thin out crowded branches, cut out water spouts, remove broken or crossing branches

Dwarf apple tree trained on espalier

and keep the tree from growing too tall or too wide. Cut it back to a main branch or you will find you have just encouraged more growth.

The same principles apply when growing trees on a trellis or a fence, except that the tree is kept flat and it sometimes does not branch where you want it to.

On heavily-bearing trees, the fruit should be thinned to every five or six inches or they will be small and possibly wormy. Stake the tree if it needs support.

5. Harvesting. When the fruit is ready it will separate easily from the branch when you lift it up and draw it away from the tree. Be careful not to knock off unready fruit or tear branches when removing the fruit.

6. Pests and diseases. Lots of things like fruit: aphids, maggots, codling moths, mites, scale, apple scab, black rot, powdery mildew, fire blight, rust and whatever else is peculiar to your area. For some people unblemished fruit is important. This requires a full spraying program since dusts are generally not as effective as sprays.

When spraying, always precisely follow the directions on the chemical's label. Because of changes in the federal, state and local regulations, check with your extension service for proper pest and disease sprays. For small areas, the trombone or slide type sprayers or the three- to five-gallon compressed air sprayers do a good job. The sprayers that attach to a garden hose do not always give an even distribution of spray because they do not always produce a uniform mix.

Here are some important points to remember about using sprays on trees.
- DO NOT APPLY INSECTICIDE WHEN THE TREES ARE IN FULL BLOOM. It will kill the bees that pollinate the flowers. Do not spray when it is windy or immediately before, during or after a rain.
- Prepare a fresh mixture each time you spray. A five- to eight-foot tree will take a half to one gallon of spray; an eight- to twelve-foot tree will take one to three gallons. It is a good idea to wear goggles and protective clothing when spraying any but the smallest trees.
- When spraying be sure to cover all parts of the tree and keep on

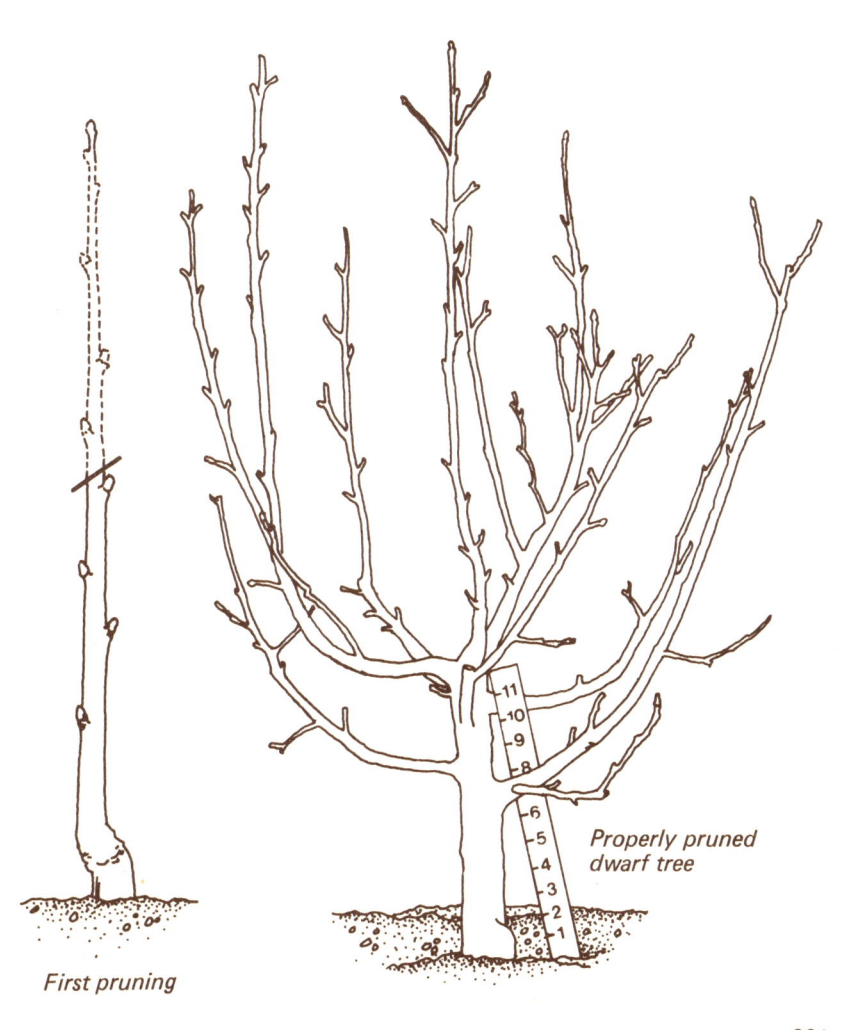

Properly pruned dwarf tree

First pruning

261

spraying until the spray starts to drip off the tree.
- For early spraying, start when the branch tips begin to show green and spray once or twice a week until the tree blooms.
- For spring spraying, start spraying when the petals fall. Spray once a week until summer.
- For summer spraying, continue spraying every ten days to two weeks until a week before harvest.

Collect all dropped fruit twice a week. The early dropped fruits are usually infested with something you do not want more of, and the later dropped fruits attract insects and diseases. The June fruit drop is usually due to the plant thinning some out so the rest will grow better. Each spring remove any dried fruit that is still hanging in the tree.

Questions and Possible Answers

Why didn't tree bear fruit?
 Tree too young.
 Only bears every other year.
 Flower buds damaged by extreme cold.
 No bees or other pollinating insects.
 Tree self-unfertile and needs pollen from another variety.
 Disease such as fire blight caused blossoms to drop.
 Fruit spurs were all pruned off.

Why was fruit scabby, wormy or spotted?
 Spray schedule not followed faithfully.
 No spraying.
 Spray did not cover all the leaves to the point of dripping off.
 Trees sprayed when wet or just before rain.

Why was fruit small?
 Differences in varieties.
 Fruit not thinned, too much competition.

Why did tree split?
 Poor shape due to improper pruning.
 Too heavy a fruit load.
 Winter injury.

Why did dwarf tree grow tall, regular size?
 Graft or bud was below the soil and the top rooted so it was no longer affected by the dwarfing roots or stock.
 Plant was incorrectly labeled at nursery.

262

Glossary of Gardening Terms

annual: A plant that grows only one season; a plant that produces its flowers and seeds and dies within one year.

aromatic: Fragrant.

biennial: A plant that usually grows one season and then flowers and fruits the second. If conditions are right, it can do it all in one season.

blanch: To bleach plants or plant parts by excluding light in order to enhance palatability of edible portions. Also, to dip vegetables in boiling water to remove skin or to prepare for freezing.

bolt, bolting: Vegetable such as lettuce or spinach going to seed and sending up a flower stalk thus ending its use as an eatable.

broadcast sowing: Seed scattered or thrown evenly on the soil, not being grown in rows or hills.

bulb: Modified underground stem and shoot surrounded by food-storing modified leaves.

burpless: A cucumber for those people with whom ordinary cucumbers do not agree.

clay: A soil made up mostly of particles that are less than 1/31,750 inch (1/200 mm) in diameter; clay, therefore, can hold more water and pack more closely than other soils.

companion cropping: Planting together two or more crops, each requiring a different length of time to mature. As short-season crops are harvested, the vacated space may be replanted with a new crop or left unplanted so that slower-maturing plants have more space in which to grow.

companion planting: See *companion cropping*. Also, the planting of pest-repellent plants with more vulnerable plants in the hope of preventing pest infestations.

complete fertilizer: Fertilizer containing nitrogen, phosphorus, and potassium.

compost: Decomposing organic matter.

cool crop: Crops that do not do well in hot weather such as members of the cabbage family, lettuce, and peas.

crop rotation: Practice of alternating crops grown in a given planting area to enhance soil fertility, to control pests and diseases, or to increase crop yields.

cross-pollination: Fertilization by transfer of pollen from one flower to another by wind, insects, or people.

cultivation: The scratching of the soil to frustrate weeds and to improve the penetration of water.

drainage: Condition that permits water to flow through the root areas of plants leaving air spaces behind. When drainage is poor, the water stands in the air spaces causing root rot.

drill: A straight trench in which seed is planted. A row.

early: A variety that matures faster (earlier) than others of its kind.

extension service: A cooperative federal, state, and county service whose purpose is to disseminate expert agricultural and home management information to the public at large through publications, correspondence, and other educational activities.

fertilizer: Organic or inorganic materials usually added to soil to provide plants with increased usable amounts of nitrogen, phosphate, potash and trace elements.

flat: A shallow, rectangular container used for starting seeds or cuttings.

forcing: Bringing a plant to maturity out of season. Speeding up the growth process by providing ideal conditions for growth.

forking: The dividing of a root, such as parsnip, upon meeting an obstruction in the soil. Turning over soil with a fork.

friable: Refers to soil that crumbles easily and is ready to work.

frost: Freezing condition in which temperature falls below the dew point and plants are covered with tiny ice particles.

fungicide: A material used to prevent, slow down, or kill fungi.

germination: The beginning of seed growth; the sprouting of seeds; the starting of plants from seeds.

growing season: The period between the last killing frost in spring and the first killing frost in fall.

guano: Undiluted bat or bird droppings; used as a high-nitrogen fertilizer.

half-hardy: Refers to plants unreliably resistant to cold.

harden, hardening: The process of gradually moving plants from a sheltered or indoor environment to an open or outdoor location. It aids their adjustment to new growing conditions and improves the odds of their survival.

hardy: Plants resistant to cold.

harvest: A crop; the picking or gathering of a crop; the season for gathering a crop.

heavy soil: Clay or other soil that is hard to work.

herbicide: Plant killer. Some are selective and can kill either narrow-leaved plants such as grasses and corn or broad-leaved plants such as most weeds and vegetables. Herbicides cannot distinguish between a vegetable and a weed.

hill: Several seeds planted in a circle rather than in a row or block. Eight to ten seeds planted in a hill will be thinned to three or four plants during the course of the growing season by people, pests, or other factors.

hilling: The covering of lower plant parts with a mound of soil for winter protection, for blanching, or for supporting weak stems.

humus: Decayed or partially decayed vegetation or recycled organic matter added to soil to improve water retention and to supply nutrients.

hybrid: A plant produced by dissimilar parent plants of the same kind in an effort to bring together the best features of each parent.

improved hybrid: Same as above, only better.

inoculant: Material dusted on pea and bean seeds to provide or increase amounts of nitrogen-fixing bacteria in the soil. Recommended whenever peas and bean crops are being sown in a given area for the first time.

insecticide: Insect killer. The most common insecticides kill in one of two ways: (1) *contact poisons* kill upon contact with some external portion of the insect's body; (2) *stomach poisons* kill by attacking internal organs after the insect has eaten from insecticide-treated plant.

intercropping (interplanting): Planting fast-growing eatables between slower-growing kinds. See also *companion cropping*.

irrigation: Watering by artificial means to provide soil moisture at a level sufficient for maximum plant growth.

loam: Soil. A good growing soil consisting of clay, silt, and sand particles spiked with a good supply of humus.

long-season crop: A crop that requires a long frost-free period to produce a harvest.

manure: Excretion from animals used as fertilizer or mulch.

mulch: Material placed around plants to cut down soil erosion, to conserve soil moisture, to insulate the soil, and to help keep weeds under control.

organic fertilizer: Complex fertilizer of plant or animal origin usually insoluble in water. Since it has to be broken down by microorganisms before nutrients are available to plants, nutrients are released slowly over a long period of time.

perennial: A plant that can grow more than one season, producing flowers and seeds each year.

pesticide: Pest killer. A general term for those materials used to control diseases (fungicides), insects (insecticides), weeds (herbicides) and other pests.

pH: p (potential of) H (hydrogen). The symbol used to express the acidity (sourness) or alkalinity (sweetness) of soils and other substances.

pollen: Dustlike material, usually yellow or white, produced on the male sexual organs of flowering plants.

pollination: Fertilization by transfer of pollen from the male flower or flower part to the female flower or flower part by wind, insects, or people.

propagation: Growing of plants from seeds, divisions, or cuttings.

ripe: Refers to mature eatables, ready to harvest and enjoy.

sand: A soil made of particles over 1/3,175 inch (1/20 mm) in diameter. These particles are irregular in shape and do not pack as tightly or hold as much water as soils with smaller particles.

seed: Embryo that forms a new plant.

self-fertile: Refers to plants whose flowers cannot be fertilized by their own pollen.

set: To plant, "set out"; to develop after pollination, "set fruit," "set seed"; seedling, cutting or bulb ready to plant, "onion set."

shoot: A sprout; new growth from seed or plant.

side-dressing: Fertilizer applied just beyond the roots of young plants, on either side of a row or in a circle around individual plants.

silt: A soil in which particles range in size between those of clay and sand. May act like either depending on the size of the particles.

sod: Grass-covered ground; a section of grass-covered soil held together by matted roots.

soil: The precious top layer of the earth's surface containing minerals, organic material, moisture and air. The substance that plants are grown in — even when it contains no real soil.

staking: Inserting a stake or pole in the ground next to a plant to which the plant will be attached for support as it grows.

stalk: A stem, usually the main stem.

starter solution: Liquid solution of fertilizer that is poured into the hole or around freshly transplanted plants to reduce shock and speed development.

stress: Environmental factors that affect plant health and cause less than perfect growth.

succession cropping: Replacing crops with the same or different crops at intervals to increase the harvest.

synthetic fertilizer: Fertilizer manufactured from organic and inorganic substances. Generally, synthetic fertilizers are water soluble and provide instantly available nutrients because they do not need soil organisms and special temperatures to make them available to plants. Usually they do nothing to improve the physical condition of soils. Synthetic fertilizers are always labeled to show percentage by weight of active ingredients.

tender: Refers to a plant that is hurt or killed by too much heat or cold (tender green bean). Not tough.

till: To prepare soil for growing crops.

tilth: The cultivation of soil; soil that has been prepared to support seed germination and healthy plant growth.

trace elements: Elements such as copper, iron, and manganese needed in minute amounts for plant growth and usually supplied by the soil.

true leaves: The real leaves; the leaves that appear after the first leaves.

tuber: A swollen storage root or stem, usually growing underground.

viable: Capable of living and growing.

vintage manure: Well-rotted manure.

Planting Dates for 68 Eatables

The detailed chart which fills the next several pages gives the planting dates for all 68 of the eatables discussed in this book. All these columns of numbers may seem overwhelming. But take heart. You need be concerned with only two columns, one column in the "Spring Planting Dates" and one column in the "Fall Planting Dates." In the section labeled "Spring Planting Dates" the date in heavy type at the top of each column stands for an average frost-free date; in the section labeled "Fall Planting Dates" the date at the top stands for an average first frost date. The date ranges which follow in each column suggest when different crops can be planted.

To use this chart, first get the average dates of the last spring freeze and the first fall freeze. This information is available at your public library or local weather bureau. Then look for your dates on the chart. For example, if the average date of the last spring freeze in your area is April 10, you will find the column headed April 10. Then look down that column to find the range of planting dates for each of the eatables you want to grow. It is quite possible, however, that your spring frost-free date will not exactly match one of the dates at the top of the chart, but rather fall between two dates. If this happens, find the two dates immediately before and after your local date and then adjust the range of planting dates in those two columns to your own situation. Go through the same process with the "Fall Planting Dates."

To make best use of this chart, jot down the eatables you are interested in growing. Then note the range of planting dates for each of them as shown in the appropriate columns. What you will have then is an overall picture of when to plant your garden. If you like to do all your planting at one time, look for overlaps in the planting date ranges for your eatables. These overlaps may reveal a block of time during which you can plant most of your garden. Though the middle date in each range is the safest, most eatables can be put out a little early or a little late. Just remember that the closer you get to the earliest date in the spring and the latest date in the fall, the more of a gamble you run.

Spring Planting Dates

	Jan. 30	Feb. 8	Feb. 18	Feb. 28	Mar. 10	Mar. 20	Mar. 30
Artichoke, Globe	2/15-3/15	2/20-4/1	3/1-4/15	3/15-4/15	3/20-4/15	4/1-5/1	4/10-5/15
Artichoke, Jerusalem	1/1-2/15	1/1-2/15	1/1-3/1	1/15-3/1	1/15-3/15	2/1-3/15	2/10-3/20
Asparagus (transplants)	—	—	—	—	1/1-3/1	2/1-3/10	2/15-3/20
Basil	2/15-4/1	2/15-4/15	3/1-6/1	3/10-6/1	3/20-6/1	4/1-6/15	4/10-6/15
Bean, Four-Angled	2/1-4/15	2/10-5/1	3/1-5/1	3/15-6/1	3/20-6/1	4/1-6/15	4/15-6/20
Bean, Lima	2/1-4/15	2/10-5/1	3/1-5/1	3/15-6/1	3/20-6/1	4/1-6/15	4/15-6/20
Bean, Mung	2/1-4/1	2/1-5/1	3/1-5/1	3/10-5/15	3/15-5/15	3/15-5/25	4/1-6/1
Bean, Snap	1/1-4/1	2/1-5/1	3/1-5/1	3/10-5/15	3/15-5/15	3/15-5/25	4/1-6/1
Beet	1/1-3/15	1/10-3/15	1/20-4/1	2/1-4/15	2/15-5/1	2/15-5/15	3/1-6/1
Broad Bean	1/1-2/15	1/1-2/15	1/1-3/1	1/15-3/1	1/15-3/15	2/1-3/10	2/10-3/20
Broccoli (transplants)	1/1-1/30	1/1-1/30	1/15-2/15	2/1-3/1	2/15-3/15	2/15-3/15	3/1-3/20
Brussels Sprout (transplants)	1/1-1/30	1/1-1/30	1/15-2/15	2/1-3/1	2/15-3/15	2/15-3/15	3/1-3/20
Cabbage (transplants)	1/1-1/15	1/1-2/10	1/1-2/25	1/15-2/25	1/25-3/1	2/1-3/1	2/15-3/10
Cabbage, Chinese	—	Plant for Fall Crop Only	—	—	—	—	—
Carrot	1/1-3/1	1/1-3/1	1/15-3/15	1/15-3/1	2/10-3/15	2/15-3/20	3/1-4/10
Cauliflower (transplants)	1/1-2/1	1/1-2/1	1/10-2/10	1/20-2/20	2/1-3/1	2/10-3/10	2/20-3/20
Celeriac	1/1-2/1	1/1-2/10	1/20-2/20	2/1-3/1	2/20-3/20	3/1-4/1	3/15-4/15
Celery	1/1-2/1	1/1-2/10	1/20-2/20	2/1-3/1	2/20-3/20	3/1-4/1	3/15-4/15
Chard	1/1-4/1	1/10-4/1	1/20-4/15	2/1-4/15	2/15-4/15	2/20-5/15	3/1-5/25
Chayote	2/15-3/15	2/15-4/1	2/20-4/15	3/1-4/15	3/15-4/15	4/1-5/1	4/10-5/15
Chicory	—	—	—	—	6/1-7/1	6/1-7/1	6/1-7/1
Chive	1/1-2/1	1/1-2/1	1/1-2/1	1/15-2/15	2/1-3/1	2/10-3/10	2/15-3/15
Collard (transplants)	1/1-2/15	1/1-2/15	1/1-3/15	1/15-3/15	2/1-4/1	2/15-5/1	3/1-6/1
Corn	2/1-3/15	2/10-4/1	2/20-4/15	3/1-4/15	3/10-4/15	3/15-5/1	3/25-5/15

	Apr. 10	Apr. 20	Apr. 30	May 10	May 20	May 30	June 10
Artichoke, Globe	4/20-6/1	5/1-6/15	5/15-6/15	5/20-6/15	6/1-6/15	—	—
Artichoke, Jerusalem	2/20-3/20	3/10-4/10	3/20-5/1	4/1-5/15	4/15-6/1	5/1-6/15	5/10-6/15
Asparagus (transplants)	3/10-4/10	3/15-4/15	3/20-4/15	4/10-4/30	4/20-5/15	5/1-6/1	5/15-6/1
Basil	4/20-6/15	5/1-6/1	5/10-6/1	5/20-6/10	6/1-6/20	6/10-6/30	6/20-6/30
Bean, Four-Angled	4/15-6/30	5/1-6/20	5/15-6/15	5/25-6/15	—	—	—
Bean, Lima	4/15-6/30	5/1-6/20	5/15-6/15	5/25-6/15	—	—	—
Bean, Mung	4/10-6/30	4/25-6/30	5/10-6/30	5/10-6/30	5/15-6/30	5/25-6/15	—
Bean, Snap	4/10-6/30	4/25-6/30	5/10-6/30	5/10-6/30	5/15-6/30	5/25-6/15	—
Beet	3/10-6/1	3/20-6/1	4/1-6/15	4/15-6/15	4/25-6/15	5/1-6/15	5/15-6/15
Broad Bean	2/10-3/20	3/10-4/10	3/20-5/1	4/1-5/15	4/15-6/1	5/1-6/15	5/10-6/15
Broccoli (transplants)	3/15-4/15	3/25-4/20	4/1-4/30	4/15-6/1	5/1-6/15	5/10-6/10	5/20-6/10
Brussels Sprout (transplants)	3/15-4/15	3/25-4/20	4/1-4/30	4/1-5/15	5/1-6/15	5/10-6/10	5/20-6/10
Cabbage (transplants)	3/1-4/1	3/10-4/1	3/15-4/10	4/1-5/15	5/1-6/15	5/10-6/15	5/20-6/1
Cabbage, Chinese	—	Plant for Fall Crop Only		—	—	—	—
Carrot	3/10-4/20	4/1-5/15	4/10-6/1	4/20-6/15	5/1-6/1	5/10-6/1	5/20-6/1
Cauliflower (transplants)	3/1-3/20	3/15-4/20	4/10-5/10	4/15-5/15	5/10-6/15	5/20-6/15	6/1-6/15
Celeriac	4/1-4/20	4/10-5/1	4/15-5/1	4/20-6/15	5/10-6/15	5/20-6/15	6/1-6/15
Celery (transplants)	4/1-4/20	4/10-5/1	4/15-5/1	4/20-6/15	5/10-6/15	5/20-6/15	6/1-6/15
Chard	3/15-6/15	4/1-6/15	4/15-6/15	4/20-6/15	5/10-6/15	5/20-6/15	6/1-6/15
Chayote	4/20-6/1	5/1-6/15	5/15-6/15	5/20-6/15	6/1-6/15	—	—
Chicory	6/10-7/1	6/15-7/1	6/15-7/1	6/1-6/20	6/1-6/15	6/1-6/15	6/1-6/15
Chive	3/1-4/1	3/10-4/10	3/20-4/20	4/1-5/1	4/15-5/15	5/1-6/1	5/15-6/1
Collard (transplants)	3/1-6/1	3/10-6/1	4/1-6/1	4/15-6/1	5/1-6/1	5/10-6/1	5/20-6/1
Corn	4/10-6/1	4/25-6/15	5/10-6/15	5/10-6/15	5/15-6/15	5/20-6/15	—

Spring Planting Dates

	Jan. 30	Feb. 8	Feb. 18	Feb. 28	Mar. 10	Mar. 20	Mar. 30
Cress	1/1-2/1	1/1-2/15	1/15-2/15	2/1-3/1	2/10-3/15	2/20-3/15	3/1-4/1
Cucumber	2/15-3/15	2/15-4/1	2/15-4/15	3/1-4/15	3/15-4/15	4/1-5/1	4/10-5/15
Dill	1/1-1/30	1/1-1/30	1/1-1/30	1/15-3/1	2/1-3/10	2/15-3/15	3/1-4/1
Eggplant (transplants)	2/1-3/1	2/10-3/15	2/20-4/1	3/10-4/15	3/15-4/15	4/1-5/1	4/15-5/15
Endive	1/1-3/1	1/1-3/1	1/15-3/1	2/1-3/1	2/15-3/15	3/1-4/1	3/10-4/10
Fennel	1/1-3/1	1/1-3/1	1/15-3/1	2/1-3/1	2/15-3/15	3/1-4/1	3/10-4/10
Fruit Trees	—	—	—	—	1/1-3/1	2/1-3/10	2/15-3/20
Garlic	—	—	Plant in Fall	—	—	2/1-3/1	2/10-3/10
Grape	—	—	—	—	1/1-3/1	2/1-3/10	2/15-3/20
Horseradish	—	—	Plant in Fall	—	—	—	3/1-4/1
Kale	1/1-2/1	1/10-2/1	1/20-2/10	2/1-2/20	2/10-3/1	2/20-3/10	3/1-3/20
Kohlrabi	1/1-2/1	1/10-2/1	1/20-2/10	2/1-2/20	2/10-3/1	2/20-3/10	3/1-4/1
Leek	1/1-2/1	1/1-2/1	1/1-2/15	1/15-2/15	1/25-3/1	2/1-3/1	2/15-3/15
Lettuce, Head (transplants)	1/1-2/1	1/1-2/1	1/1-2/1	1/15-2/15	2/1-2/20	2/1-3/1	3/1-3/20
Lettuce, Leaf	1/1-2/1	1/1-2/1	1/1-3/15	1/1-3/15	1/15-4/1	2/1-4/1	2/15-4/15
Marjoram	2/15-4/1	2/15-4/15	3/1-6/1	3/10-6/1	3/20-6/1	4/1-6/15	4/10-6/15
Muskmelon	2/15-3/15	2/15-4/1	3/15-4/15	3/15-4/15	3/15-4/15	4/1-5/1	4/10-5/15
Mustard	1/1-3/1	1/1-3/1	1/1-3/15	2/1-3/15	2/10-3/15	2/20-4/1	3/1-4/15
Okra	2/15-4/15	2/15-4/15	3/10-6/1	3/15-6/1	3/20-6/1	4/1-6/15	4/10-6/15
Onion (transplants)	1/1-1/15	1/1-1/15	1/1-2/1	1/1-2/1	1/15-2/15	2/10-3/10	2/15-3/15
Onion (seed)	1/1-1/15	1/1-1/15	1/1-2/15	1/1-2/15	2/1-3/1	2/20-3/10	2/20-3/15
Onion (sets)	1/1-1/15	1/1-1/15	1/1-3/1	1/1-3/1	1/15-3/10	2/1-3/20	2/15-3/20
Parsley	1/1-1/30	1/1-1/30	1/1-1/30	1/15-3/1	2/1-3/10	2/15-3/15	3/1-4/1
Parsnip	—	—	1/1-2/1	1/15-2/15	1/15-3/1	2/15-3/15	3/1-4/1

	Apr. 10	Apr. 20	Apr. 30	May 10	May 20	May 30	June 10
Cress	3/10-4/15	3/20-5/1	4/10-5/15	4/20-5/20	5/1-6/1	5/15-6/1	5/15-6/15
Cucumber	4/20-6/1	5/1-6/15	5/15-6/15	5/20-6/15	6/1-6/15	—	—
Dill	3/10-4/10	3/20-4/20	4/1-5/1	4/15-5/15	5/1-5/20	5/10-5/30	5/20-6/10
Eggplant (transplants)	5/1-6/1	5/10-6/1	5/15-6/10	5/20-6/15	6/1-6/15	—	—
Endive	3/15-4/15	3/25-4/15	4/1-5/1	4/15-5/15	5/1-5/30	5/1-5/30	5/1-5/30
Fennel	3/15-4/15	3/25-4/15	4/1-5/1	4/15-5/15	5/1-5/30	5/1-5/30	5/1-5/30
Fruit Trees	3/10-4/1	3/15-4/15	3/20-4/15	4/10-4/30	4/20-5/15	5/1-5/20	5/15-6/1
Garlic	2/20-3/20	3/10-4/1	3/15-4/15	4/1-5/1	4/15-5/15	5/1-5/30	5/1-5/30
Grape	3/10-4/1	3/15-4/15	3/20-4/15	—	—	—	—
Horseradish	3/10-4/10	3/20-4/20	4/1-4/30	4/15-5/15	4/20-5/20	5/1-5/30	5/1-5/30
Kale	3/10-4/1	3/20-4/10	4/1-4/20	4/10-5/1	4/20-5/10	5/1-5/30	5/1-5/30
Kohlrabi	3/10-4/10	3/20-5/1	4/1-5/10	4/10-5/15	4/20-5/20	5/1-5/30	5/1-5/30
Leek	3/1-4/1	3/15-4/15	4/1-5/1	4/15-5/15	5/1-5/15	5/1-5/15	5/1-5/15
Lettuce, Head (transplants)	3/10-4/1	3/20-4/15	4/1-5/1	4/15-5/15	5/1-6/30	5/10-6/30	5/20-6/30
Lettuce, Leaf	3/15-5/15	3/20-5/15	4/1-6/1	4/15-6/15	5/1-6/30	5/10-6/30	5/20-6/30
Marjoram	4/20-6/15	5/1-6/15	5/10-6/15	5/20-6/15	6/1-6/20	6/10-6/30	6/20-6/30
Muskmelon	4/20-6/1	5/1-6/15	5/15-6/15	5/20-6/15	6/1-6/15	—	—
Mustard	3/10-4/20	3/20-5/1	4/1-5/10	4/15-6/1	5/1-6/30	5/10-6/30	5/20-6/30
Okra	4/20-6/15	4/20-6/1	5/10-6/1	5/20-6/10	6/1-6/20	—	—
Onion (transplants)	3/1-4/1	3/15-5/1	4/1-5/1	4/10-5/1	4/20-5/15	5/1-5/30	5/10-6/10
Onion (seeds)	3/1-4/1	3/15-4/10	3/15-4/15	4/1-5/1	4/20-5/15	5/1-5/30	5/10-6/10
Onion (sets)	3/1-4/1	3/10-4/1	3/10-4/10	4/10-5/1	4/20-5/15	5/1-5/30	5/10-6/10
Parsley	3/10-4/10	3/20-4/20	4/1-5/1	4/15-5/15	5/1-5/20	5/10-5/30	5/20-6/10
Parsnip	3/10-4/10	3/20-4/20	4/1-5/1	4/15-5/15	5/1-5/20	5/10-5/30	5/20-6/10

Spring Planting Dates

	Jan. 30	Feb. 8	Feb. 18	Feb. 28	Mar. 10	Mar. 20	Mar. 30
Pea, Black-eye	2/15-5/1	2/15-5/15	3/1-6/15	3/10-6/20	3/15-7/1	4/1-7/1	4/15-7/1
Pea, Sweet	1/1-2/15	1/1-2/15	1/1-3/1	1/15-3/1	1/15-3/15	2/1-3/15	2/10-3/20
Peanut	2/1-4/1	2/1-5/1	3/1-5/1	3/10-5/15	3/15-5/15	3/15-5/25	4/1-6/1
Pepper (transplants)	2/1-4/1	2/15-4/15	3/1-5/1	3/15-5/1	4/1-6/1	4/10-6/1	4/15-6/1
Potato, Sweet (transplants)	2/15-5/15	3/1-5/15	3/20-6/1	3/20-6/1	4/1-6/1	4/10-6/1	4/20-6/1
Potato, White	1/1-2/15	1/1-2/15	1/15-3/1	1/15-3/1	2/1-3/1	2/10-3/15	2/20-3/20
Pumpkin	2/15-3/15	2/15-4/1	2/20-4/15	3/1-4/15	3/15-4/15	4/1-5/1	4/10-5/15
Radish	1/1-4/1	1/1-4/1	1/1-4/1	1/1-4/1	1/1-4/15	1/20-5/1	2/15-5/1
Rhubarb	—	—	—	—	—	—	—
Rosemary	1/1-1/30	1/1-1/30	1/1-1/30	1/15-3/1	2/1-3/10	2/15-3/15	3/1-4/1
Rutabaga	—	—	—	1/1-2/1	1/15-2/15	1/15-3/1	2/1-3/1
Sage	1/1-1/30	1/1-1/30	1/1-1/30	1/15-3/1	2/1-3/10	2/15-3/15	3/1-4/1
Salsify	—	—	1/1-2/1	1/15-2/15	1/15-3/1	2/15-3/15	3/1-4/1
Soybean	3/1-6/30	3/1-6/30	3/10-6/30	3/20-6/30	4/10-6/30	4/10-6/30	4/20-6/30
Spinach	1/1-2/15	1/1-2/15	1/1-3/1	1/1-3/1	1/15-3/10	1/15-3/15	2/1-3/20
Spinach, New Zealand	2/1-4/15	2/15-4/15	3/1-4/15	3/15-5/15	3/20-5/15	4/1-5/15	4/10-6/1
Squash, Summer	2/1-4/15	2/15-4/15	3/1-4/15	3/15-5/15	3/15-5/15	4/1-5/15	4/10-6/1
Squash, Winter	2/15-3/15	2/15-4/1	2/20-4/15	3/1-4/15	3/15-4/15	4/1-5/1	4/10-6/1
Strawberry (transplants)	Plant in Fall	—	—	—	2/1-3/1	2/10-3/10	
Tarragon	1/1-1/30	1/1-1/30	1/1-1/30	1/15-3/1	2/1-3/10	2/15-3/15	3/1-4/1
Thyme	1/1-1/30	1/1-1/30	1/1-1/30	1/15-3/1	2/1-2/10	2/15-3/15	3/1-4/1
Tomato (transplants)	2/1-4/1	2/20-4/10	3/1-4/20	3/10-5/1	3/20-5/10	4/1-5/20	4/10-6/1
Turnip	1/1-3/1	1/1-3/1	1/1-3/1	1/20-3/1	2/1-3/1	2/10-3/10	2/20-3/20
Watermelon	2/15-3/15	2/15-4/1	2/20-4/15	3/1-4/15	3/15-4/15	3/25-5/1	4/10-5/15

	Apr. 10	Apr. 20	Apr. 30	May 10	May 20	May 30	June 10
Pea, Black-Eyed	5/1-7/1	5/10-6/15	5/15-6/1	—	—	—	—
Pea, Sweet	2/20-3/20	3/10-4/10	3/20-5/1	4/1-5/15	4/15-6/1	5/1-6/15	5/10-6/15
Peanut	4/10-6/15	4/25-6/10	5/10-5/30	—	—	—	—
Pepper (transplants)	5/1-6/1	5/1-6/1	5/15-6/10	5/20-6/10	5/25-6/15	6/1-6/15	—
Potato, Sweet (transplants)	5/1-6/1	5/10-6/10	5/20-6/10	—	—	—	—
Potato, White	3/10-4/1	3/15-4/10	3/20-5/10	4/1-6/1	4/15-6/15	5/1-6/15	5/15-6/15
Pumpkin	4/20-6/1	5/1-6/15	5/15-6/15	5/10-6/15	6/1-6/15	—	—
Radish	3/1-5/1	3/10-5/10	3/20-5/10	4/1-6/1	4/15-6/15	5/1-6/15	5/15-6/15
Rhubarb	3/1-4/1	3/10-4/10	3/20-4/15	4/1-5/1	4/15-5/10	5/1-5/20	5/15-6/15
Rosemary	3/10-4/10	3/20-4/20	4/1-5/1	4/15-5/15	5/1-5/20	5/10-5/30	5/20-6/15
Rutabaga	—	—	5/1-6/1	5/1-6/1	5/1-5/20	5/10-5/20	5/20-5/30
Sage	3/10-4/10	3/20-4/20	4/1-5/1	4/15-5/15	5/1-5/20	5/10-5/30	5/20-6/10
Salsify	3/10-4/10	3/20-4/20	4/1-5/1	4/15-5/15	5/1-5/20	5/10-5/30	5/20-6/10
Soybean	5/1-6/30	5/10-6/20	5/15-6/15	5/25-6/10	—	—	—
Spinach	2/1-4/1	3/1-4/15	3/20-4/20	4/1-6/15	4/10-6/15	4/20-6/15	5/1-6/15
Spinach, New Zealand	4/20-6/1	5/1-6/15	5/1-6/15	5/10-6/15	5/20-6/15	6/1-6/15	—
Squash, Summer	4/20-6/1	5/1-6/15	5/1-6/15	5/10-6/15	5/20-6/15	6/1-6/20	6/10-6/20
Squash, Winter	4/20-6/1	5/1-6/15	5/15-6/15	5/20-6/15	6/1-6/15	—	—
Strawberry (transplants)	3/1-4/1	3/10-4/10	3/20-4/20	4/1-5/1	4/15-5/15	5/1-6/1	5/15-6/1
Tarragon	3/10-4/10	3/20-4/20	4/1-5/1	4/15-5/15	5/1-5/20	5/10-5/30	5/20-6/10
Thyme	3/10-4/10	3/20-4/20	4/1-5/1	4/15-5/15	5/1-5/20	5/10-5/30	5/20-6/10
Tomato (transplants)	4/20-6/1	5/5-6/10	5/10-6/15	5/15-6/15	5/25-6/15	6/5-6/20	6/15-6/30
Turnip	3/1-4/1	3/10-4/10	3/20-5/1	4/1-6/1	4/15-6/1	5/1-6/15	5/15-6/15
Watermelon	4/20-6/1	5/1-6/15	5/15-6/15	5/20-6/15	6/1-6/15	—	—

Fall Planting Dates

Aug. 30	Sept. 10	Sept. 20	Sept. 30	Oct. 10	Oct. 20
Artichoke, Globe					
Plant in Spring	—	—	—	—	—
Artichoke, Jerusalem					
Plant in Spring	—	—	—	—	—
Asparagus					
—	—	—	—	10/20-11/15	11/1-12/15
Basil					
5/20-6/1	6/1-6/10	6/10-6/20	6/10-6/30	6/10-7/15	6/10-8/1
Bean, Four-Angled					
—	—	—	6/1-6/15	6/1-6/15	6/15-6/30
Bean, Lima					
—	—	—	6/1-6/15	6/1-6/15	6/15-6/30
Bean, Mung					
—	5/15-6/15	6/1-7/1	6/1-7/10	6/15-7/20	7/1-8/1
Bean, Snap					
—	5/15-6/15	6/1-7/1	6/1-7/10	6/15-7/20	7/1-8/1
Beet					
5/15-6/15	5/15-6/15	6/1-7/1	6/1-7/10	6/15-7/25	7/1-8/5
Broad Bean					
5/10-6/15	5/1-7/1	6/1-7/15	6/1-8/1	Usually Spring Planted Only	
Broccoli					
5/1-6/1	5/1-6/1	5/1-6/15	6/1-7/10	6/15-7/15	7/1-8/1
Brussels Sprout					
5/1-6/1	5/1-6/1	5/1-6/15	6/1-6/30	6/15-7/15	7/1-8/1
Cabbage (transplants)					
5/1-6/1	5/1-6/1	5/1-6/15	6/1-7/10	6/1-7/15	7/1-8/1
Cabbage, Chinese					
5/15-6/15	5/15-6/15	6/1-7/1	6/1-7/15	6/15-8/1	7/15-8/15
Carrot					
5/15-6/15	5/15-6/15	6/1-7/1	6/1-7/15	6/1-7/25	6/15-8/1
Cauliflower (transplants)					
5/1-6/1	5/1-7/1	5/1-7/1	5/10-7/15	6/1-7/25	7/1-8/15
Celeriac					
5/1-6/1	5/15-6/15	5/15-7/1	6/1-7/15	6/1-7/15	6/1-8/1
Celery (transplants)					
5/1-6/1	5/15-6/15	5/15-7/1	6/1-7/15	6/1-7/15	6/1-8/1
Chard					
5/15-6/15	5/15-7/1	6/1-7/1	6/1-7/15	6/1-7/20	6/1-8/1
Chayote					
Plant in Spring	—	—	—	—	—
Chicory					
5/15-6/15	5/15-6/15	5/15-6/15	6/1-7/1	6/1-7/1	6/15-7/15
Chive					
5/10-6/10	5/15-6/15	5/15-6/15	Plant in Spring	—	—
Collard (transplants)					
5/15-6/15	5/15-6/15	5/15-6/15	6/15-7/15	7/1-8/1	7/15-8/15
Corn					
—	—	6/1-7/1	6/1-7/1	6/1-7/10	6/1-7/20

	Oct. 30	Nov. 10	Nov. 20	Nov. 30	Dec. 10	Dec. 20
Artichoke, Globe						
Plant in Spring	—	—	—	—	—	
Artichoke, Jerusalem						
Plant in Spring	—	—	—	—	—	
Asparagus						
	11/15-1/1	12/1-1/1	—	—	—	—
Basil						
	6/1-8/10	6/1-8/20	6/1-9/10	6/1-9/20	8/1-10/1	8/1-10/1
Bean, Four-Angled						
	7/1-8/1	7/1-8/15	7/15-9/1	8/1-9/15	9/1-9/30	9/1-10/1
Bean, Lima						
	7/1-8/1	7/1-8/15	7/15-9/1	8/1-9/15	9/1-9/30	9/1-10/1
Bean, Mung						
	7/1-8/15	7/1-9/1	7/1-9/10	8/15-9/20	9/1-9/30	9/1-11/1
Bean, Snap						
	7/1-8/15	7/1-9/1	7/1-9/10	8/15-9/20	9/1-9/30	9/1-11/1
Beet						
	8/1-9/1	8/1-10/1	9/1-12/1	9/1-12/15	9/1-12/31	9/1-12/31
Broad Bean						
	8/1-9/15	9/1-11/1	10/1-12/1	10/1-12/31	10/1-12/31	10/1-12/31
Broccoli						
	7/1-8/15	8/1-9/1	8/1-9/15	8/1-10/1	8/1-11/1	9/1-12/31
Brussels Sprout						
	7/1-8/15	8/1-9/1	8/1-9/15	8/1-10/1	8/1-11/1	9/1-12/31
Cabbage (transplants)						
	8/1-9/1	9/1-9/15	9/1-12/1	9/1-12/31	9/1-12/31	9/1-12/31
Cabbage, Chinese						
	8/1-9/1	8/15-10/1	9/1-10/15	9/1-11/1	9/1-11/15	9/1-12/1
Carrot						
	7/1-8/15	8/1-9/1	9/1-11/1	9/15-12/1	9/15-12/1	9/15-12/1
Cauliflower (transplants)						
	7/15-8/15	8/1-9/1	8/1-9/15	8/15-10/10	9/1-10/20	9/15-11/1
Celeriac						
	6/15-8/15	7/1-8/15	7/15-9/1	8/1-12/1	9/1-12/31	10/1-12/31
Celery (transplants)						
	6/15-8/15	7/1-8/15	7/15-9/1	8/1-12/1	9/1-12/31	10/1-12/31
Chard						
	6/1-9/10	6/1-9/15	6/1-10/1	6/1-11/1	6/1-12/1	6/1-12/1
Chayote						
Plant in Spring	—	—	—	—	—	
Chicory						
	7/1-8/10	7/10-8/20	7/20-9/1	8/15-9/30	8/15-10/15	8/15-10/15
Chive						
Plant in Spring	—	11/1-12/31	11/1-12/31	11/1-12/31	11/1-12/31	
Collard (transplants)						
	8/1-9/15	8/15-10/1	8/25-11/1	9/1-12/1	9/1-12/31	9/1-12/31
Corn						
	6/1-8/1	6/1-8/15	6/1-9/1	—	—	—

277

Fall Planting Dates

	Aug. 30	Sept. 10	Sept. 20	Sept. 30	Oct. 10	Oct. 20
Cress	5/15-6/15	5/15-7/1	6/16-8/1	7/15-9/1	8/15-9/15	9/1-10/15
Cucumber	—	—	6/1-6/15	6/1-7/1	6/1-7/1	6/1-7/15
Dill	5/15-6/15	5/15-6/15	6/1-7/1	6/1-7/15	6/15-8/1	7/15-8/15
Eggplant	—	—	—	5/20-6/10	5/15-6/15	6/1-7/1
Endive	6/1-7/1	6/1-7/1	6/15-7/15	6/15-8/1	7/1-8/15	7/15-8/15
Fennel	5/15-6/15	5/15-7/15	6/1-7/15	6/15-7/15	6/15-7/15	6/15-8/1
Fruit Trees	—	—	—	—	10/20-11/15	11/1-12/15
Garlic	Usually Planted in Spring		—	—	Plant in Spring	—
Grape	—	—	—	—	10/20-11/15	11/1-12/15
Horseradish	Usually Planted in Spring		—	—	Plant in Spring	—
Kale	5/15-6/15	5/15-6/15	6/1-7/1	6/15-7/15	7/1-8/1	7/15-8/15
Kohlrabi	5/15-6/15	6/1-7/1	6/1-7/15	6/15-7/15	7/1-8/1	7/15-8/15
Leek	5/1-6/1	5/1-6/1	Usually Planted in Spring		—	—
Lettuce, Head	5/15-7/1	5/15-7/15	6/1-7/15	6/15-8/1	7/15-8/15	8/1-8/30
Lettuce, Leaf	5/15-7/15	5/15-7/15	6/1-8/1	6/1-8/1	7/15-9/1	8/15-9/1
Marjoram	5/20-6/1	6/1-6/10	6/10-6/20	6/10-6/30	6/10-7/15	6/10-8/1
Muskmelon	—	—	6/1-6/15	6/1-7/1	—	—
Mustard	5/15-7/15	5/15-7/15	6/1-8/1	6/15-8/1	7/15-8/15	8/1-9/1
Okra	—	—	6/1-6/20	6/1-7/1	6/1-7/15	6/1-8/1
Onion (transplants)	5/10-6/10	5/10-6/10	Plant in Spring	—	Plant in Spring	—
Onion (seed)	5/1-6/1	5/1-6/1	Plant in Spring	—	Plant in Spring	—
Onion (sets)	5/1-6/1	5/1-6/1	Plant in Spring	—	Plant in Spring (except for green onions)	
Parsley	5/15-6/15	5/15-6/15	6/1-7/1	6/1-7/15	6/15-8/1	7/15-8/15
Parsnip	5/15-6/1	5/15-6/15	5/15-6/15	6/1-7/1	6/1-7/10	—

	Oct. 30	Nov. 10	Nov. 20	Nov. 30	Dec. 10	Dec. 20
Cress	9/15-11/1	10/1-12/1	10/1-12/1	10/1-12/31	10/1-12/31	10/1-12/31
Cucumber	6/1-8/1	6/1-8/15	6/1-8/15	7/15-9/15	8/15-10/1	8/15-10/1
Dill	8/1-9/15	9/1-11/15	9/1-12/31	9/1-12/31	9/15-12/31	9/15-12/31
Eggplant	6/1-7/1	6/1-7/15	6/1-8/1	7/1-9/1	8/1-9/30	8/1-9/30
Endive	7/15-8/15	8/1-9/1	9/1-10/1	9/1-11/15	9/1-12/31	9/1-12/31
Fennel	7/1-8/1	7/15-8/15	8/15-9/15	9/1-11/15	9/1-12/1	9/1-12/1
Fruit Trees	11/15-1/1	12/1-1/1	—	—	—	—
Garlic Plant in Spring	8/1-10/1	8/15-10/1	9/1-11/15	9/15-11/15	9/15-11/15	
Grape	11/15-1/1	12/1-1/1	—	—	—	—
Horseradish Plant in Spring	—	—	—	—	—	
Kale	7/15-9/1	8/1-9/15	8/15-10/5	9/1-12/1	9/1-12/31	9/1-12/31
Kohlrabi	8/1-9/1	8/15-9/15	9/1-10/15	9/1-12/1	9/1-12/31	9/1-12/31
Leek Plant in Spring	—	9/1-11/1	9/1-11/1	9/1-11/1	9/15-11/1	
Lettuce, Head	8/1-9/15	8/15-10/15	9/1-11/1	9/1-12/1	9/15-12/31	9/15-12/31
Lettuce, Leaf	8/15-10/1	8/25-10/1	9/1-11/1	9/1-12/1	9/15-12/31	9/15-12/31
Marjoram	6/10-8/10	6/10-8/20	6/10-9/10	6/10-9/20	8/1-10/1	8/1-10/1
Muskmelon	—	—	6/1-8/15	7/15-9/15	8/15-10/1	8/15-10/1
Mustard	8/15-10/15	8/15-11/1	9/1-12/1	9/1-12/1	9/1-12/1	9/15-12/1
Okra	6/1-8/10	6/1-8/20	6/1-9/10	6/1-9/20	8/1-10/1	10/1-12/31
Onion (transplants)	—	9/1-10/15	10/1-12/31	10/1-12/31	10/1-12/31	10/1-12/31
Onion (seed)	—	—	9/1-11/1	9/1-11/1	9/1-11/1	9/15-11/1
Onion (sets)	—	10/1-12/1	11/1-12/31	11/1-12/31	11/1-12/31	11/1-12/31
Parsley	8/1-9/15	9/1-11/15	9/1-12/31	9/1-12/31	9/15-12/31	9/15-12/31
Parsnip Spring Planted	—	8/1-9/1	9/1-11/15	9/1-12/1	9/1-12/1	

Fall Planting Dates

Aug. 30	Sept. 10	Sept. 20	Sept. 30	Oct. 10	Oct. 20
Pea, Black-Eyed					
—	—	—	—	6/1-7/1	6/1-7/1
Pea, Sweet					
5/10-6/15	5/15-7/1	6/1-7/15	6/1-8/1	Usually Spring Planted Only	
Peanut					
—	—	—	—	Plant in Spring	—
Pepper (transplants)					
—	—	6/1-6/20	6/1-7/1	6/1-7/1	6/1-7/10
Potato, Sweet (transplants)					
—	—	—	—	5/20-6/10	6/1-6/15
Potato, White					
5/15-6/1	5/15-6/15	5/15-6/15	5/15-6/15	5/15-6/15	6/15-7/15
Pumpkin					
—	—	6/1-6/15	6/1-7/1	6/1-7/1	6/1-7/15
Radish					
5/1-7/15	5/1-8/1	6/1-8/15	7/1-9/1	7/15-9/15	8/1-10/1
Rhubarb					
9/1-10/1	9/15-10/15	9/15-11/1	10/1-11/1	10/15-11/15	10/15-12/1
Rosemary					
5/15-6/15	5/20-6/15	6/1-7/1	6/1-7/15	6/15-8/1	7/15-8/15
Rutabaga					
5/15-6/15	5/15-6/15	6/1-7/1	6/1-7/1	6/15-7/15	7/1-7/20
Sage					
5/15-6/15	5/20-6/15	6/1-7/1	6/1-7/15	6/15-8/1	7/15-8/15
Salsify					
5/15-6/1	5/15-6/10	5/20-6/20	6/1-6/20	6/1-7/1	6/1-7/1
Soybean					
—	—	—	5/25-6/10	6/1-6/25	6/1-7/5
Spinach					
5/15-7/1	6/1-7/15	6/1-8/1	7/1-8/15	8/1-9/1	8/20-9/10
Spinach, New Zealand					
—	—	—	5/15-7/1	6/1-7/15	6/1-8/1
Squash, Summer					
6/10-6/20	6/1-6/20	6/1-7/1	6/1-7/1	6/1-7/10	6/1-7/20
Squash, Winter					
—	—	5/20-6/10	6/1-6/15	6/1-7/1	6/1-7/15
Strawberry (transplants)					
—	—	—	Plant in Spring	—	—
Tarragon					
5/1-6/15	5/1-6/15	6/1-7/1	6/1-7/15	6/15-8/1	7/15-8/15
Thyme					
5/1-6/1	5/1-6/15	6/1-7/1	6/1-7/15	6/15-8/1	7/15-8/15
Tomato (transplants)					
6/20-6/30	6/10-6/20	6/1-6/20	6/1-6/20	6/1-6/20	6/1-7/1
Turnip					
5/15-6/15	6/1-7/1	6/1-7/15	6/1-8/1	7/1-8/1	7/15-8/15
Watermelon					
—	—	6/1-7/15	6/1-7/1	—	—

	Oct. 30	Nov. 10	Nov. 20	Nov. 30	Dec. 10	Dec. 20
Pea, Black-Eyed	6/1-8/1	6/15-8/15	7/1-9/1	7/1-9/10	7/1-9/20	7/1-9/20
Pea, Sweet	8/1-9/15	9/1-11/1	10/1-12/1	10/1-12/31	10/1-12/31	10/1-12/31
Peanut	—	—	Plant in Spring	—	—	—
Pepper (transplants)	6/1-7/20	6/1-8/1	6/1-8/15	6/15-9/1	8/15-10/1	8/15-10/1
Potato, Sweet (transplants)	6/1-6/15	6/1-7/1	6/1-7/1	6/1-7/1	6/1-7/1	6/1-7/1
Potato, White	7/20-8/10	7/25-8/20	8/1-9/15	8/1-9/15	8/1-9/15	8/1-9/15
Pumpkin	6/1-8/1	6/1-8/15	6/1-8/15	7/15-9/15	8/15-10/1	8/15-10/1
Radish	8/15-10/15	9/1-11/15	9/1-12/1	9/1-12/31	9/1-12/31	10/1-12/31
Rhubarb	11/1-12/1	—	—	—	—	—
Rosemary	8/1-9/15	9/1-11/15	9/1-12/31	9/1-12/31	9/15-12/31	9/15-12/31
Rutabaga	7/15-8/1	7/15-8/15	8/1-9/1	9/1-11/15	10/1-11/15	10/15-11/15
Sage	8/1-9/15	9/1-11/15	9/1-12/31	9/1-12/31	9/15-12/31	9/15-12/31
Salsify	6/1-7/10	6/15-7/20	7/15-8/15	8/15-9/30	8/15-10/15	9/1-10/31
Soybean	6/1-7/15	6/1-7/25	6/1-7/30	6/1-7/30	6/1-7/30	6/1-7/30
Spinach	9/1-10/1	9/15-11/1	10/1-12/1	10/1-12/31	10/1-12/31	10/1-12/31
Spinach, New Zealand	6/1-8/1	6/1-8/15	6/1-8/15	—	—	—
Squash, Summer	6/1-8/1	6/1-8/10	6/1-8/20	6/1-9/1	6/1-9/15	6/1-10/1
Squash, Winter	6/1-8/1	6/1-8/15	6/1-8/15	7/15-9/15	8/15-10/1	8/15-10/1
Strawberry (transplants)	Plant in Spring	—	11/1-12/31	11/1-12/31	11/1-12/31	11/1-12/31
Tarragon	8/1-9/15	9/1-11/15	9/1-12/31	9/1-12/31	9/15-12/31	9/15-12/31
Thyme	8/1-9/15	9/1-11/15	9/1-12/31	9/1-12/31	9/15-12/31	9/15-12/31
Tomato (transplants)	6/1-7/1	6/1-7/15	6/1-8/1	8/1-9/1	8/15-10/1	9/1-11/1
Turnip	8/1-9/15	9/1-10/15	9/1-11/15	9/1-11/15	10/1-12/1	10/1-12/31
Watermelon	—	—	—	—	—	—

Personal Gardening Calendar

USE THIS CALENDAR TO PLAN YOUR GARDENING ACTIVITIES	MARCH	APRIL	MAY	JUNE	JULY	AUGUST	SEPTEMBER	OCTOBER	NOVEMBER	DECEMBER	JANUARY	FEBRUARY
Start of growing season (average date of last spring freeze)												
End of growing season (average date of first fall freeze)												
Length of growing season												
Start hardy plants indoors (7 weeks before date to set out)												
Start tender plants indoors (7 weeks before date to set out)												
Plant hardy plants and seeds outdoors (2 weeks before average date of last spring freeze)												
Plant tender plants and seeds outdoors (2 weeks after average date of last spring freeze)												
Clean up garden												
Plan next year's garden, order seeds												
Leave garden for vacation												

Index

A

Allium cepa. See onion
Allium porrum. See leek
Allium sativum. See garlic
Allium schoenoprasum. See chive
Amaranthus retroflexus. See pigweed
Anethum graveolens. See dill
Anthracnose, 90
Ants, 86, 87
Aphids, 84, 86, 89
Apium graveolens dulce. See celery
Apium graveolens rapaceum. See celeriac
Apple, 110-11. See also tree fruit
Arachis hypogea. See peanut
Arctium species. See burdock
Armoracia rusticana. See horseradish
Artemisia dracunulus. See tarragon
Artichoke, globe, 16, 43, 111-12, 270-71, 276-77
Artichoke, Jerusalem, 16, 43, 112-14, 270-71, 276-77
Artificial light, 36-37
Asparagus, 16, 43, 114-15, 270-71, 276-77
Asparagus bean. See bean, four-angled
Asparagus officinalis. See asparagus
Asparagus pea. See bean, four-angled
Aubergine. See eggplant

B

Basil, 16, 43, 116-17, 270-71, 276-77. See also herbs, 224-27
Bean crops, 208-10. See also bean, lima; bean, mung; bean,snap; pea, black-eyed; soybean
Bean, four-angled, 16, 43, 117-18, 270-71, 276-77
Bean, lima, 16, 43, 118-20, 270-71, 276-77. See also bean, 208-10
Bean, mung, 16, 38, 43, 120-21, 270-71, 276-77. See also bean, 208-10
Bean, snap, 16, 43, 121-23, 270-71, 276-77. See also bean, 208-10
Bean sprouts, 38
Beet, 16, 43, 123-24, 270-71, 276-77. See also root crops, 237-40
Beetles, 84, 86, 87
Belgian endive. See chicory
Bell pepper. See pepper
Bermuda onion. See onion
Beta vulgaris. See beet
Beta vulgaris cicla. See chard
Bindweed, 76, 77
Bird pepper. See pepper
Black-eyed beans. See pea, black-eyed
Black-eyed peas. See pea, black-eyed
Blights, 91
Blossom end rot, 91
Borecole. See kale
Borers, 84, 86, 87
Bouquet garni, 225-26
Brassica caulorapa. See kohlrabi
Brassica chinensis. See cabbage, Chinese
Brassica juncea. See mustard
Brassica napobrassica. See rutabaga
Brassica nigra. See mustard, black
Brassica oleracea acephala. See collard; kale
Brassica oleracea botrytis. See cauliflower
Brassica oleracea capitata. See cabbage
Brassica oleracea gemmifera. See Brussels sprouts
Brassica oleracea italica. See broccoli
Brassica rapa. See turnip
Broad bean, 16, 43, 124-25, 270-71, 276-77
Broadcasting, 24
Broccoli, 16, 43, 126-27, 270-71, 276-77. See also cabbage, 210-14
Brocks. See broccoli

283

Brussels sprouts, 16, 43, 127-28, 270-71, 276-77. See also cabbage, 210-14
Buckhorn, 79
Bullnose pepper. See pepper
Burdock, 76, 77
Bush bean. See bean, snap
Butter bean. See bean, lima
Butterhead lettuce. See lettuce

C

Cabbage, 16, 43, 128-30, 210-14, 270-71, 276-77. See also broccoli; Brussels sprouts; cabbage, Chinese; cauliflower; collard; kale; kohlrabi; mustard
Cabbage, Chinese, 16, 43, 130-31, 270-71, 276-77. See also cabbage, 210-14
Cabbage looper, 84, 86, 87
Cabbage worms, 86
Calabrese. See broccoli
Cantaloupe. See muskmelon
Capsicum annuum. See pepper
Capsicum frutescens. See pepper
Carrot, 16, 43, 131-32, 270-71, 276-77. See also root crops, 237-40
Catalogs, seed, 68-69
Caterpillars, parsley, 88
Cauliflower, 16, 43, 132-34, 270-71, 276-77. See also cabbage, 210-14
Celeriac, 16, 43, 134-35, 270-71, 276-71. See also root crops, 237-40
Celery, 16, 43, 135-37, 270-71, 276-77
Celery cabbage. See cabbage, Chinese
Celery root. See celeriac
Celtuce. See lettuce
Chard, 16, 43, 137-39, 270-71, 276-77
Chayote, 16, 43, 139-40, 270-71, 276-77
Chenopodium album. See lamb's quarters
Chenopodium bonus henricus. See lamb's quarters
Cherry tomato. See tomato
Chichorium endivia. See endive
Chichorium intybus. See chicory
Chickweed, 76, 77
Chicons, 141
Chicory, 16, 43, 140-42, 270-71, 276-77
Chili pepper. See pepper
China beans. See peas, black-eyed

Chinese cabbage. See cabbage, Chinese
Chinese mustard. See mustard
Chive, 16, 43, 142-43, 270-71, 276-77. See also herbs, 224-27
Cho-cho. See chayote
Chowder peas. See pea, black-eyed
Chuchu. See chayote
Citrullus vulgaris. See watermelon
Civit bean. See bean, lima
Clay soil, 44, 49-50
Cold frame, 34-35
Cole family, 210
Collard, 16, 43, 143-44, 270-71, 276-77. See also cabbage, 210-14; kale, 158-59
Compost, 55-58, 59, 60
Container growing, 29-33, 36-38
Convolvulus species. See bindweed
Cool-season crops, 42-43
Cooperative Extension Service, 71-74
Corn, 16, 43, 144-46, 214-17, 270-71, 276-77
Corn borers, 84, 85
Corn earworms, 86, 87, 88
Cornell Peat-Lite Mix, 51
Cos. See lettuce
Cowpeas. See pea, black-eyed
Cress, 16, 43, 146-47, 272-73, 278-79
Crisphead lettuce. See lettuce
Cucumber, 16, 43, 147-48, 218-20, 272-73, 278-79
Cucumis sativus. See cucumber
Cucurbita maxima. See pumpkin; squash
Cucurbita moschata. See pumpkin; squash
Cucurbita pepo. See pumpkin; squash
Cuke. See cucumber
Currant tomato. See tomato
Cutworms, 84, 85
Cynara scolymus. See artichoke, globe

D

Dandelion, 76, 77
Daucus carota. See carrot
Day length, 40-41
Devil pepper. See pepper
Dill, 16, 43, 149-50, 272-73, 278-79. See also herbs, 224-27
Diseases, 90-97
Dolmades, 156
Dry onion. See onion

E

Eggplant, 16, 43, 150-51, 272-73, 278-79. *See also* tomato, 248-54
Endive, 16, 43, 151-52, 272-73, 278-79. *See also* lettuce, 228-30
English peas. *See* pea, sweet
Escarole. *See* endive
Extension service. *See* Cooperative Extension Service

F

Fava bean. *See* broad bean
Fennel, 16, 43, 152-54, 272-73, 278-79. *See also* herbs, 224-27
Fertilizer, 23, 33, 36, 50, 53-55, 58, 94-95, 96
Fines herbes, 225
Finnochio. *See* fennel
Florence fennel. *See* fennel
Flowering cabbage. *See* cabbage, Chinese
Foeniculum vulgare dulce. See fennel
Four-angled bean. *See* bean, four-angled
Fragaria chiloensis. See strawberry
Fragaria virginiana. See strawberry
French bean. *See* bean, snap
French endive. *See* chicory
Fruit trees. *See* tree fruit
Fruitworms, tomato, 88

G

Garden cress. *See* cress
Garden pea. *See* pea, sweet
Garlic, 16, 43, 154-55, 272-73, 278-79. *See also* onion, 230-34
German greens. *See* kale
Glycine max. See soybean
Golden gram. *See* bean, mung
Goosefoot, 78
Gourd, 240
Grape, 16, 43, 155-56, 220-24, 272-73, 278-79
Grass (weed), 76, 78
Grasshoppers, 86
Green bean. *See* bean, snap
Green cabbage. *See* kale
Green gram. *See* bean, mung
Green onion. *See* onion
Greens. *See* mustard
Green shell bean. *See* bean, snap
Growing season, 13-17, 34-35, 42-43, 99, 269-81
Grubs, 85
Guinea squash. *See* eggplant
Gumbo. *See* okra

H

Hakusai, 131
Hardening, 24-26
Hardy crops, 14-16
Helianthus tuberosus. See artichoke, Jerusalem
Herbicides, 81-82, 96
Herbs, 16, 43, 224-27. *See also* basil; chive; dill; fennel; marjoram; parsley; rosemary; sage; tarragon; thyme
Hibiscus esculentus. See okra
Hill planting, 24
Fines herbes, 225
Hornworms, 88
Horsebean. *See* broad bean
Horseradish, 16, 43, 156-58, 272-73, 278-79
Hosta, 79
Hot frame, 35
Hot pepper. *See* pepper

I

Inorganic mulches, 60-61
Ipomoea batatas. See potato, sweet
Irish potato. *See* potato, white
Italian broccoli. *See* broccoli

K

Kale, 16, 43, 158-59, 272-73, 278-79. *See also* cabbage, 210-14; collard, 143-44
Kidney bean. *See* bean, snap
Knob celery. *See* celeriac
Kohlrabi, 16, 43, 159-61, 272-73, 278-79. *See also* cabbage, 210-14

L

Lactuca sativa. See lettuce
Lady's fingers. *See* okra
Lamb's quarters, 78
Land-grant institutions, 71-74
Lavandula officinalis, 224
Leafhoppers, 84, 89
Leaf lettuce. *See* lettuce
Leaf mustard. *See* mustard

Leek, 16, 43, 161-62, 272-73, 278-79.
  See also onion, 230-34
Legume, 208
Lepidium sativum. See cress
Lettuce, 16, 43, 162-64, 228-30,
  272-73, 278-79
Light, 38-42
Light gardening, 36-37
Lima bean. *See* bean, lima
Lotus tetragonolobus. See bean,
  four-angled
Love apple. *See* tomato
Lycopersicon esculentum. See tomato

M

Maggots, root, 85
Mailing specimens, 72
Malus pumila. See apple
Mango pepper. *See* pepper
Manure, 23, 53-54, 60
Marjoram, 16, 43, 164-65, 272-73,
  278-79. *See also* herbs, 224-27
Marjorana hortensis. See marjoram
Merliton. *See* chayote
Michihli. *See* cabbage, Chinese
Mildews, 91
Mulch, 44, 58-62
Mung bean. *See* bean, mung
Muskmelon, 16, 43, 166-67, 272-73,
  278-79. *See also* cucumber, 218-20
Mustard, 16, 43, 167-69, 272-73,
  278-79. *See also* cabbage, 210-14
Mustard, black, 78, 79
Mustard spinach. *See* mustard

N

Napa cabbage. *See* cabbage, Chinese
Navy bean. *See* bean, snap
New Zealand spinach. *See* spinach,
  New Zealand
Nitrogen, 54-55, 95, 96

O

Ocimum basilicum. See basil
Ocimum crispum. See basil
Ocimum minimum. See basil
Okra, 16, 43, 169-70, 272-73, 278-79
One-seeded cucumber. *See* chayote
Onion, 16, 43, 170-72, 230-34, 272-73,
  278-79
Organic matter, 23, 44

Organic mulches, 59-60
Oyster plant. *See* salsify
Oxalis stricta. See sour grass

P

Pak-choy. *See* cabbage, Chinese
Parsley, 16, 43, 172-73, 272-73,
  278-79. *See also* herbs, 224-27
Parsnip, 16, 43, 173- 75, 272-73,
  278-79. *See also* root crops, 237-40
Partial shade, partial crop, 41
Pastinaca sativa. See parsnip
Pea, black-eyed, 16, 43, 175-76,
  274-75, 280-81. *See also* bean,
  208-10
Pea, sweet, 16, 43, 176-77, 274-75,
  280-81
Peanut, 16, 43, 177-79, 274-75,
  280-81
Pear tomato. *See* tomato
Pepper, 16, 43, 179-80, 234-37,
  274-75, 280-81
Peppergrass. *See* cress
Pepperweed, 80
Pesticides, 91, 93, 95, 96
Pests, 82-90, 94-97
Pe-tsai, 131
Phaseolus aureus. See bean, mung
Phaseolus lunatus. See bean, lima
Phaseolus vulgaris. See bean, snap
Ph of soil, 49, 55, 64, 97
Phosphorus, 55, 97
Pie plant. *See* rhubarb
Pigweed, 78-79
Piper nigrum, 234
Pisum sativum. See pea, sweet
Plantago lanceolata. See plantain
Plantago major. See plantain
Plantain, 79, 80
Planting, 13-18, 23, 24-26, 269-81
Plastic mulch, 61-62
Plum tomato. *See tomato*
Pole bean. *See* bean, snap
Polygonum hydropiper. See
  smartweed
Polygonum species. *See* smartweed
Portulaca oleracea. See purslane
Potassium, 55
Potato, sweet, 16, 43, 181-82, 274-75,
  280-81
Potato, white, 16, 43, 182-83, 274-75,
  280-81
Protecting plants, 26, 34-35
Psophocarpus tetragonolobus. See
  bean, four-angled

Pumpkin, 16, 43, 184-85, 274-75, 280-81. *See also* squash, 240-43
Purslane, 79-80

R

Radish, 16, 43, 185-86, 274-75, 280-81. *See also* root crops, 237-40
Raphanus sativus. See radish
Raphanus sativus longipinnatus. See radish
Record keeping, 27
Rheum rhaponticum. See rhubarb
Rhubarb, 16, 43, 187-88, 274-75, 280-81
Ringo, 254
Romaine. *See* lettuce
Root crops, 237-40. *See also* beet; carrot; celeriac; parsnip; radish; rutabaga; salsify; turnip
Root maggots, 85
Rosemary, 16, 43, 188-89, 274-75, 280-81. *See also* herbs, 224-27
Rosmarinus officinalis. See rosemary
Rots, 91, 94
Russian turnip. *See* rutabaga
Rusts, 91
Rutabaga, 16, 43, 189-90, 274-75, 280-81. *See also* root crops, 237-40

S

Sage, 16, 43, 191-92, 274-75, 280-81. *See also* herbs, 224-27
Salsify, 16, 43, 192-93, 274-75, 280-81. *See also* root crops, 237-40
Salvia officinalis. See sage
Sandy soil, 44, 49-50
Santolina chamaecyparissus, 224
Santolina virens, 224
Savoy cabbage. *See* cabbage
Scale, 86
Scallion. *See* onion
Scotch bean. *See* broad bean
Sea kale. *See* chard
Seakale beet. *See* chard
Sechium edule. See chayote
Seeds, 18-22, 24, 68-70
Slugs, 88
Smartweed, 80
Smuts, 91-92
Snails, 88
Snap bean. *See* bean, snap
Soil, 48-51, 53, 62-64
Soilless mix, 33, 36, 50-51

Solanum melongena. See eggplant
Solanum tuberosum. See potato, white
Sour grass, 80-81
Sou-sou. *See* chayote
Southern peas. *See* pea, black-eyed
Soybean, 16, 43, 193-94, 274-75, 280-81. *See also* bean, 208-10
Spacing, 26
Spanish onion. *See* onion
Spider mites, 84, 89
Spinach, 16, 43, 194-95, 274-75, 280-81
Spinach, New Zealand, 16, 43, 196-97, 274-75, 280-81
Spinacia oleracea. See spinach
Spittlebugs, 90
Spring onion. *See* onion
Sprouts. *See* bean sprouts; Brussels sprouts
Squash, 16, 43, 197-98, 240-43, 274-75, 280-81
Squash vine borers, 86, 87
Stellaria media. See chickweed
Stem lettuce. *See* lettuce
Stem turnip. *See* kohlrabi
Strawberry, 16, 43, 198-200, 243-48, 274-75, 280-81
String bean. *See* bean, snap
Stringless bean. *See* bean, snap
Succory. *See* chicory
Sugar pea. *See* pea, sweet
Summer squash. *See* squash
Sunscald (sunburn), 92
Swede. *See* rutabaga
Swedish turnip. *See* rutabaga
Sweet corn. *See* corn
Sweet pepper. *See* pepper
Sweet potato. *See* potato sweet
Sweet marjoram. *See* marjoram
Swiss beet. *See* chard
Swiss chard. *See* chard

T

Taraxacum officinale. See dandelion
Tarragon, 16, 43, 200-201, 274-75, 280-81. *See also* herbs, 224-27
Temperature, 42-43
Tender crops, 14-16
Tetragonia expansa. See spinach, New Zealand
Teucrium chamaedrys, 224
Thrips, 89, 90
Thyme, 16, 43, 201-2, 274-75, 280-81. *See also* herbs, 224-27
Thymus vulgaris. See thyme

287

Tire planter, 30-32
Tomato, 16, 43, 202-3, 248-54, 274-75, 280-81
Tools, 45-48, 64-67
Tragopogon porrifolius. See salsify
Transplanting seedlings, 19, 21-22
Transplants, 18, 24
Tree fruit, 16, 43, 254-62, 272-73, 278-79. *See also* apple, 110-11
True leaves, 21
Turnip, 16, 43, 204-5, 274-75, 280-81. *See also* root crops, 237-40
Turnip cabbage. *See* kohlrabi
Turnip-rooted cabbage. *See* kohlrabi
Turnip-rooted celery. *See* celeriac

U

University of California Mix, 50-51

V

Vegetable pear. *See* chayote
Vicia faba. See broad bean
Vigna sinensis. See pea, black-eyed
Viola species. *See* violet
Violet (weed), 81
Viruses, 92, 96
Vitis varieties and hybrids. *See* grape

W

Warm-season crops, 42-43
Water, 43-48
Watermelon, 16, 43, 205-6, 274-75, 280-81. *See also* squash, 240-43
Wax bean. *See* bean, snap
Weeds, 75-82
White cabbage. *See* cabbage, Chinese
Whiteflies, 84, 89, 90
White potato. *See* potato, white
Wilts, 92, 97
Windsor bean. *See* broad bean
Winged bean. *See* bean, four-angled
Winter squash. *See* squash
Wireworms, 85-86
Witloof. *See* chicory

Y

Yam. *See* potato, sweet
Yellow turnip. *See* rutabaga

Z

Zea mays. See corn
Zucchini. *See* squash